Dónall Mac Amhlaigh (1926-1989) was one of the most important Irish-language writers of the 20th century. A native of County Galway, he is best known for his novels and short stories concerning the lives of the more than half-a-million Irish people who left Ireland for post-war Britain.

A prolific journalist and a committed socialist in the Christian Socialist tradition, Mac Amhlaigh, whose diaries and notebooks are held in the National Library of Ireland, was a member of the Connolly Association in Northampton and contributed regularly to newspapers such as the Irish Press and a range of journals on both sides of the water throughout the 1970s and 1980s. In his writings, Mac Amhlaigh often provided the perspectives of the Irish in Britain on issues such as class, economy, emigrant life in England, the conflict in Northern Ireland and civil rights-related issues.

Mícheál Ó hAodha is an Irish-language poet from Galway in the west of Ireland. He has written poetry, short stories, journalism and academic books on Irish social history, particularly relating to the Irish working-class experience, and the Irish who emigrated to Britain. He is one of the very few poets since Ó Ríordáin to explore the metaphysical in the Irish language, his work encompassing themes of loss, longing, memory, love and forgetting in collections such as *Leabhar na nAistear (The Book of Journeys)* and *Leabhar na nAistear II*.

With Support from

FREEDOM
TO **WRITE**
FREEDOM
TO **READ**

Supported using public funding by
**ARTS COUNCIL
ENGLAND**

CYNGOR LLYFRAU CYMRU
BOOKS COUNCIL of WALES

PARTHIAN

Praise for *A Soldier's Song*

Dónall Mac Amhlaigh's contribution to Irish literature has been long neglected. He is the greatest chronicler of the Irish navvy slaving on English building sites. It is quite amazing that of all our emigrant millions the best that has been writ and said of their lives and times has been written in Irish. But before he joined the great exodus to the digging holes of England, Mac Amhlaigh was an Irish soldier. Not being a military people, the Irish people have little respect for their army. The author's account, ostensibly autobiographical, but undoubtedly with some fictional flourishes as would befit a novelist, makes for a great read. This soldier's story does not include great wars, but just the fun and competition and camaraderie and happenstances of young men who end up in uniform. It is funny and sad and wistful, and a portrait of a time and experience which has never been captured quite like this. Mícheál Ó hAodha's translation brings us right into his world, giving the original Irish a new life with style and with verve.

Alan Titley, translator: *The Dirty Dust: Cré na Cille*

Mícheál Ó hAodha has done the literary world a huge service by translating Dónall Mac Amhlaigh into English. It is one of the few novels (in either Irish or English) which explores the 'silent generation' of Irish who emigrated, primarily to Britain, to find employment in the post war years. Originally written in a minority language which is fading fast, it explores Ireland's urban environment as opposed to a rural one. As such, it is a unique and important part of Ireland's social history.

Gillian Mawson, author of *Britain's Wartime Evacuees – Voices from the Past*

Dónall Mac Amhlaigh's *A Soldier's Song* is a work that exudes authenticity and immediacy. It bears the stamp of the author's distinctive voice and companionable persona, the idiosyncrasies of which translator Mícheál Ó hAodha has deftly captured in this fine translation that gives fresh, twenty-first-century life to a lost literary treasure.

Liam Harte, Professor of Irish Literature, University of Manchester. Author of *Reading the Contemporary Irish Novel 1987-2007* (2014) and *The Literature of the Irish in Britain: Autobiography and Memoir, 1725-2001* (2009).

Dónall Mac Amhlaigh's *A Soldier's Song* demonstrates why Irish is one of the oldest written vernaculars in the world. In a language vibrant to its very core, Mac Amhlaigh gives a picture of a country and a people that have been central to the European imagination for centuries. He captures precisely the psychoses, the sadnesses, the joys and the prejudices of a people forced into the music of survival. This novel is as much about the change from rural to urban in Irish life as it is about a young man's hopes and dreams in a post-war Europe just coming-of-age. Written just before he left Ireland for a new life in Britain, Mac Amhlaigh's novel is a paean to the city of his birth – Galway – its people, pubs and streets. Like Joyce, Mac Amhlaigh sought to record every pub and dancehall, every sunset, stone wall and rainbow in his mind, to pack the city in his suitcase so that she remained with him forever, so he could all at once hear her lost voice everywhere.

Colum McCann, U.S. National Book Award Winner

# A Soldier's Song

## *Saol Saighdiúra*

*Dónall Mac Amhlaigh*

Translated by

Mícheál Ó hAodha

PARTHIAN

Parthian, Cardigan SA43 1ED
www.parthianbooks.com
*Saol Saighdiúra / A Soldier's Song* by Dónal Mac Amhlaigh:
First published in Irish in Ireland in 1962 by An Clóchomhar, Dublin.
This edition in English in 2023 by Parthian Books.
This translation by Mícheál Ó hAodha 2023 with permission of
Cló Iar-Chonnacht, An Spidéal, Galway, Ireland.
© Cló Iar-Chonnacht 2022
©This translation by Mícheál Ó hAodha 2023
This book has been selected to receive financial assistance from English PEN's PEN
Translates programme, supported by Arts Council England. English PEN exists to
promote literature and our understanding of it, to uphold writers' freedoms around the
world, to campaign against the persecution and imprisonment of writers for stating
their views, and to promote the friendly co-operation of writers and the free exchange
of ideas. www.englishpen.org

Published with the support of the Books Council of Wales

CYNGOR LLYFRAU CYMRU
BOOKS COUNCIL of WALES

*ISBN: 978-1-914595-03-5*
*ISBN ebook: 978-1-914595-36-3*
*Editor: Gina Harrison*
*Cover Image: Sunset in Connemara, County Galway, Ireland, MNStudio / Alamy*
*Cover design Lyn Davies*
*Typeset by Elaine Sharples*
*Printed by 4Edge UK*
*A cataloguing record for this book is available from the British Library*

# A Soldier's Song

## *Saol Saighdiúra*

# Chapter 1

It is my last day working for the O'Neill's in Salthill. It's Monday, the 3rd of November, 1947. I've spent four months working as a waiter in the hotel here, but the tourist season is over now and I can't expect them to keep paying me for the winter when there's nothing to do around the place anymore. Myself and Maitias Ó Conghaile from *Doire Fhatharta*[1] are enlisting in the army tomorrow – if we're accepted that is; and then it's goodbye to Galway for the next six months. We'll be training up on the Curragh, in Kildare.

But then when I went down to Joe's house, they thought that I'd lost the plot. I told them what I was doing and Joe says: 'What the hell would you want to join the army for?' grabbing the tongs and giving the fire a poke. His wife Meaig arrived in just then too carrying two buckets of water. She was just back from the well.

'What's this about the army? Who's joining the army? It's not that lazy little good-for-nothing of ours Peadar is it? He's not going on about joining the army again, is he! As if it'd do him any good! All the young crowd today is the same. All they care about is soldiering – either that or leaving for England.'

'Arah, keep quiet you, you divvy, and mind your own business, will you?' says Joe gruffly, the same as always. 'Peadar hasn't a notion of joining the army. It's Danny here who's thinking of joining up.'

'And that's his choice too,' says Meaig, once she realised that it wasn't her own son that was joining. 'Let him be let you. Shur, can't the young lad do whatever he likes? There's nothing wrong with the army at all, you know – shur wasn't his own father in the army? I don't know why people are always telling others what to do anyway – instead of just listening to them for a change. There's no fear that they'd mind their own business anyway!'

Meaig was thick that she'd to go to the well when her husband and son were in warming their arses by the fire.

'Eh? What's this I hear about our Danny joining the army?' says Daideo[2] shifting beneath his quilt.

'Hey – this lad here's hoping to enlist in the soldiers the same as thousands before him. I don't see what you're all worked up about. God knows, you lot are worse than a pack of children, the lot of ye,' says my cousin Peadar, chipping in.

'Still, I think you'd be mad to tie yourself down like that Danny,' says Joe.

'The army? – There's never any of God's luck where there's soldiers,' says Daideo, gobbing into the fire. The 'Tans' came within a whisker of shooting him dead during the Troubles, the same man he's had it in for soldiers since then – not that I can blame him in fairness. Joe shook his head ruefully: 'I never passed that (i.e. Renmore Barracks) beyond that a chill didn't go up my spine at the sight of the high walls and giant iron gates. It'd remind you of a prison more than anything else.'

Meaig opened her mouth to say something else, but Peadar got in before her. 'Will you make us a cup of tea there Mam? Suit you better than spouting off about stuff that you know feck-all about!'

I stayed there with them until I'd my tea drank and left them to it. I could tell by him that Joe'd try and knock some work out of me if I hung around much longer. Maybe that's the reason he's not keen on me enlisting either. Many's the day's work that he's got out of me for free. I don't care anymore, though. I'll do my own thing from now on, and I'll be back here in spring again wearing my green soldier's uniform with the help of God.

I felt a kind of sad leaving Joe's house, especially when I looked across at the Burren Hills on the far side of the bay and the Aran Islands at the edge of the horizon – like something that'd emerged from the sea. Rahoon and Letteragh to the north of me and Barna Woods to the west, the entire landscape shrouded in that strange and beautiful silence that permeates autumn in this part of the world. I thought back to those days long ago when we arrived home from school, autumn afternoons just like this one, when we arrived in starved with the hunger. And no matter how hungry we were, we'd pray that our mother hadn't made stew that day. Anything but stew!

I walked over to Salthill and called into the hotel to see whether they'd anything for me to do. They'd no jobs for me though and told me to take the rest of the day off instead. I'll sleep in the hotel tonight, but from tomorrow on, I'll be up in the Curragh of Kildare probably. I'll be sorry to say goodbye to Seán and his wife after this long with them. They were always very nice and kind to me even if we got on each other's nerves the odd time when things were hectic at the height of the tourist season; it was always worth it. They always treated me as just another member of their family and not like a boy who was working for them.

I went down to Micilín's house (Maitias' brother) in Buttermilk Lane and I stayed chatting with Micilín and his wife until Maitias arrived in from Tirellan where he's working for a local farmer. God, but we've had some great nights in that house there, listening to the gramophone and dancing the 'Stack of Barley' and the 'Half-set'. The Carraroe and the Eanach Mheáin[3] people are the ones who go there most and you'd hear many fine songs sung in the real 'sean-nós' style in that place. Mugs of tea and big hunks of currant cake passed around the room then by Micilín's wife and a nice long chat once the dancing was over and she told us all to go home for ourselves. Maitias and I went for a wander around Galway town then and we met the girls. The two girls we met had just finished work for the day – Juleen and

Margaret – and they work over in the hospital laundry. Maitias and I started going out with them – him with Joyce and me with Margaret. We were going out with these girls ever since Race Week.[4] I was only just back in Galway from Kilkenny when I met Margaret and I'd lost most of my Irish by then because of the length of time I'd spent away from Galway. Once I started going out with Margaret, my Irish came back to me again quickly as she has no English worth talking about. She's a fine-looking girl with beautiful long black hair and she loves slagging and joking and having the crack. Mind you, she was a bit sad in herself tonight. She said she'd miss me when I'm gone. She told me she'll be waiting eagerly for me to return to Galway again. I feel the same way about her as well, of course.

Just after we were saying goodbye to the girls at the hospital gates they called us back again and told us to call to them again tomorrow afternoon again before we leave – that they've a message for us to do downtown for them. Then they ran quickly back inside into the hospital.

Maitias and I stayed chatting down near the bridge until fairly-late and to make matters worse again, Seán Ó Néill was still awake when I got back to barracks and insisted that we drink a few bottles of beer together to mark the occasion of our departure from here. Well – that's me finished with the work in O'Neill's pub now although they said that they'd welcome me back with open arms anytime I wanted a job there again. A hundred farewells to my small box-room at the top of their house and the stunning view of Galway Bay all laid out before you on a moonlit night. If I get on as well in the future as I did when I was working in Salthill, I'll have no complaints. It's time for me to stop writing this now and go to sleep.

# Chapter 2

Maitias met me at the corner of Eyre Square the next day and we went over to the hospital to see the girls one last time. We got through the main gate without too many questions and into the laundry where the girls work. Oh little brother, but you couldn't see your hand in front of you with the steam that was in the room and you couldn't hear yourself think with the racket and spinning of the huge washing machines there. Once the steam cleared somewhat, we saw the giant vat of soap and water and the Connemara girls up to their elbows in water. We called over to the girls, but they just giggled and waved some old pairs of drawers in our direction. Margaret and Juleen emerged from the steam in the end, laughing and giggling at the antics of the other girls. They couldn't talk to us for long though and we said goodbye quickly again. Believe it or not, they gave us a half-sovereign each as a parting gift! God knows, this was a very kind gesture on their part, especially when they aren't very well off themselves at all; they only got paid one pound, one crown per month in addition to their food. I was lonelier leaving Margaret than I thought I'd be, but we're going to write to one another every week until I'm back home again.

Maitias and I went over to Renmore again, but at the barracks gate, they told us that there'd be no doctors available for the next few days. We were better off heading down to Athlone ourselves we said, because there'd be a doctor there who could do the medical immediately. We got the three o'clock train, even if we were a bit quiet passing over the bridge at Loch an tSáile and on past Baile Locháin. When we enquired at the gate of the barracks in Athlone, the army policeman gruffly told us go away first, for some reason. It's not as if we looked rough or untidy at all or that we were flat broke or whatever either. He let us in eventually and we followed the barracks assistant to the storeroom where we were each given a mattress, two pillows, and sheets and blankets. We were led into a long wooden cabin and told to pick where we wanted to sleep until the exam the following morning. Maitias showed me how to dress a bed the way that a soldier's supposed to do it – (he spent a while in the Preparatory Corps so he knows these things) and then we went over to the canteen for a cup of tea. There were a good few soldiers there already, some of them drinking tea or playing billiards or just listening to the radio. I couldn't but envy these lads who've their training done already, not that I'd want to be stationed in this barracks here, however. We're lucky that we're Irish speakers, otherwise, we wouldn't be sent back down to Renmore again at all, once our training's done.

We bought tea and scones and sat at the table nearest the fire, and one of the soldiers wasn't long coming over to us, a big block of a lad with fair hair. He asked us where we were from and whether we'd been accepted for training yet and once we told him that we were joining the Irish-speaking *An Chéad Chath*, what do you know but didn't he switch to Irish! He'd good Irish too, by my soul, other than that he had a strange dialect. He was from Turbot Island out from Clifden and he'd a year done in the Army already. I got the feeling that Maitias wasn't over the moon that this fellow had joined us. I offered him a drop of tea and a few scones, and he kicked me in the ankle under the table unknown to the other fellow. This Clifden lad was broke; he didn't even have a cigarette on him, but tomorrow's pay-day – and so before he said goodbye again, he made sure to bum a few cigarettes off Maitias.

We headed out the town then and spent an hour or so hanging around. To be honest, the place didn't seem like much to us. It wasn't a very lively spot – not compared to Galway anyway. Back in Galway, you'd be meeting girls and boys from Connemara every few minutes as you walked down the street, but this place was different. It was strange to our eyes.

'You'd be a long time waiting for someone to speak a bit of Irish to you here,' Maitias says, 'you might as well be out in Hong Kong for all the chances of that happening.'

I slept like a baby the first night even though the bed was as hard as a rock. In the morning, we ate breakfast in the canteen with the soldiers and then put the bed-frames and the bedclothes back to the store. We were brought down for our exams then – tests in numeracy, writing and geography – after which we'd to go to the doctor's for the medical. Before this exam took place at all however, the Recruiting Officer asked us whether we'd still be happy to join the army even if one of our friends was refused admission on medical grounds. Maitias and I looked at one another momentarily before responding as neither of us was quite sure what to say to this. We told the Officer that it'd benefit neither of us to turn down our chance in the army just because another lad was rejected and so they went ahead with the medical. We needn't have worried though because we were both out again two minutes later. We'd got through. Next, we were instructed to take the oath. We did that and then we were given our travel passes for the journey down to Kildare. One minute we were two ordinary civilians and the next we were fully-fledged members of the Irish Army! My heart swelled with pride and joy at my new status and I told Maitias as much too as we left the barracks again, seeing as I knew he felt the same way about it. He told me to cop on to myself though and that there'd be time enough for me to be talking pride and all the rest of it once I'd actually completed my army training and had my proper qualifications.

The train we boarded had just arrived in from Galway and by chance, we ran into a group of boxers from *An Chéad Chath*. They were on their way up to the Curragh for a boxing tournament. The lads all looked manly and neat in their fine-polished uniforms and shoes and their bright-shining brass – and the insignia of *An Chéad Chath* prominent on their uniforms. I can't wait for my training to be done here so that I'll be as well as qualified and as well turned-out a soldier as any of them. They all spoke Irish to a man and you'd go a long way before you'd find a finer-looking body of men anywhere, I'd say. On reaching Kildare, there was an army lorry waiting for us and Maitias and I were given our instructions straight away by an army sergeant there. We climbed into the back of the lorry and travelled out along the narrow road that splits the green sward of the Curragh Plain.

\* \* \*

Our work today in McDonagh barracks – or the 'General Training Depot', as they call it – was the same as yesterday. After we'd collected our mattress and sleeping gear from the store we were brought over to a big barracks-room full of new recruits, all of whom were getting their beds ready for the night. There was a big turf fire at the top of the room, but the beds nearest the fire were all taken already by the lads who were ahead of us and so we'd to be happy with two beds far away from the heat. It doesn't matter though, because we'll only be in this room for a few days by all accounts. Once other Irish-speaking recruits arrive here, we'll get our own room at the far end of the barracks. We started to unfold the blankets, but the Sergeant stopped us. 'Don't bother with that yet,' he said, 'come with me so that you can pick out your kit.' We followed him across the square to another building and then upstairs to where the Quartermaster was dividing out the kit amongst the recruits. It was getting late and he was about to finish up for the day and he didn't look too happy at all to see us arriving in. We got in the queue and I smiled at him but he was right-grumpy.

'What's the smirking for Sonny – did you win the Sweep or something?' – he says.

The store-man who was helping the Quartermaster divide out the kit didn't look like he was too thrilled either; they just handed us whatever was at hand and it was obvious they couldn't wait to get rid of us. He handed me a uniform that I thought looked alright until Maitias told me in Irish that it was all rucked up at the back and looked ridiculous on me. Maitias was right, of course. I found a uniform that fitted me fairly well in the end, and was handed the rest of my stuff. Oh little brother, you wouldn't believe the amount of stuff that we get as our kit – shoes, shirts, socks, brushes, a wooden belt, a cap, a work uniform or fatigues, a button-stick and don't ask me what else – everything thrown into a big canvas bag. A kit-bag they call it. They give you a big wooden box to store all this stuff in and it's back from the Depot again.

I don't know how in Jesus's name I'll keep track of all this gear, especially seeing as there are a good many of the Dublin gang in the room and they've a reputation for stealing that goes back years. Maitias says that we need to buy two padlocks for our stuff now or we won't have a razor left between us after a few days.

We got tea at half past four. The canteen is directly opposite the room here and I can honestly say that I never tasted a tastier loaf of bread than the one we got this afternoon. One loaf between every five of us is what we get here, but it's not nearly enough really. I know that I could eat a full loaf myself, no problem. We'll have supper in a while, but this is just a mug of porridge, the others tell us. What harm? We're not broke yet. Shur, we can always pay a visit to the canteen later.

We were woken with a start this morning by the loud blast of the bugle announcing *Reveille*. Next minute, the big sergeant arrives into the room, walking stick in hand. He raps his stick on the edge of the door and makes a racket loud enough to wake the dead, then he's down through the room prodding and poking everyone with the stick and bellowing at the top of his voice:

'Rise and shine, beds in line. Sluggards arise and greet the day! Any man not out on parade in five minutes gets put up on a 117. That, for your information gentlemen, is an Army Charge Sheet and something you'd rather not get acquainted with too soon. Shake a leg there, now, everyone up!'

I nearly fell out of bed, I was in such a rush to get up! Maitias told me to take it handy and not to be making an idiot of myself in front of all these strangers here. We're given a minute or two to dress ourselves and make the beds. He was in no rush and yet he was still ready quicker than I was. I was still only half-dressed and Maitias was ready to go out on parade, his blankets carefully folded, one on top of the other. I wasn't the worst of the lads there though, as by the time I'd given my hands and face a quick rinse and went downstairs, some of the other lads were still fiddling with their laces and stuff. Others raced out to the washroom, tucking their shirts into their trousers and all the rest of it.

Breakfast was nice and tasty (pity there wasn't more of it!); we got an egg and a slice of bacon each, a big mug of sweet tea and a fifth of that fine loaf with the black crust on the end of it.

We still had a fair bit of time yet to prepare correctly for the Morning Parade and I polished the buttons on my uniform and shoes while Maitias went out to the washroom for a shave. A long slate *edge* jutting out from the wall serves as the washbasin here and there's plenty of cold water any time you want it. You use cold water for shaving. It's tough, but that's the way it is.

We were ordered out on parade then, where a different sergeant again spent a while trying to get us some way organised before the Company Lieutenant appeared. He was a very young man to be at that rank, I thought, but he walked up and down and inspected us all closely, then gave us a short lecture. You're in the Army now, he said, and we can make a good life for ourselves here if we want to. It's up to ourselves. If we do everything that we're told, no one'll find fault with us, but if we try and act all hard and that, we won't be long finding out that the Army can be ten times harder than us. And we won't be long finding out who's really in charge either, he told us. To have a fine, manly life for ourselves while we're wearing the uniform, we've to make sure we complete our duties carefully. We need to understand that the sergeants and other army personnel here, irrespective of rank, are our friends, he said. We shouldn't ever hesitate to ask them for help at any stage, especially if we're anxious or worried about anything. One lad standing behind me mumbled sarcastically under his breath all the while the Lieutenant was talking. This fellow was in the Army before by all accounts, but he left once he'd his initial training over with. I don't know what in the name of God brought him back here again because all he's done since yesterday is give out everything about the Army non-stop. This fellow has the ability to talk without moving his lips, like a ventriloquist nearly, and it's hard to tell where the muttering is coming from sometimes. Maitias says that this trick of being able to talk under your breath like this is a pure sign that he's spent time in the *glasshouse* or Military Prison, but I don't know if that's right or not. When we scattered after parade, Sergeant Sullivan came in with orders for me and Maitias. Sullivan's a wiry, tough-looking fellow with ginger hair, and he has the bluest and most piercing eyes I've ever seen. It's like he's looking right through you. I wouldn't like to draw this fellow onto me, I can tell you.

We'll have our own room shortly, he told us, as soon as other Irish speakers arrive here. We're to have our training in Irish and that's what we'd prefer too seeing as I can't see us really gelling with the crowd that we're in with right now – because of different languages. For example, Maitias and I were chatting last night after 'Lights Out' when we heard someone sniggering in the dark. The sniggering went around the room until everyone was laughing and mocking us – for speaking in Irish, of course!

Maitias' very impulsive and he jumped out into the middle of the floor and challenged them. This quietened them for a while even if there were still some smart comments from the ones who were taking the piss out of us after this too. I told them that it was a bit rich for them to be making fun of us, considering that we had two languages and they had only one – 'and that one only half-right at that.' Oho son, but that really got their goat! Next minute a big, tall fellow jumps up out of his bed in anger to tell me that I was 'out of order' saying the likes of this:

'That's a very serious thing to say about anyone, making out we're illiterate or something. I'm not forgetting that remark, mind, and I'll make a complaint to the C.O. tomorrow.'

I wouldn't mind but this fellow could tear me apart if he wanted to; he's bloody huge – never mind running off to the Company Captain with his stories.

We spent the day at various odd jobs. First, we'd to leave our civvies in the kit-bags in the store, take a bath, get a haircut and then sign various papers. We were marched up to the Medical booth this afternoon for blood tests and who was there already when we got in but the lads we'd been exchanging jibes with last night! You should have heard ventriloquist-man giving out as we moved up the line to give blood. The way he went on you'd have sworn the medical orderly was ready to stab us with a pick instead of getting the small pin-prick that we got in the end!

'There's no need for this at all,' he said, chewing the top of his thumb where they'll be taking the drop of blood from in a minute. 'There's no need for this at all. It's all just stupidity and show. I was here before and they took my bloods already. Surely that's down on paper somewhere. Wouldn't you think they'd just go and check the records they have already, instead of making a pin-cushion out of me again?' He kept whining like this until they took the blood sample from him and then went off holding his 'injured' thumb.

Group 'O' seems to be the most common blood group by all accounts, and tomorrow, I'll be given a small medal with this blood group marked on it in addition to my I.D. number. '89383, Private, Mac Amhlaigh, Dónall', is who I am now and my comrade Maitias is '89382, Private, Ó Conghaile, Maitias'. Seven-and-twenty a week is our pay until we're fully trained. Then we do a one-star or two-star trial maybe, and if that goes alright our pay's increased. You get a pay rise of seven shillings a week for every star you get.

This camp is a good and healthy place and it's no wonder, seeing as at the lowest point out the countryside here, you're as high up as the top of *Nelson's Pillar* in Dublin – or that's what they say anyway. There are thousands of sheep grazing the plains around here and strangely, they aren't a bit shy of people. In the mornings they're standing in the doorway as soon as you go outside and they sniff around the swill-barrels outside the canteen on a regular basis. There are seven barracks altogether in this Camp, each of which is named after the leaders of the Easter Rising. There are two picturehouses here too as well as one 'dry' canteen; we've plenty of opportunities to spend some of our wages here so I plan on sending a half-sovereign home every week with the help of God.

Today we were moved downstairs to the bottom room and Maitias and I grabbed the two beds closest to the fire the minute we went in, needless to say. Sergeant Red said that he expected us to keep this room as clean as snow at all times; for some reason, I felt that he was directing this instruction at me mainly. Another lad joined us today, Ó Murchú (Murphy) from Limerick, and he has excellent Irish, even if he didn't go past National School for his education. He's a small, bony but muscular fellow who always has an anxious look about him – as if he's expecting someone to play a trick on him or to cheat him out of something any minute. He and his father worked for a local farmer down in Limerick until recently and they were paid 70 pounds a year in total – this was their pay, including the use of a house, a garden, milk and the like. Isn't this a strange arrangement all the same? To give Connemara it's due, at least every man working there has his own smallholding and isn't at the mercy of some local big farmer or landlord. As the song goes:

> *Seal ag tarraingt fheamainne cur fhataí is ag baint fhéir,*
> *Is ní raibh fear ar bith dá bhoichte nach raibh áit aige dhó féin,*
> (At times cutting seaweed, sowing potatoes or saving hay, / And there was no man so poor that he didn't have his own patch for himself.)

Would you believe it? I'm only in the army a few days and I already have a 'charge' against my name! We were on parade at nine o'clock this morning and the Lieutenant doing a careful inspection of us when he asked me whether I'd shaved that morning.

'I didn't sir,' I replied.

'Oh, do you see this Sergeant,' he says turning to the ginger-haired Sergeant.

'How come you didn't shave?' the Sergeant says gruffly.

'Well, I don't ever shave to be honest', I says. 'Because I haven't started shaving yet.'

'Oh, he doesn't ever shave himself,' repeats the Lieutenant, 'have we any medicine for that one Sergeant, I wonder?'

'Yes, we do sir. I'll charge him after parade is over,' says the Sergeant.

I was sent over to the Company Captain once we were finished and charged with being 'unshaven on parade'. He let me off though when I explained that I didn't know about this rule that you'd to start shaving yourself once you enlisted. The Sergeant gave me a right dirty look as I passed him on my way out of the Company Office.

Maitias tells me that I have to be on alert about them from now on as they'll be watching me carefully to make sure I don't make any other mistakes. Maitias knows a lot about the Army and he's the great 'survivor' no matter what he does, so I'd be as well listening to him. We got a fine dinner today, a lovely piece of trout each with peas and potatoes. We were allowed just three potatoes each, but I felt full leaving the table all the same. I thought the food was fine, but the ventriloquist-fellow thought the fish was rotten. I've never come across the likes of him before. He complains about the slightest thing. Maitias calls him a 'barrack-room lawyer' and he's warned me to steer clear of him as he's trouble.

We spent the day learning how to march correctly in formation and were all fairly tired by the end. The Sergeant is witty and he's full of quips and smart-alec stuff, but if you laugh at anything he says, he gives you a right bollocking. I was nearly fit to burst a few times and at one stage I couldn't help myself and gave a snigger. He read the riot act with me. Maitias is very good on the marching and never needs correction on it.

This basement room we're in is grand and comfortable and we're at home here already, unlike the room above where the other crowd slagged us off for speaking Irish. Maitias reckons our gang will be as strong and close-knit as any soon – a lot more so than the crowd upstairs. Maitias's the type who likes a bit of rivalry methinks. He's not gone on that shower upstairs and makes it very obvious.

*Saturday, 8.11.1947*
We'd a great big parade this morning – the Leader's Parade – and it was one hell of a sight. Hundreds of soldiers in full battle-dress, spick-and-span, out on the large square, and the band playing marching tunes. All of us recruits were on parade and we looked fairly pathetic really compared to the crowd who've guns already. The Barrack Leader, a small

wiry man with a swarthy face, went around inspecting us. He'd a pair of leather boots up to the knees and a riding crop under his arm. After the parade, our rooms were inspected and everyone had to stand next to their bed, their kit-box open next to them.

The Sergeant came around first to check that everything was in order. I thought my kit-box was fine, but when he came to me, he let a shout out of him: 'The Chamber of Horrors!' he says. 'All y'need now is the Mummy!' I had to empty everything out of the kit-box onto the floor straight away and then put it all back in again as quick as I could. The Company Captain inspected us a short while later again and he didn't fault me on anything even if Sergeant Red stopped and had a good gander at me and my kit. We'd the rest of the day off and Maitias and I went for a walk around the camp. It's a hellish lonely and isolated place really when you take it all in. Please God, I won't have to stay here for good.

We'd to be back in time for tea and that Rattigan fellow, the perpetual whiner, sat at the same table as us. We'd eggs for tea, but he turned his nose up at the sight of them, like they were rotten or something. When the orderly dished out the food, he picked up one of the eggs and gave it a sniff.

'The hen who laid this egg must be drawing the pension for years,' he said.

'What's wrong?' the barracks orderly asked.

'O, nothing at all, Sarge, nothing at all,' he says.

No sooner was the orderly gone but your man was in full-flow again though:

'There y'are. You're not even allowed open your mouth in this place. You might as well be in Russia.'

Maitias says that your man is a gammon hard-chaw and that he's intent on causing trouble. Two other recruits joined our group this afternoon, a young lad from the Aran Islands, Martin Cooke and a lad from Tooreen in Mayo, by the name of Connery. I knew the pair of them to see already from Galway. The lad from Aran has hardly any English, but he's a nice lad and bright, and I've no doubt that he'll get on well here. The other lad's very polite and I'd say he's well-educated. Our number is gradually increasing. There's a big group of new recruits from Dublin down the block from us here too. None of them are that big or strong, but they're very cocky all the same. They christened me 'Dev'[5] from day one.

One of these lads asked me for a loan of my knife at tea-time. He told me he'd left his own knife back in the room, so I gave him a loan of mine. After tea I followed him out of the canteen and over to his room. Like a fool, I thought that he'd forgotten to give it back to me. When I asked him for it back, he looked at me as if like I was some sort of a nut.

'Knife? What're you on about?' he says.

'The knife I gave you there in the canteen just a few minutes ago.'

'You never gave me any knife,' he says. 'Who're you anyway? I never met you before in my life. Isn't it true for me lads?'

'True for you,' chorused the other lads. I knew then that I was only wasting my time. I'd probably have to fight every one of them to get that bloody knife back again.

'I must have made a mistake about the man I gave it to so,' I said.

'That's right Dev,' says your man.

When I told Maitias later what'd happened, he said that it was easy-known I was a 'red-arse' – a new recruit who's still learning the ropes.

Sunday really dragged that first week, especially seeing as we'd no duty after the Parade Mass. I wrote a letter home telling them what things were like here, and then another one to Margaret. I spent the afternoon relaxing on the bed and I left very lonely thinking about Galway. With God's help, it won't be long before I've completed my stint here and we'll be stationed back in Renmore. Patrick Connery here is actually a relation of Sean-Phádraig Ó Conaire, the writer, believe it or not. Signs on it too, he wrote an essay for the magazine *Ar Aghaidh* recently and it was as good as anything I've ever read in Irish. Myself and the Aran lad praised the essay to high heaven, but Maitias said that he thought that kind of work – reading and writing – is just stupidity and a waste of time really. It's a pity I don't have any small book with me here that I could pass the time with at night.

We were given our rifles the other day. They're very heavy considering how small they look. We were in the storeroom and the Quartermaster handing them out, when he says:

'Now young soldiers, take good care of these guns while you have them and you won't go wrong. A soldier's best friend is always his gun.'

Rattigan laughed sarcastically at this. 'Not at all,' he mutters under his breath. 'They're the friggin' worst friend a soldier can have.'

We were given other stuff as well as the guns – a water bottle, a tin hat or helmet, a pack, a groundsheet and a handful of straps, two pouches and a wide belt to keep everything in. This is our equipment or kit and when we got back to the room, the red-haired fellow showed us how to fold the groundsheet properly and pack everything together. I could have been there till kingdom come for all I could manage it though. I just couldn't get all the stuff packed together right. If I don't have it done fairly well by tomorrow, the red fellow's going to kill me, he says. Slowly but surely, our room's getting fuller. Three other recruits arrived today, one from Cavan and another from Dublin, a lad by the name of Begley who seems very nice. The third lad is from Newcastle West in County Limerick and his surname is Hartnett. Begley has good Irish, but the other two lads have very little. The reason that they've been assigned to the Irish-speaking group, is that there aren't enough Gaeltacht people joining as recruits, I think. These lads won't be long getting comfortable speaking Irish, I'd say.

Myself and the lad from Cavan spent a good while chatting to one another by the fire this evening. He was telling me about the wild times he had when he was at college in Dublin before this, out drinking and pawning things to get money and all that. He hadn't bothered with any study, he said, but this was what'd done for him in the end. Like me, he likes reading and he brought a book of English poetry with him from when he was in college. I felt sorry for him when I saw him trying his best polishing his uniform buttons with *brasso*. There was more *brasso* on him than there was on the uniform for a finish and so I'd to show him how to use the button-stick properly. Maitias says that he's never seen anyone as awkward as this fellow in his life before. He said that watching us two was like watching a cat trying to teach a hen how to swim.

Maitias and Murphy have no bother keeping their uniform and clothes clean, but I've a long way to go to be as good as them in this department. I watched them the other day when they were polishing their shoes. The first thing they did was scrape the shoes with a razor blade until they were white as snow. Then they spread the red dye or ink out onto the shoe-leather and let it dry for a while. Next, they poured more red ink into a box of 'Ruby' and set fire to it. The 'Ruby' melted and mixed in with the ink, after which they applied this mixture to the shoes. If you'd seen the gleam on those shoes when they were done with them! I'm so bloomin' awkward that if I tried the same trick, I'd have nothing, only red fingers by the end of it.

It's great the way that we're all getting to know one another and more used to one another's ways in the room here. We were sitting around the fire tonight having the chat. You'd have sworn we all knew each other for years. It's funny the way that both languages (Irish and English) are mixed together here too and the new lads trying to speak Irish, especially when they're talking to the lad from the Aran Islands. Martin Cooke's Irish is a bit different from the Irish the Connemara lads have also. He pronounces his words in a softer way somehow and his accent isn't as strong as theirs.

Of course, there are differences in the Irish spoken between one village and another, back home in Galway. Even where I'm from, the Irish is slightly different from further west in Barna, or further back in Connemara too. The dialect in my homeplace, Knocknacarra is closer to Menlo-Irish or Claregalway-Irish, I'd say. I've met people from Inisheer over the years and I always thought that their Irish was Munster Irish really. For example, they pronounce the word *mór* (big) as *múr*. I picked up a good bit of Munster Irish when I was at school in Kilkenny and something happened tonight that proved this. Maitias was helping me put my kit in order and when he was finished, I said to him:

'*Gura maith a'd a Mhaitias, déanfaidh mé rud ort fós.*' (Lit: 'Thanks Maitias, I'll do something for you yet.')

He gave me a confused look.

'I mean that, "I'll do you a good turn sometime",' I explained to him then.

'Oh! You'd a right to say that in the first place. I thought you were threatening me or something! What you should really say in Irish is: '*Déanfaidh mé rud duit.*' (Lit: I'll do something for you.') But sure, there isn't any good Irish where you're from!'

Next thing Limerick poked his nose into it. He said that I was the one who's Irish was correct – and that really put the cat amongst the pigeons, I can tell you! Next thing, the pair of them were slagging one another off with Maitias saying that Limerick, as with all the Munster crowd, had nothing only book-Irish really.

Maitias and I received letters from the girls today. They hand out the post at dinner-time in the canteen. As you'd expect, most of them were marked 'Mr' instead of 'Private' and the sergeant handing them out said: 'There are no "Misters" here, please – only "Privates". You leave your titles behind you when you come here.'

My letter was in Irish and Maitias's was in English. It was written kind of funny really, even if Maitias couldn't see the humour in it. You couldn't say that there wasn't poetry in it though. Here's one sentence from his letter: 'Sometimes I saunter up as far as the station, thinking that some wind will blow you down to me.'

Many Gaeltacht people have the habit of writing to each other in English, even if they always speak to one another in Irish. We spent a while drilling with our guns today. The guns are heavy, awkward-enough old pieces, to be honest. The red-haired Sergeant was on our case because we were so slow moving our guns when marching and every minute, he was: 'Pull that bloody bolt towards you, '83 McCauley! Stand up straight Hartnett!' and all the rest of it. He has an ugly habit of dragging English adjectives into his Irish when he's giving orders. His Irish is fairly fluent, but he always hesitates and has to think before he says anything – or that's what I think anyway.

Daily life here is like school in some ways. It's very regimented and everything is divided up along into the same time slots each day. A set amount of time is spent marching, learning in class, or maybe doing athletics or playing sport. I can't swim and neither can the lad from Aran, but we were brought down to the baths today all the same. Everyone jumped into the water straight away, but I just stood on the edge of the pool, hesitating. Next thing the ginger fellow sneaks up behind me and shoves me into the water. Luckily, it wasn't too deep and I managed a crab-like swim and got out of the water again. I felt really great after swimming however and on the way back for dinner, I was thinking quietly to myself. 'Here goes now Dónall; now's your chance to do what you always dreamed about since you were young – to be a soldier and to have good crack with all the other lads. Isn't this a great life really? It beats working in the mill or even working in O'Neill's hotel, good as it was.'

# Chapter 3

We're here a week now exactly. A week is just a short time and yet we've got to know lots of new people and learned new things. We received our wage packet today at half past one – we were only owed a half-week's wages, but we couldn't have been prouder the lot of us, as we walked up to the table to receive our pay. You have to take the money in your left hand and make a bowing motion with your right before turning sharply on your heel and exiting.

An old woman in a dark shawl and an old-fashioned black hat was sitting outside the front-wall of the barracks today selling sweets and fruit from a big basket. She'd a small donkey and cart from which she was also selling various provisions too. She's a throwback to the old days, that's for sure. They say that she's been selling her wares from outside the barracks here since she was a small girl. Most of us couldn't pass by without buying something from her and the minute we got paid, we all bought something off her – even though it'll be time for dinner soon. Limerick didn't bother going out to her, though. He's thrifty and he went back to the room without spending so much as a halfpenny. Everyone's entitled to their opinion, but if we were all that tight, the poor old sweet-woman would never make a living!

You've never seen the like of Big Reaney before in your life. He'd eat a rake of sweets and then go straight back out for more. Today's a sort of a half-day really and we spent the afternoon playing cards or athletics; even if you don't take part in the sports, you still have to go down to the playing pitches with the others so we were all marched down there after the two o'clock parade. A small group of us didn't bother with sport and spent the rest of the afternoon wandering around. Cooke, Maitias, Limerick and myself; none of us have the slightest interest in sports or boasting about how good we are at them either – unlike some of the other lads here. Limerick is already old and worn-out from too much heavy physical labour. His joints are all so swollen and stiff that I doubt he ever played sport when he was younger. Tonight, when we were tidying up, '06 Reaney whispered in my ear and we headed down to the wet canteen for a drink. You can't buy pints in the canteen so we made do with bottled beer. A bottle of beer is sixpence. That's a mark-up of one penny on every bottle – compared to buying beer out in a hotel or a pub outside somewhere. The place was packed with recruits, some of whom were drinking beer for the first time, I'd say. I had a real thirst on me as I've barely had a drink since I first started hanging around with Maitias. '06 and I were birds of a feather though, and when the barracks orderly came in to close up for the night, the pair of us were still sitting there and nice and well-on-it, the same as the others there. We got to our feet straight away though and returned to our quarters in a nice orderly fashion as befits new soldiers.

# Chapter 4

I was given three days C.B.[6] today and it was stupid how it happened. We were just back in barracks after a spot of training on taking up positions. We'd to come indoors because it was lashing rain outside. It was fairly dark when we got back to the room, and the Sergeant reached for the light-switch to turn it on. The brass cover for the switch wasn't back on properly because someone'd been messing with it this morning. And when the Sergeant reached over to it, the cover fell onto his hand and hurt him. I was closest to him when it happened and so he turned on me, those piercing eyes of his drilling right through me. 'Who took the cover off the *switch*?' he bawled out. And for some bizarre reason, it was right then and there that all good sense abandoned me. 'Me' I says, inexplicably. I don't know what got into me, it must have been a rush of blood to the head or because I got a sudden fright or something. Whatever it was, I blurted this out anyway, and the lads stared over at me like I'd just lost my mind.

'What'd you do that for?' the Sergeant asks.

'Just for the crack,' I says, like the fool of long ago. You might as well be hanged for a penny as for a pound. Oh God! That's when he went ballistic altogether! He stormed out of the room in a fury and wrote a charge out against me straight away. Next, I was ushered in to face the Company Captain for the second time since our arrival here and as you imagine, he didn't go as soft on me this time. He read out the charge to me and said:

'Guilty or not guilty?'

'Not guilty, sir,' I replied.

He looked over in confusion at Sergeant Sullivan but Sullivan confirmed that I'd admitted to doing it earlier. The Captain looked back at me again and asked whether what Sergeant said was the truth. I was getting a bit sick of this crack at this stage.

'Well, Sir, it's true that I told the Sergeant that I removed the cover from the switch, but the truth is that I had nothing to do with it really.'

The Captain went quiet for a second and then asked whether I usually made false statements like this. The charge against me was pronounced in English and the Captain says very eloquently then:

'Most extraordinary. I see endless possibilities in this, and most of them, I fear, rather disastrous for you, Private McCauley. For instance, you might confess to a theft, or a murder or some other misdemeanour of which you were entirely innocent. Or—'

It was obvious that he didn't believe me one bit though, and he fell serious just as quickly again:

'Do you accept my penalty?' he says.

'I do sir,' I says, seeing as I couldn't very well say anything else.

'Well, you're confined to barracks for the next three days,' he says, and I was marched back out again. Later, when we got a break for a smoke, Maitias pulled me aside by the sleeve and whispers:

'What in hell's name possessed you to say that you loosened the cover?'

'Oh, don't ask me little brother,' I says, 'I can't tell you why to be honest.' He stared at me and shook his head ruefully.

We were sitting next to the fire relaxing after tea when the bugle sounded outside on the square. 'That's your call now,' says Maitias, and unfortunately, he was right. '*Faillitheoirí*' ('Dossers')[7] was the tune, and the men who're confined to barracks have to run across to the guard-room immediately on hearing this sound. It can sound every half an hour until it's time for lights out. If the bugle sounds, you've to drop whatever you are doing straight away. A handful of Dubliners appeared the same as me and we were left standing outside the guard-room for quite a while before the Barracks Police showed any interest in us. These Barracks Police are different from the others; they don't have the same status as the Military Police and they're a lot tougher on us in reality. One of them eventually came out to us and ordered us to 'Stand to Attention'. He looked us over suspiciously for a minute, and pronounced as follows:

'Gammon hard-chaws and real-live muck-birds!' He 'quick-marched' us then down to the officers' canteen where an elderly and sleepy-looking cook took charge and we were put scouring pots and dishes. And that old cook gets plenty of work out of us, you can be sure of it! He sat up on the kitchen table mumbling to himself and half-dozing as we worked. No sooner were we finished with one task, but he quickly roused himself and found something else for us to do. I felt like shit, the way we were working our arses off down there and the other lads back in the room relaxing and having the crack. There was no getting out of it though. He kept us there for hours and it was ten o'clock that night before he let us go again. We were only just out the canteen door when the Dublin lads produced all the stuff they'd robbed while we were in the kitchen – eggs, slices of bacon, prunes and God knows what else. How they siphoned all this food away without the cook noticing is beyond me … but anyway! Worse luck, this idiot here had nothing for himself at the end of it either!

I was exhausted by the time we got back to the room, but I still had to polish my leggings and boots for the morning, shine my uniform buttons on, and brass up the rest of my kit. I was delighted to find that the other lads had already done this for me, fair play to them! Everything was polished and gleaming – the shoes and the buttons – even the gun looked brand-new. All the lads were asleep in their beds except for '06 Reaney. He came in just a few minutes after me, humming to himself, half-drunk after the pub. He came over the minute he spotted me and sat on the edge of the bed. I told him how grateful I was to all the lads for the way that they'd looked after my stuff while I was gone, but he'd no interest in this. '*A small gesture to a fellow soldier, surely, old boy?*' he says, as he put his hand inside his uniform and produced two bottles of beer. We drank to one another's health and the health of our army company. '06 got all sentimental then and told me about home and about the girl that he was going out with before he went to college. He didn't go on too long at this crack though because he gives a big yawn and quickly falls asleep.

It has to be one of the nicest things in the world, lying there snug and warm in your bunk, the rest of the company sleeping peacefully around you. Giant shadows climbing the walls as the cinders in the fireplace glow red and then die away. You hear the lonely cry of the wind outside and you feel a special connection with the world and with your fellow soldiers. And even if some of them are still strangers to you, an invisible bond links you with this unique brotherhood of men, something strong and indivisible. This is one of the hidden riches of the military life, in my opinion. And then, despite your best efforts to dwell in the moment, you soon find yourself falling asleep too, the same as everyone else.

We practise endless foot-drills here. 'Square-bashing' is what some of the English-speakers call it and this is a very appropriate term for the perennial sound of hobnailed boots striking the square. 'Left, right, left, right; right-turn, left-turn, about-turn and forward march'; over and over again. Sergeant Red barking out the instructions at the top of his voice. They say that he's always in a bad mood on Thursdays and Fridays because he's hungover and has a sore head. I'm not sure about this, but he was definitely in a foul mood today, whatever was bugging him. His face turned dark red from all the shouting and those hawk-like eyes of his going through us for a shortcut, for the slightest mistake or misdemeanour. Some of these marching drills are hard enough to remember, but when they're done right, they're some sight – no doubt about it. The opening and closing of the ranks and the changes of direction while marching; when perfectly performed, they're a real joy to watch. When they announce, 'Change direction on the right', the man who's leading the line there has to switch direction and strike time hard on the ground with his boots until the rest of the company come into line with him. '*Deasaíonn siad*' ('They do a right') then before moving on. I'm not sure who invented the Irish-language terms for some of these drills, but some of them could be easier or clearer I think. Take the phrase '*Adbhansóidh an Complacht*' (The Company will Advance'), for example. This phrase smacks too much of English-language influence if you ask me. '06 Ó Reaney was in a bad way today, sweating profusely and dehydrated after the drink last night. And even if the Sergeant has a lot of time for him, he showed him no mercy today – and it was the same for everyone else. We marched up, down and across, and over and back, endlessly repeating the same movements, our boots knocking sparks from the rock-hard surface of the square. And just when we thought the Sergeant was slowing down to give us a break – with his 'walk' for a while, he'd quickly pick up the pace again. 'Forward march. Lift them up, up, I say. Raise them and they'll fall themselves!'

'Raise those legs of yours Private Reaney. Hey you McCauley, take that smirk off your mug and raise those legs of yours, you're worse than an old wan.' He barked out the instructions over and over again, until his voice was nearly gone.

I might be bad but Hartnett from Abbeyfeale and the lad from Tooreen will never cut out for this marching lark; they're worse than each other, the pair of them; they can't get the hang of this crack at all. They can't keep time with the marching and get confused on turning left and right. They got confused today and the whole thing was a mess.

Some of the lads behind them went right and some went left and Sergeant Red went crazy. He was fit to explode, that big ropey vein in his neck bulging with anger.

'God Almighty,' he says. 'Why have I – above all others – been punished like this? How was I unlucky enough to get this bunch of old wans and incompetents assigned to me – I've never seen a shower the likes of you ever before!'

We spent a while this afternoon learning how to assume 'a flat position lying on the ground while holding the gun' and this exercise certainly didn't do anything for the Sergeant's temper either. At one stage, he compared poor Hartnett to a cow that was about to calve, he was that awkward!

I couldn't help it and burst out laughing at this, and he made me perform the drill three times in a row as punishment: '*You, McCauley, are like a crow balancing on the edge of a swill-barrel*.' I was hard-pressed not to explode again at this but I managed to keep a lid on it. I couldn't draw him on me anymore than I'd already done. Thank God, we were left to our own devices tonight after presenting for guard-duty as we've to get ready for the Leader's Parade tomorrow. I've just one more night of C.B. left and once it's over with, I'll make sure never to get punished like this ever again.

There are two other lads from Connemara here in McDonagh Barracks except that they're not in the same company as us. They were here before the Irish-speaking company was formed at all, but they'll still have to learn all the Irish-speaking orders and terms once they're assigned to our C company – which'll be very soon. Seán Ó Neachtain (John Delia) from Camus Íochtair is one of the lads and Tomás Ó Cualáin (Tom Mheata Mhóir) from Carna is the other. They often call into our company and we usually have great chat and banter with them. John Delia would eat a cow, he's always that hungry, and when he realised that Cooke was gone out tonight, he raided his kit-box and took whatever food he'd stashed away. By the time poor Martin returned from shaving himself in the wash-house, there wasn't a crumb of his bread left and not so much as a tailor's thimbleful of jam either. Martin noticed that his stuff had been raided the minute he opened his kit-box to leave his towel and his razor back in. He didn't let on anything at first though, but sat himself down by the fire where John Delia was already warming himself instead. 'Oh! A thousand welcomes to you Seán,' Martin says, 'I didn't see you there until now.'

'No worries' says Maitias, recalling the raid the Camus man had made on Martin's stuff earlier.

'God knows, I'm big enough not to go unnoticed anyway.'

'By my soul, but that's the truth too, God bless you,' Martin agreed.

'You wouldn't want to be feeding that fellow anyway Martin,' added Maitias for good measure.

'How d'ya mean?' says the Aran Islander, letting on to be surprised. 'Does he eat a lot or what?'

'Oh shur, that fella would eat an old shoe so he would,' replied Maitias. 'It's no surprise really, I suppose. The Curragh's a place that increases your appetite a lot. It's the strong air here, y'see …'

'Oh, feck you all anyway, you shower of bastards,' says the Camus man; he couldn't take any more of it. I never heard such a big deal about a bit of an old loaf of bread and a spoonful of jam. I've often had a small biteen like that between one meal and the next, and nothing else for God's sake!

Another Connemara lad has joined this company, Máirtín Nee from Gleann Catha in Rosmuc. He was stationed down in the hospital for the past few months and his company is almost fully trained now. He isn't a lad who has any real interest in soldiering as a career though and says that he's going to 'work his ticket' if he can.

Maitias and a few other lads went to the photographer's house in the centre of the camp this afternoon to get a shot of themselves wearing their uniforms. If getting your picture in uniform isn't enough for them, the photographer also has a cowboy outfit that you can get your photo taken in also! This cowboy outfit is very popular for the photos. If you have a picture of a girl you're fond of, you can get that added to your photo and the photographer can even place an image of two hands entwined beneath the two faces and add whatever caption or phrase you like to it. '06 Reaney was shocked when he heard how much the photos cost though, and he immediately calculated how many bottles of porter you could get for the same money down in the wet canteen. I have to agree with him on this; you'd probably get more for your money having a few drinks than you would making faces and posing for a photo. I'll probably go down to get my photo taken next week, all the same. I got a letter from Margaret today; herself and Juleen find Galway very lonely since we left. They rarely go out at night now, she says; they don't even bother going down to *Micilín's* pub much these days. Juleen's hoping that Maitias will return to Galway on a visit at Christmas, but Margaret knows that I'll probably head home to Kilkenny then myself.

The Christmas spirit in the air already – even here in this wild and windswept place. Everyone's talking about holidays now and getting their passes ready to go on leave. To be honest, I can't wait for next spring when we'll return to Galway. My heart was broken this evening watching all the others getting ready to go out to the Pictures and myself and the chancers from Dublin confined to barracks. Luckily for us, there was a nice lad on guard-duty this evening; either that or he didn't have anything for us to do. We were left to our own devices anyway, and were happy-out about it. All the new recruits go for a walk around the camp on Saturday afternoons whereas the soldiers who've been here longer tend to head off to bed for a sleep; it's as if they want to forget that they're stationed here at all. I think that this is probably the last place in Ireland that most people want to be stationed in really; there's so little to do here. There are two cinemas here alright – the Curragh Picture House that's at the crossroads between McDonagh Barracks and McDermott Barracks. The other one, Sandes House, is at the far end of the camp. This latter cinema has a fine big canteen attached to it and is very popular as a consequence.

The Sandes family are Protestants who've been here since when the British were still in charge, and some people claim that the army chaplains are always worried that they'll try and convert some of the soldiers here to Protestantism – using their cups of tea and sweet-cakes as inducements. The chaplains needn't worry their heads about this, however. It's not as if many of the recruits have much interest in their own religion anyway – other than attending Mass on a Sunday – never mind having an interest in other religions. There's one recruit here who's always down in that cinema, a fellow who loves making up bits of old poems. The same lad composed a short poem about a ballerina he saw on a visit to Dublin once. I can't remember it now, but it went something like this: 'O Swan-like creature.' Well, after he'd been going to Sandes House regularly for a while, the older women there started inviting this fellow in for a cup of tea and a chat. He usually sits in their kitchen for the tea rather than staying outside in the canteen. He's the only one you could possibly claim might be targeted for conversion! At one stage, this same fellow, who's as cute as a fox, changed his ballerina poem to a religious verse in praise of God.

All he did was change the secular terms of his poem to religious ones and the job was done. There's no telling how many, buns, cakes and other treats he's brought back for himself from his visits there ever since!

* * *

This morning the Mass Parade was held before breakfast and I felt like a new man to be honest. It was like I'd had a great weight lifted from my shoulders now that my C.B.'s over with. The Dublin crew are very friendly with me now since we were all 'incarcerated' together during C.B., but I wouldn't trust any of them – as far as I'd trust Judas himself! Maitias and I went out for a walk after breakfast. We're not as pally now as we were when we first enlisted. This is what happens in the army life. 'Familiarity breeds contempt' and all that. We can see one another's faults more clearly now than before, I suppose, and can get on each other nerves more that we're in such close proximity to one another here. I spend more time having the crack with '06 Reaney these days than I do with my old buddy.

The other lads in the room here are all very friendly too, even if they're a bit younger than me and even if most of them don't have much interest in world affairs or books like me. Begley is very different from the other Dublin city lads. You can tell that his family are better off than the others and he has a more refined or mannerly way about him than them. You hear many people praising poverty and what it does for you, but I'm not sure about that at all. Most people who praise the virtues of poverty are rich themselves, I notice. You'd be waiting a long time before you'd hear any of the poor citing the advantages of their poverty. You can't blame these poor lads if they're a bit rough in their ways either. Some of them have had it really tough in the grim back-streets of the inner cities. And all of us – even those of us who were fortunate enough to be born into slightly better circumstances – can be a bit ignorant or 'rough-around-the-edges' at times – if we were honest about it. '06 and I walked the entire camp today and there's no doubting how exposed and wild this place looks at this time of the year. '06 is always hungry – the poor lad.

* * *

I learnt something new today when we were cleaning our guns! The mouth of a water bottle is a small bit wider than the mouth of the tiny oil bottle that we've to force down the muzzle of the gun. And the oil bottle is very difficult to get back up again once you've pushed it into the bloody gun-muzzle! I learned this lesson the hard way today and ended up having to pay for both a new water bottle and a new bottle of oil. What happened was that I was messing around the other night and shoved the bottle of oil down into an empty water bottle. Why! Because I was making an imaginary Molotov cocktail to fling across the room at '90 Murphy. But the bottle of oil went right down into the bigger bottle and the bloody thing jammed and I couldn't get it out again! I was in right bloody state then, I can tell you! I tried a lot of different tricks to unjam it, but I had to give up in the end. I left the water bottle up on the rack above the bed with the rest of my kit. I can always get a drop of oil from one of the other lads for cleaning the gun, and the lack of an oil bottle won't be noticed anyway until we have another kit inspection. I thought I'd get away with it, but I was wrong. Wouldn't you know it but they'd have to have a kit inspection today! They just sprung it on us all of a sudden, and I was caught straight away. For the inspection, I laid out my kit as neatly as possible and prayed that the missing oil bottle wouldn't be noticed. Each man stood next to his bed as the Lieutenant circuited the room. He looked at my stuff and made as if to move away, and for a second, I thought I'd got away with it. But then, he smirked and said in a mocking voice, nice and slow:

'The oil bottle, McCauley, where's your oil bottle?'

'Oh, the oil bottle Sir, is it?' I said, letting on to be surprised and he stared at me.

'Yes, Private McCauley, the oil bottle, where you keep the oil for cleaning the musket. Where is it?'

'It's up there, Sir,' I says, inclining my head towards the rack. He looked up but shur, there was no sign of the bottle.

'Where up there?' he says, more impatiently this time.

'It's in the water bottle, sir,' I says, trying to suppress a nervous giggle. He looked shocked and glanced from me to Sergeant Red as much as to say – 'Did you just hear what this fellow is after saying?'

Then, more sternly: 'Do you mind me asking you what that bottle is doing stuffed into the water bottle?'

'Well, it's not exactly ...'

He cut me short and grabbed the bottle from the rack then gave it a shake before passing it to the Sergeant so that he could do the same. They looked at one another momentarily and nodded:

'It's in here alright; no doubt about it, the oil bottle's inside it alright.' The Lieutenant handed me the bottle with a pained expression.

'Give Private McCauley two new bottles on credit,' he instructed the Quartermaster. They moved on to Maitias then, Sergeant Red throwing me a filthy look as he went past! The Lieutenant had taken just a few steps when he turned back to me and says:

'Do you mind me asking again how the oil bottle got jammed down into the water like that?'

Then, before I could respond – 'Don't bother,' he says dismissively before moving on. '*Sufficient for the day is the evil thereof*, eh?' he says to the two soldiers accompanying him on the inspection.

I wasn't the only one who'd made a shit of things though because when he reached Hartnett he got a right land altogether. You never saw such as a mess in your life, everything thrown higgledy-piggledy all over the place, and half his kit missing. And Hartnett standing to attention next to the bed, as relaxed as ever, a picture of all innocence. You'd swear he hadn't a care in the world, the same man! The Sergeant would've bawled him out of it – I'd say – only the Lieutenant was present. We could see that he was raging though, especially after all he'd taught us on preparing the kit for inspection, the veins in his jaw bulging with anger. They spent a good while checking Hartnett's stuff, the Quartermaster listing everything that was missing. They were just done when the Lieutenant turned back suddenly and asked Hartnett what books he had at the bottom of his bag. The Sergeant took out one of them and all three men had a good gawk at it. It was a small booklet entitled *Enlisted; or, My Story*, one of those small Protestant pamphlets that was published during the Victorian era, then exchanged quick glances as much as to say: 'we had to find one of them now, didn't we – God help us!' They were gone then again, faces clouded with that tormented and long-suffering look of theirs.

# Chapter 5

It's a fortnight now since we left Galway, Maitias and I, and we've adapted fairly well to life here in that short space of time. I think I'd die now if they kicked me out of the army; not that we're fully safe here yet either, as we've to be 'finally approved' in another week's time. Anyone who isn't 'finally approved' gets the road. There are a good few lads here who couldn't care less really whether they're kicked out or not, but I know that I'd be really upset if I'm not kept on. I'm not sure that the lad from Tooreen or Hartnett will ever do any good here as they're really struggling with all the different drills. It's strange really because both of them are bright lads; it's just that they can't seem to get the hang of the drills no matter how often they do them. All the same, I think Sergeant Red is harder on me than he is on either of them, even if I'm not the worst here at drilling by any means. Today, we were learning how to shoot at particular positions and targets with the gun perched on a three-sided rest. 'The "top" of the front-sight needs to be set directly in line with the "U" on the back-sight and level with the shoulders' – as the book says. I thought my first shot was fairly accurate, but when Sergeant Red looked through the sight, he said: 'If it was just you and a giant elephant in a small room McCauley, I'd put money on it that you still wouldn't hit it.' Another Irish speaker has just arrived here, a lad named Hynes from Claregalway, but he won't be assigned to our company. He's up on the next floor above, but he was down to us for a visit this evening. He spent a good while chatting to us and warned us not to let any of the officers or the O.N.C.'s hear that he speaks Irish in case they decide to put his name down for *An Chéad Chath*.[8] He doesn't want to be sent to Galway after he's trained, for some reason. I have to pick out a small present to send on to Margaret for Christmas. She's far too kind, the creature. The Abbeyfeale man is 'confined to barracks' for the next week now. Not that he minds too much. He's a sort of a philosopher-type, the same fellow, and he's always very relaxed and easy-going. Nothing stresses him unduly and he's always in good form. When 'Faillitheoirí' ('Dossers') sounded on the bugle there a while ago, it didn't knock a stir out of him. He just laid the book he was reading aside and slowly ambled off to the guard-room where he's on duty. I've never once heard him utter a rude word to anyone in the room, even if some of the other lads, especially Maitias, are often hard on him. The Limerick-man has a dignity about him despite his awkwardness as a soldier and you can't help but like him. He's a funny-looking fellow really, low-sized and sturdy – a small butt of man. And he's always untidy and thrown-together, even when in uniform. He'd remind you of a poor rural person from the Ukraine or somewhere, someone who'd been taken prisoner by the Germans and forced to join their army during the war. We had to run a couple of miles today in those light athletics shoes called *gym shoes* – to give them their official Army name – but this is nothing to what lies ahead. We'll soon have to run five miles in full battle-dress in under fifty minutes. We have to complete this before we're allowed to pass out and complete our stint here officially. Each recruit is given three chances at this and if he fails on the third attempt, he's not kept on and has to leave the army. Rattigan, from the room above, was running beside me today and giving out stink non-stop, even if he was gasping for breath at the same time. The fact that he was suffering so badly yet still whining gave me hope in a way. If he can finish the run within the allotted time, then so can I, except that I'll be keeping my mouth firmly shut.

He might be an officer, but the Lieutenant of our platoon is the nicest fellow you could ever meet. It's not that he won't give you a hard time when you need it because he will; it's just that he has a really good way about him and is very good at talking to us recruits. He lets you know that he's an officer, but that he's human at the same time – and that he cares about the men under his command. From what I've seen so far, these younger officers who're just straight out of Military College are much nicer than the older crowd. They say that the training the officers do is much tougher and more intensive than what we regular soldiers do. That's only right too, of course. As with Fionn Mac Cumhaill and the Fianna long ago – it's not like they can ask the foot soldiers to do anything that they can't do themselves.

I've to get my stuff ready now for the morning – especially if I'm to have any chance of getting out for a drink tonight. '06 has had a wash earlier and has 'thrown a bit of a shape' on himself and I can see him licking his lips already. He has the look of a man who has a thirst on him.

# Chapter 6

I drank too much porter last night and, signs on it, I'm fit for nothing today. '06 was grand. The only thing bothering him this morning was that he was hungry, but I barely ate anything at breakfast, I was in such a bad way. I'd nearly swear the Sergeant knew what was on me because he tore into the marching when the parade was over as if his life depended on it, and I felt like I was going to collapse at any moment.

Although the morning was cold outside, I was sweating and my legs were weak as water. We got some nice soup to eat around eleven o'clock and I felt better after that. By dinner-time, I was back to my normal self again – or nearly anyway. There's a lad in the company here from County Leitrim and he must have the *craos deamhain* ('demon of gluttony') or the *alp luachra*⁹ inside him because he's always hungry, the poor lad. He hangs around the canteen until everyone's left hoping to get a bit of leftover *buckshee*,¹⁰ and it doesn't matter how much he gets of it, he can eat it. He has a great store of old songs and the lads in the room have him tormented asking him to sing different songs. He's shy at first but once he gets going, there's no stopping him. He sang 'The Woods of Drumboe', 'Down by Lough Sheelin's Side', 'The Star of Donegal' and God knows how many other songs for us today and to give him his due, he's a good singer. There's no harm in that lad at all and it doesn't bother him in the slightest that the lads are always badgering him to sing for them. *An Bhadhbh* (The Banshee) is what '06 calls him.

One task that I haven't managed to get the hang of at all yet is folding the groundsheet correctly. You have to spread it out on the floor first and fold it really neatly and tightly, so perfectly that it'll fit into the small pack that acts as a cover for it. Maitias and '90 Murphy do a nice job of this but myself, Hartnett and '06 just can't get a handle on it at all. I tried it a couple of times the other day but with no success and the Sergeant said to me:

'The way you throw it out, it's like you're throwing something at a hen or shooing it out the door. There are two ways of doing something McCauley – the right way and the wrong way – and leave it to you to do it the wrong way.' The Sergeant has no confidence in me as regards my soldiering skills at all. He says that he feels himself aging since he began training our platoon and he'll be older again by the time he's finished training me, I'm afraid! I've to leave this folding of the groundsheet routine aside for the moment now and start cleaning. '06 is across from me now eating sweet-cakes as fast as he can stuff them into his gob. I've never seen a man to eat food like him before.

Our Company (One Company) had a long slow-march in full battle-dress today. Every man brought an extra pair of socks in his pack and a piece of soap. The soap is to rub on the socks in case your shoes blister your feet at any stage. We were all full of energy and determination setting out. Once we'd covered the first couple of miles, we were given permission to speak and the lads were all chat and jokes. The further we walked though, the less the conversation. The weight of all the battle-gear and the muskets began to kick in and no one had the energy for chat anymore. As for myself, although I'm not that athletic really, there's one thing I can do and that's keep walking. I could walk forever. And, whatever it is, I forget about the weight of the musket and all the kit, the further I walk. After a while, I forget that I'm carrying all that heavy stuff at all. The other lads might have been getting quieter and quieter but not Rattigan! He was as mouthy as ever!

'This is ridiculous I'm telling you,' he says. 'This makes no sense whatsoever. We've done these long marches loads of times already and there's absolutely no need for us to do it again. The Company Captain is just working up his appetite for dinner, that's all. It's just an excuse for him to go wandering halfway around the county, but we're the ones who've pay for it with sore feet and numb shoulders. That fellow will have pheasant and roast steak and a big bottle of wine for his dinner, I guarantee you, but what'll we get? We'll have feck-all, that's what – just whatever's left over from that bunch of hooligans in Company Two – because it'll be too bloody late by the time we're finished this march.'

He went on and on like this for ages and there was no part of the training here that he didn't slate. There was no officer or O.N.C. here who escaped his censure either. In the end, the Platoon Commander told him to shut up.

'Giving out again, Rattigan, are we?' I've never once seen you that you weren't complaining about something or other. I can't for the life of me understand what brought you back to the army again, seeing as you hate military life so much.' This wound up Rattigan even more, it goes without saying.

'I was lured back in, that's what happened,' he shouted out crankily. 'I was lured back in. There wasn't a day that I went down to sign on or collect the *dole* that I didn't see posters everywhere telling me to join the army again. 'Join the Irish Army today', 'Join the Forces'. You couldn't spit but hit one of those bloody posters. They were everywhere. In the end, they brainwashed me so much that I went all the way to Castlebar, nearly thirty miles away, to enlist.'

'It's a pity you ever bothered,' says the Commander, 'the Defence Forces wouldn't have missed out on much if you'd never re-enlisted.' Rattigan was raging by then and retorted bitterly – 'Well, no offence Commander, but I was in the Defence Forces before you even knew what end of a gun the bullets came out of,' he says. We all burst out laughing at this, and the poor Platoon Commander had to shut it. He couldn't say nothing to this because that's what counts most in the army when it boils right down to it – how much time you've spent in the forces. The way the old-timer who's spent more than twenty years in the army sees it, the red-arsed new recruit has little standing or importance; how long you've spent in the army is everything. And it's the exact same with the recruits who've just completed their initial training; they look down their noses on the latest batch of recruits just in the door.

We were allowed rest after a while and the air was full of groans and the sound of pack-straps being undone and guns and other heavy gear being left down on the ground; that and the sound of a dozen cigarettes sparking into life. Our break didn't last too long however, and we were on our way soon again. Of all the lads in our platoon, I was one of the lads who suffered least on this march – even if I say so myself. Maitias and '90 Murphy were the other two. Maitias has great stamina and even if Murphy isn't as strong as him, he's hardy and stubborn and hates to see anyone get the better of him in a competition. We were wrestling in the room the other night, myself and himself, and I managed to get the better of him in the end. Not because I was physically stronger than him – but just that I was a bit cuter about it and took full advantage of a few mistakes he made. You should've seen the look of disappointment on his face when I let him up off the floor after he'd given in. We'd have to have another bout later on again because he wasn't at all happy that I'd beaten him so easily. '06 Reaney and I were talking about it later and '06 reckons that '90 Murphy is just one of those types who has to confront every challenge that comes his way in life head-on. He can't let anything go in that regard, not until he's managed to overcome it. There's always fierce competition between himself and Maitias to see which of them has the cleanest shoes, and whose uniform brass is shining brightest on parade. If you were to see the pair of them arranging their kit, you wouldn't hold out much hope for yourself, that's for sure. They both use wooden 'clothes-horses' inside their shirts and underwear when they hang them up to make sure that their clothes are absolutely perfect and stiff for inspection. When they lay out their uniforms and other clothes on the bed, you'd swear that they're even neater and more perfect than the official regulations as outlined on the wall-charts of every military barracks in the country. I think Maitias is probably even more perfect when it comes to neatness than the other man, although there's little between them. '90 is probably better than Maitias when it comes to remembering all the 'fine print' of the regulations we've been issued with and this is because of the schooling he's received. The National Schools in Munster obviously provide the children with a really good education, maybe better than in other parts of the country. For example, I've yet to meet anyone from County Limerick who hasn't had a really good knowledge of history, geography and mathematics etc. My own father didn't go past National School himself, but there were very few questions about maths or geography that he didn't know the answer to.[11]

We've school here once a week, by the way. I had to laugh the other day watching '06 Reaney, a man who's been to University, having to sit down and write an essay entitled 'A Day by the Sea.' Talking of school, the Irish-speaking platoon has the reputation for learning, and not without reason either. After all, three lads in our platoon were attending university before they joined – '06 Reaney, Begley, and another lad who joined just recently, Maurice O'Riordan[12] from Cork. O'Riordan's a very nice lad altogether and thousands of people know of him because he played hurling for Cork – they'd know him as 'Mossy' O'Riordan, of course. And the fact that I wear glasses now means that lots of them here think I'm as educated as these other lads!

They call me 'Dev' or 'Professor' here a lot. And things have changed a bit in relation to the Irish too. Before this, some of the recruits were teasing us Irish speakers about the language but now they've a lot more respect for us in this regard. Actually, the English-speakers in the company are kind of proud now of the fact that they have an Irish-speaking platoon amongst them.

A good few lads had to drop out of the slow march today before the end and they'd to send the ambulance out for them as far as I know. Rattigan himself would have dropped out only that he wouldn't have it said that the Platoon Commander had got the better of him. Incredibly, he never let up with his carping and whining all day. Even when the lads were returning to camp again, he was still moaning about sore feet and cut shoulders and all the rest of it.

We're stretched out on our beds now relaxing after dinner and tea – we got the two meals nearly one after another today – and '06 is munching away on his biscuits and sweets now 'as happy as Larry'. There's no fear but that Martin Nee will work his ticket once we're finished here as he hasn't the slightest interest in army life. He's on C.B. nearly all the time these days and the poor devil doesn't seem to care one way or another either. He cleans his gun about once a century and as Sergeant Red says, he has old moss growing on his brass buttons. If he'd already been 'finally approved', there's no way he'd get away with any of this crack. He'd be shoved into the guard-room until he came to his senses and that'd be the end of that. The way things are at the moment though, he'll just be let away with his mistakes for another while before they release him completely from the army. There's a good few mornings where he tells the sergeant that he wants his name put down on the doctor's list. If you want to 'go to bed sick', the doctor or the orderly will come and see you immediately. This is a dangerous game though! If they decide that you're not really that sick, they may give you a light 'duty' to do, a few small jobs as a room orderly or whatever. If they decide that you're not really sick at all, they'll give you 'medicine and duty' which means a big spoon of some awful-tasting stuff and out with you on parade then. You can be charged too with letting on to be sick and if you're found guilty of this, the punishment's a harsh one. Because

Martin's been in hospital quite often over the past year however, it'd be a tough one for them to say that he's only pretending to be sick. They aren't too hard on him as a consequence and he's regularly assigned to the position of Room Orderly for our room. I never met anyone who's more wary of strangers than him and Martin. He keeps to himself and I'd say he's barely spoken more than two words to any of the other lads who've little Irish here. He does talk to '90 Murphy the odd time alright, but the latter is still 'a stranger' in his eyes. The fact that Martin has very little English is probably the main reason for his shyness in this regard, I'd say.

There's another lad in this platoon for the last short while whose spoken-Irish is very fluent altogether – wherever he learned it – especially for a lad who's not from the Gaeltacht. Gerry Gavanly's his name. I'll never forget the first night that he arrived to our platoon. A young lad, he has curly blonde hair, which gives him an innocent and baby-faced look. Most new lads walk into the room shyly, kit-bag in hand. Not Gerry though! He burst into the room like a tornado and flung his kit-bag down onto an empty bed, then launched himself up the room spouting Irish to beat the band! Old wise sayings and phrases on the necessity of reviving the ancestral language and all the rest of it. He had them all! Sidling up next to the fire and scanned the room and then launched into a lecture on the cowardice of all who profess to be in favour of the Irish language but who never speak it – in addition to those who are simply against the Irish language full-stop. Gerry said that his father was in this army camp previously.

'I'll leave and enlist in the Irish-speaking *An Chéad Chath*' he announces to one and all. 'I'll have my own language and I'll have nationalism and culture and the ancestral wisdom of the Gaels all in one.'

'Where'll you get all those things now little brother – in *An Chéad Chath First Battalion* is it?' asked a bemused-looking Martin Nee.

'Definitely' says Gerry, his eyes scanning the rest of us again as if in challenge:

'How many native speakers are here? I don't like English, I'll have you know, and I don't intend speaking it either.'

It was as if he'd the lot of us under his command already because no man was brave enough to contradict him. Me and '90 Murphy told him that there were a few people who'd Irish from the cradle in the platoon and Hynes from Claregalway included himself in this category. Gerry rejected Hynes' claim with a dismissive wave of his hand, however. 'I don't include you,' he said, 'you don't have the right accent. You're from the Breac-Ghaeltacht[13] I'm sure, aren't you?' Hynes isn't someone who has a great love for Irish and nor would you ever assign the label of 'patriot' to him, but Gerry's dismissal of him stung him badly.

(*'Ara droch-rath ort a chunúis…'*) 'Arah, bad luck to you, you useless f——r,' he says. 'Shur, I've better Irish than you any day of the week,' he says with a pus on his face.

'*Cunús, cunús*' – now there's a word I don't have. I'll have to note that one down,' Gerry says, completely unfazed by Hynes, and delighted that he was already enriching his Irish and he only barely in the door. He gave a wide smile and addressed the room again:

'To speak a language is to make it live,' he said, 'well, it's about time we introduced ourselves. Gearóid Gabhlanlaigh (Gerard Gavanly) is my name.'

'What's the English for that?' said Maitias.

'Gavanly's what they call me in English, but I don't use that version of my surname,' he responded solemnly.

'So it's an English surname originally then?' says Maitias testily.

'No it's not. Not at all. It's an old Spanish surname originally,' says Gerry, unhappy at this turn in the conversation.

'We used to have Spaniards coming into our island long ago,' added Martin Cooke. 'They were a contemptible shower.'

'Yes, they're a brutal shower alright,' I said, joining in for the crack. 'What about the Spanish Inquisition?'

'They were a noble bunch when they stood with us in our time of need. What about the Battle of Kinsale?' Gerry countered, more subdued now.

'Arah, sure didn't the bastards let us down that time?' I says.

'I see that you have a habit of interpreting history in your own way,' your man retorted sarcastically. The attacks were coming in thick and fast now and Gerry decided to call time on the debate, if possible:

'Well, I'm no *apologia* for the Spanish anyway,' he says, 'and they've nothing to do with us in the army here anyway.'

'What's the social life like here lads? What d'you get up to here?' Gerry says, Little Hartnett staring perplexed at our newcomer all the while. It was as if he'd just come across a new specimen of humanity for the first time. The same went for '06 Reaney; he was so taken aback that he momentarily forgot the bun that he was stuffing his face with.

'What do we get up to?' Maitias said. 'I'll tell you what we get up to. We go marching and drilling and do slow marches and kit inspections, that's what we get up to.'

'Never mind that. Games and pastimes is what I mean. Do you put on dramas or musicals or anything like that? Man does not live on bread alone, you know,' says Gerry, looking in '06's direction. Before he'd a chance to discuss cultural matters any further though, he was called out to get sheets and blankets.

'Something tells me that we won't have it as peaceful in this room from now on,' says '06 with a sigh, after Gerry was gone. He's right, of course. There'll be sparks flying every night now I'd say, as we debate every aspect of Irish language and culture. All the talk of the revival of the Irish language reminded me of the Gaelic League meetings we used to have back in Kilkenny at one time. Gerry has a real fire and energy in him that the rest of us are lacking. He can't stay quiet for two minutes but is always giving his opinion on something or kicking off a new debate on some controversial question or other. He's not the best soldier in the world mind you; he's no better than any of the rest of us here. He doesn't do his training with us of course, since we're too far ahead of him now; he's in one of the most recently created platoons. He might well turn '06 Reaney off the Irish language altogether, I'm afraid.

# Chapter 7

We're training very hard these days. It looks as if they want to have us ready and out of here sooner than they'd originally planned. The recruitment campaign that began last year has proven very successful by all accounts as there are more new recruits coming in all the time, and they've to find places for them all. We were out on the range today firing live rounds and I didn't do too bad this time. I've never been that good when it comes to shooting at stationary targets before this, but I got 85 marks out of 120 this time while Maitias and Murphy both scored above 100. They'll both be gunners in the future and so they'll be allowed to sew a gunner's badge onto the sleeves of their uniform. It's a very nice badge too, this one. It's got an image of a bow-and-arrow on it and we'd all love to have one of them. All of us, except '06 Reaney that is. He's sick of it and couldn't care less at this stage. All he wants is to get this training over with and he'll be happy enough at that.

We reached the firing range fairly early today, but didn't start the shooting for a good while. You'd swear that they were deliberately delaying the start of it because they knew we couldn't wait to start the shooting practice. In the meantime, the targets were being raised and lowered in the booths and the officers and O.N.C.'s were having long conversations on their phones. Some of the lads got a bit impatient after a while and started complaining and next thing, we were ordered out for a long bout of drilling with the muskets! Finally … the order came through for us to begin firing the live rounds and we were allowed to lay out the ground-sheets and get ourselves into position. You jam the bolt of your musket firmly against your shoulder and wait for the order to be given – 'Loading five bullets'. It's a really strange feeling, I have to admit, when you load the live bullets into the breach! I nearly began to shake when I thought for a moment of the power that I now had – power held right there in my own two hands! Prior to this, the dummy bullets had been nothing more than toys really, harmless things that you got used to the same as someone'd get used to a pencil when writing. Now that there was live ammunition in the musket however, the gun had changed nature; it was no longer the innocuous object that I'd carried around with me as my permanent companion for the guts of two months. Even Sergeant Red himself – he'd changed too. Instead of giving out as normal, he was more understanding and went around now advising everyone about what to do and making sure that all the men were nice and relaxed.

'Take it nice and handy now; you've plenty of time. Get yourself settled nice and comfortable on the ground first. That's it. Remember now that you don't pull the trigger at all, you tighten it. The first squeeze and then the second. The front of the muzzle should line up with the centre of the rear-sight 'U' and directly in line with the shoulders. And keep the butt of the gun pressed tightly against the shoulders.'

This last bit of advice is particularly important as the gun gives a hell of a recoil when you fire it and if you don't have a very firm grip on the butt, your shoulder-bone will know all about it!

No sooner had I fired the first shot but the white wheel came back towards me indicating that I'd got a *bull*. I kept the burst of joy that coursed through me to myself, removed the empty cartridge and replaced it with another live round. Sergeant Red was next to me, advising me on technique, and I took quite a while before I fired a second time. I'd barely released the trigger when the white wheel returned again, and I'd got a second *bull*!

I felt like a gambler on a roll then, and I barely registered surprise when I got two *bulls* in a row with my next two shots! I had just one bullet left now and I was absolutely convinced that I could get the centre of target with this last shot. The red-haired fellow was singing my praises now, but it was as if he was trying to dampen my high expectations somehow also. I could barely hear him anymore though, I was on such a high by then. My heart was pounding in my ears and I was absolutely focused on getting that last bull. I fired my last shot and waited. The orderly in charge of the target was a bit slow feeding back the results this time, I thought, and when the small puff of smoke cleared, I was disappointed to find that my shot had gone completely astray. Not only had I not hit the red bullseye but I hadn't even hit the target! He waved the flag over and back to indicate same! I was really disappointed and embarrassed, but I could tell by the look on the faces of the platoon leaders that I wasn't the first recruit who'd been taken down a peg or two on the firing range.

We withdrew now to another firing area about 300 yards from the targets where we began quick-firing and slow-firing while wearing gas masks. This last form of training is the one that really kills the likes of me – someone who wears glasses. They have some stuff that you can rub on the inside of the gas mask to prevent them from fogging up, but it doesn't really work. You'd nearly be better off taking your glasses off altogether than trying to wear them beneath the gas mask. I only got a very low score on this drill – surprise, surprise! But Sergeant Red and the Lieutenant of our platoon were very happy with how we got on today overall. As soon as we got back to McDonagh Barracks, we'd to clean the muskets out with boiling water and plenty of 'four-by-two'. You do this by pulling a soft cloth through the barrel of the gun and applying the different liquids to it. This cleaning kept us busy for quite a while because water-tanks were brought out from the store and we poured of gallons of water (or so it seemed to me anyway) down the barrels of the muskets until they looked halfway-clean. They're going to do a strict inspection of the guns tomorrow morning and if there's anything wrong, we're in big trouble apparently. Like most other tasks they undertake here, Maitias and Murphy were finished way quicker than the rest of us and their guns way cleaner than ours, you can be sure of it. '06 Reaney was last back into the room here and you'd hardly have recognised him, his face was so filthy looking after cleaning his gun. He's sitting across from me on the bed opposite now drawing from the well of poetry – *Palgrave's Golden Treasury*, a big paper-bag of sweets beside him, and he's as happy as a piper.

Maitias has gone very quiet and withdrawn recently, whatever's up with him. He's also got very cranky too and never stops hassling poor Hartnett. He recently nicknamed him 'Blackpool', a name he uses as a form of insult. I don't know where this nickname came from or why Maitias deems it derogatory, but whatever the reason, Maitias's able to get any amount of sarcasm and derision into the word whenever he uses it. I can't understand for the life of me why Maitias has it in for Hartnett because you couldn't meet a nicer or more humble fellow anywhere.

Hartnett's Irish isn't good and it will never be either, even if he understands everything that's said to him in Irish. It's a pity really because he'd love to have better Irish and he has an unbelievable store of history and lore in that head of his. He reads *Ireland's Own*[14] and *Our Boys*[15] from cover to cover and his kit-box is full of Brian O'Higgins[16] publications and magazines and song-books. The other night he was telling us about something that he read recently. It was about the old people in County Tipperary who are the last Irish speakers there. A man was travelling through that county on foot around nightfall, and passing through the Comeragh Mountains came across a small group of people reciting the Rosary together in Irish at a crossroads there recently.

'It was in the most backward part of the county,' said Hartnett, although he didn't mean anything by this, I'm absolutely certain of it. But, oh little brother, he'd barely uttered those words when Maitias jumped up off his bed and went for him bald-headed. '*Bhoil, a Blackpool na buinní, a gheancacháin lofa*' ('Well, Blackpool of the scutters,[17] you rotten pointy-nosed yoke you'), he says, raging. 'If I hear you mocking the Irish language or the places where it's spoken ever again, I'll throw you out of the room here head-first. There's nothing "backward" about Irish or the people who speak it; not like the other crowd who can only speak pigeon-English, and that only half-properly anyway – the likes of that shower upstairs that Dónall was on about recently. Mind yourself now son or it'll be the worse for you; take it from me!'

The lad from Abbeyfeale got a fright and apologised profusely to us. It'd never been his intention to cause any offence to anyone or to demean the Irish language in any way, he said. Sure, how could he look down on Irish when he was as keen as anyone on becoming as fluent as possible in it? That was the end of the discussion that night, even if there was more than one lad there who wasn't a bit happy at the way Hartnett had been treated and that was '06 Reaney. He propped himself up on his elbow in the bed and gave Maitias a cold stare. He didn't say a word but gave him a filthy look instead. He was seriously pissed-off with him and rightly so because that was really nasty attacking Hartnett like that – especially seeing as he probably won't be in our platoon here for much longer either. Unlike the rest of us, '06 is not keen to have his stint here over with because he loves going horse-racing at the Curragh. He loves dog-racing too and says that this is the only part of Galway life that he really likes whenever he goes home. Still, I'd be surprised if he didn't get sick of a place like this eventually, especially when he realises properly what it's like here all-year round. A bare and isolated area like this that's cut off from most of the rest of the world is grand for someone who isn't the brightest or who's got very few hobbies. Say, the likes of an older soldier whose only interest in life is collecting his pay and spending it within a night or two on drink and cards. The type of fellow who's happy enough the rest of the week stretched out on his bed and staring up at the bare walls of the barracks. Any man interested in drama or other cultural-related activities would soon get sick of a place like this though. Lads like Begley and O'Riordan are the types who want to get ahead in the army, but I don't think '06 Reaney thinks the same way they do.

Hartnett from Abbeyfeale, as well as Connery, and Nee were released and sent home today. The first two lads made a sorry sight as they gathered their kit together and put it back in the store, and it felt strange when they arrived back in again wearing their civvies. It was as if an unseen barrier had already gone up between them and the rest of us who were still in our army uniforms. The Quartermaster gave each of them a suit, a shirt and a cap. Hartnett put his cap on straight away and it made him look like a right country bumpkin, even if the poor man thought he was the bee's knees! Martin Nee arrived in next, a smirk on his face, and he dressed from head to toe in one of those *Martin Henry*[18] suits as they're known. This suit didn't do much for poor Martin though. He had his cap perched sideways on his head and it was obvious that he didn't care how he looked really – anything, so long as he didn't have to wear the Army uniform anymore. Poor Hartnett went around and shook hands with each of us – even Maitias – and you could tell that he was close to crying when he left the room. Connery was too shy to go around shaking everyone's hand, but even a blind man could tell that he was really upset at having to leave. As for Nee, he couldn't get out of here fast enough. He was blue in the face telling the others to get a move on so they wouldn't be late for the train in Kildare.

The room seemed strangely empty when the lads were gone even if it's not that long ago really since that first day when Maitias and I were the only two here. There are seven of us left now only one of whom will still be here in a few days' time seeing as everyone's going home for Christmas – everyone except '06 Reaney that is. He'll find it lonely here by himself, I'll bet.

# Chapter 8

They're pushing us hard these days, no doubt about it. The rumour is that we'll be leaving here in the first week of March. The sooner the better as far as I'm concerned. I'm more impatient now to be finished since we came back from the holidays. Maitias went back to Galway of course, and he told me that Margaret was very disappointed that I didn't go back on a visit, especially as she's thinking of going to England if she doesn't get a better job soon. She finished up in the hospital a while back and has been working in a private house out in Salthill since. She doesn't like it much there though as the people who own the house aren't very nice to her and they think it's funny that she doesn't speak much English as well.

Of course, I was sad that I couldn't go down to Galway during the break but my parents would've thought it strange if I didn't spend some time down in Kilkenny with them, especially given that they're just two hours away from here. The train to Kilkenny was jam-packed with people returning for Christmas, most of whom were back home from England. They were all dressed in their poshest clothes and had loads of money, or so it seemed anyway. Half of them were putting on a bit of an English accent and as you'd expect, these were the ones who'd only just recently moved to England. I met a fellow who was at school with me and although it's less than a year since I last met him, he nearly had me deafened with all his: 'D'you remember him?' and 'Where d'you think he's gone to now?' and 'I'll hardly return home now – only for the holidays …' He had a fine suit on and a gold-strap wristwatch that he consulted every two minutes. The fact that the train was delayed really bothered him he said, and the sub-text of his conversation was that things are way better across the water than they are here. Everything worked better over there – according to him anyway – and there were never any delays like this. I felt like saying to him that he was a bigger fool to waste money on a trip home so, especially if it's as backward here as he's making out. It won't be long before the shine of his new life across the water wears off; the more he gets used to life over there, I thought to myself, the more it'll seem the same as everywhere else.

I was telling another lad about this fellow on the train when I was in Kilkenny over the Christmas and he said to me that your man was at the same crack when he was talking to him as well – just the day before I met him on the train! They were standing on the steps of the Tolsel in High Street when your man glanced down at his watch:

'Oh I say,' he announced. 'There used to be an old clock around here someplace at one time, wasn't there?' He was referring to the clock that stands on top of the Tolsel, of course.

'Well, there used to be and there still is,' the other lad said to him. 'It was here when your great-grandfather ran around here as a child and it'll still be here when our children's children are grown up too, I'd say.'

It's hard enough putting up with the posing and shite-hawking of someone who's back from Australia, never mind England!

Something's really bugging Maitias for the past while. He's not the same man at all. He doesn't go out at night anymore but just stays in, sitting on his bed, polishing his shoes and organising his gear. He has a full kit-box now and it's really something to behold. He keeps it as neat as a pin and he's even added a small wooden shelf to it where he keeps his *brasso*, his *blanco*, and different polishes. You have to wet the *blanco* before applying it to different types of equipment. It comes in a small block and has a round hole at the top of it. You wet it first and then you apply it and polish it in using a small brush. And whatever it's applied

57

to has to be washed beforehand too so that when the *blanco* dries in, you use a dry brush for the polishing. It looks great when the job is done correctly, but there are plenty of us here who can't seem to apply the *blanco* evenly enough; when it's not applied evenly, you end up with bright and dark patches all over whatever you're polishing instead of a nice even polish. Nothing ruins parade more than if all the equipment isn't the same colour and it drives Sergeant Red mad as well.

Gerry Gavanly's being trained in an English-speaking platoon now and he's not too happy about this arrangement at all. If he isn't mixing with us during the day, he's in our company every evening and when he starts talking there's no stopping him. Politics, the language issue, how to dance the different Irish dance-steps correctly, how much he hates the Shoneens;[19] these are his favourite subjects of conversation. I don't mind listening to him, but his constant chatter is really getting on '06 Reaney's nerves at this stage. Maitias has started slagging Gavanly off a bit now too, now that he doesn't have the small man from Abbeyfeale to tease anymore, but Gerry's well able to look after himself. Needless to say, you'd get tired of Gerry's antics sometimes even if he wouldn't annoy you for long. When you think of it, Gerry's still barely out of his teens and still trying to figure this world out for himself.

\* \* \*

God help us, but I nearly shot the head off Sergeant Red today by accident. We were shooting small mortars from our guns, and I was a bit jittery, and pulled the trigger before the Sergeant had stepped back fully out of the way. He'd just slotted the mortar into position and it nearly singed him, it went that close to his face. Jesus, I nearly died when I realised how close I came to killing him! I was sure that he was going to kill me for this but, strangely enough, he didn't say too much to me at all. I think he probably took one look at me and saw how shaken I was myself, and decided there was no point. This is always the way with Sergeant Red, though. He's unpredictable and you never know what he's going to do next. He could give out yards to you one minute for something small and the next minute, you could really feck-up and he wouldn't say anything at all to you.

There's another Irish speaker in the room with us now, Darach Ó Maoilbhríde from Carna. He enlisted in Athlone yesterday and was sent down here by train the same as ourselves. He's a well-built and handsome lad and he even has a trace of moustache already. That'll be duly shaved off by tomorrow, I'm sure. He has the real Connemara 'look' about him and he's a bit of a 'man-about-town' by all accounts, seeing as he's as fluent in English as he is in his native language Irish. He's not a bit shy like the other lads, but then why should he be? This isn't his first time in an army barracks. He's already spent a few years in the English airforce and a while in the Irish Navy too. And prior to that again, he spent a time in the Manufacturing Unit of the Irish Army. He's picked up a bit of an English accent so that even when he talks to you in Irish, he's using words like 'blimey' or 'blow me'. I took to him straight away – even if there's probably a bit of the 'Jack the Lad' about him. Maitias didn't like him from the very beginning though, for some strange reason. Darach Ó Maoilbhríde's a very able individual and reads people well. The minute he realised that Gerry Gavanly was a committed Gael, he was straight over to him and the pair of them debating the preservation of the Irish language and other similar things – subjects that are close to Gerry's heart. Next thing, the two of them headed out to the canteen to continue their discussion. I'll put money on it that Gerry'll be paying for whatever treats they get there! I've never really liked that canteen much for some reason and other than to have the odd cup of tea there, I wouldn't bother with it all really. Some recruits play billiards in there and others just sit around listening to the radio. I much prefer to stay here in the room or head out to the Pictures every now and then. I don't understand why they don't have a library in this barracks though, because there'd be a big demand for it, I've no doubt.

'06 Reaney's sitting across from me now and he's trying to catch my attention. He probably wants to go out for a few jars tonight, I suppose. We went into Newbridge last night where we'd a good few drinks. It's alright for him though; unlike me, he doesn't have to send any few pence home.

'90 Murphy's busy writing again. He's writing home, as he often does. I've never seen anyone here to get as many letters as he does; not that you'd begrudge him them, seeing as he's such a good correspondent himself. Maitias's polishing his shoes with the tip of his index finger. You'd nearly see yourself reflected in those shoes now, they're that shiny. Not that Maitias'd take any heed of you if you said this to him. He'd just keep polishing away. He gets letters often from Juleen, but it's a good while now since I last got one from Margaret. She hated it working in that private house in Salthill and the chances are that she's left that now.

No doubt about it but that Darach Ó Maoilbhríde is a funny son of a gun. He's so confident in himself that you'd swear he'd been in this barracks for years and considers every other recruit here a bit of a joke. I don't understand this cocky attitude of his or where he gets his confidence from though. It's not as if he's the greatest soldier the world has ever seen either. He's good at the foot-drills and the musket drills but other than that, there's no other obvious reason for him to be so full of himself. His kit-box is a disgrace and he's always looking to borrow *brasso*, shoe polish and 'four-by-two' from others. He annoys the hell out of poor Maitias too with his 'You're the love of my heart Maitias; could you give me a small drop of *Ruby*' or 'just the shell's shite of a bit of toothpaste there please, Maitias'. Now Maitias's not miserly or mean by any means; he just likes for every man to have his own supplies. He's the type who'd go and buy his own stuff rather than constantly asking someone else for the loan of this, that and the other. You wouldn't mind if Darach showed Maitias a bit of respect after he borrows stuff from him but he doesn't. He'll even come over and take a look at Maitias's kit-bag and tell him that it's a right disgrace, a total mess.

'Blimey, Maitias boy, if you think that you've packed that kit-bag properly there, you're badly mistaken. If you check the diagram down on the door there below ...'

'Ara, would you ever give over, you'd swear your own manky box was nice and neat; you'd be better off now minding your own business, so you would,' Maitias says. He's at the end of his tether with your man.

'Alright, matey cock, I was only trying to help you,' your man says then, not a bit fazed by Maitias's telling him where to go. The next time, Ó Maoilbhríde's stuck for something, and Maitias won't give it to him, he'll be over to me probably ...

Gavanly was his most loyal worshipper in the beginning and they were great friends, heading off together to Newbridge or to céilí's and Irish-language classes in Kildare. Gerry was as happy as a sand-boy with all this talk about the promotion of the Irish language, nationalism, and the sharing of ancient wisdom ...

Mind you, he had to give Ó Maoilbhríde a lot of *brasso*, shoe polish and 'Mac's Smiles' in return for this exchange of Gaelic culture. This only lasted a while, though. They're not as good friends anymore, though – especially since Gerry became more open about lending his stuff to others and not just Ó Maoilbhríde. Darach still goes out every night funnily enough, even if no one's too sure where he goes. I know that he's really obsessed with the Pictures – but unless he's going to see the same film two or three nights a week, he must be disappearing off somewhere else. I wouldn't put it past him that he's made friends with people living out in Brownstown or one of those other villages, and that he heads out there drinking tea and eating slices of bread in the evenings.

He's got a hard neck anyway and he can spout lies for Ireland. It's true that he spent some time in the RAF and in the Irish Navy but other than that, I'm not sure I'd believe a word he tells us. Still and all, he's a very nice fellow and I'd rather him here than not. Maitias claims that I only see the good in people for some reason – even in cute hoors and oddballs.

* * *

We ran five miles today in full battle-dress, carrying our packs – all our equipment including helmet, musket and dagger, and we were all completely exhausted by the end of it. Everyone in First Company did the run. We set off from Pearse Barracks and down by the old graveyard and followed along the edge of the plain and the southern end of the firing range. From there, we followed the back-road until we'd done a semi-circle and then back along the main road on the Newbridge side. It was five miles in total and it was tough. I felt so bad after the first mile that I was sure there was no way I'd finish it. I was gasping for air and my feet felt like two massive lumps of lead, I was really struggling. The bloody musket was as heavy as a rail-track, and like Rattigan on that slow march a while back, my pack was cutting into my shoulders. I kept going somehow and after a while, I began to feel a bit stronger. My breathing became more regular so that I was even able to exchange a few words of conversation with '06 who was closest to me. The last mile was brutal altogether though, and by the time we were finished, everyone was shattered. Maurice O'Riordan, who's as fit and lean as a wolf, just flew along the road effortlessly. He could have left us all behind easily, if he wanted to – but he's not a show-off like that. Maitias managed to keep slightly ahead of '90 Murphy for the duration of the run and that really bothered the Limerick-man, I'd say, he's got such a strong competitive streak in him. That five miles would break most men, and I was really happy once it was over. We left all our equipment back in the room and made for the baths. A change of clothes and a bath, and everyone felt much better again. Everyone demolished their afternoon meal I can tell you.

Ó Maoilbhríde is some boyo! Today, he asked me for a 'loan' of a half-crown and would you believe it – he invited me and Gerry to the Pictures with it? They were showing *Great Expectations*, and it was a great film in my opinion. Given the solemnity with which Darach directed proceedings as we took our four-penny seats, you'd have sworn we were sitting in the dearest seats in Covent Garden over in London! He went off at one stage to buy ice cream and a handful of sweets for us, and then doled them out to us with a formality that'd have put you in mind of one of the gentry long ago dividing out alms amongst his subjects. He's a cheeky, ignorant fecker in ways too though, especially the way he constantly demeans the new recruits and takes the piss out of them for no reason. Actually, he'd a brief argument with one of these new recruits down in the Picture house tonight when he told this one fellow to get his big head out of the way of the screen! When your man didn't oblige straight away, Darach started taunting him and calling him a 'ploughboy'.

'There are far too many rednecks being brought into the Army these days, I'm afraid,' he says in English at the top of his voice – just in case the lad he'd called 'ploughboy' hadn't heard him already! Your man didn't take too well to this though. Not that this fazed Darach one bit. On our way out the door, what does he do but turn around to all and sundry and announce in a loud voice in English again:

'That was a good Picture young lads. Boy, but I got one hell of a "sensation" when that old witch frightened the young lad inside in the room that time.' I wouldn't mind, but Darach has the richest Irish of anyone in the platoon when he sets his mind to it. He just has a slight lisp when he speaks. I'd say he's the type of fellow that lives for today and doesn't give a toss about what happened yesterday or what might happen tomorrow. He has his wages spent very quickly which is strange really because he doesn't drink at all. I think poor Maitias has aged a bit more since Darach's arrival; that hangdog look comes over him for some reason every time he runs into the man from Carna.

\* \* \*

## Renmore Barracks

Well, we know now that we won't be here too much longer. We've completed nearly all our training and Sergeant Red says that we weren't the worst platoon he's ever trained either. That's a bit of a compliment really, coming from him! Strangely, now that I know we're finishing up, I'm not half as impatient to get out of here as before. Who knows? Maybe, I'll even miss this place a bit after a while.

'*Ar Churrach Chill Dara sea scar mé le mo grá mo chroí*' ('On the Curragh of Kildare is where I separated from the love of my heart') the old song goes, but there will be no one here who'll be missing the Curragh that much! Not unless their 'first love' are the green plains of Kildare and the constant pangs of hunger – even if the food we get is very good here – or the loneliness that haunts the place every Saturday and Sunday afternoon when the newest recruits take their long aimless walks and are the only ones who stir from their rooms. Even if I remember this place more fondly once I'm gone, that doesn't mean I'm not looking forward to going west across the Shannon again. I don't know whether I'll meet Margaret when I'm in Galway again as I haven't heard from her for a good while and Juleen hasn't mentioned her in any recent letters of hers either. One way or another, we'll have a nice time over the summer as there's nowhere nicer in the world than Galway when the weather's fine. We've been in the Curragh here the guts of nine months now, and we're much tougher and healthier now than when we first enlisted. And even if the majority of us are always hungry, we haven't lost weight – except '06 that is – and he needed to lose some weight. We're experts on every type of marching and drilling with guns now. Even our Army uniforms sit better on us now, I think. We won't be deemed 'rookies' anymore either please God, once we've left the Curragh.

The room is very quiet these days. This is because Gerry Gavanly is in the Military Hospital at the moment and Darach Ó Maoilbhríde is gone out on his ticket. We went down to see Gerry a few times and the only thing bothering him is how soon he'll be back with us here in the Curragh. I don't know exactly why Ó Maoilbhríde was given his ticket. All I know is that he was summoned before the Company Captain a few days ago and when he came out, he'd had a change of heart about a lot of things. Before this he never stopped going on about his knowledge and military skills but now he's cynical about everything to do with the army and wonders why anyone would even bother enlisting. 'It's a funny life in ways, the army life,' he says, 'when you think about it. You've to accept orders from a bunch of mutton-heads who aren't much better than yourself. You wouldn't mind if they were brilliant at what they do, but as I said to the Captain when I was in talking to him, I've forgotten more about soldiering than some of them ever learned in the first place. God knows, it'd be a fine thing to be free and not to have to worry anymore about stupidity like polishing shoes and brass buttons and the like!' Maitias' eyes widened at this and he whispers across to me:

'I hope to the dutiful Son of God that they're releasing him. I'd say that's what's finally happening.' Maitias was right, sure enough – and more's the pity. He's very astute about stuff like this and has probably seen this sort of thing before when he was in the Manufacturing or

Engineering Corps. Anyway, Darach said goodbye and God bless to everyone and as far as we could tell, he wasn't too put out at all at being released. I know that I, for one, will definitely miss his lively presence in the room. The day's coming soon when we're all finally done here. We're to be sent by train to Renmore Barracks, Galway the day after tomorrow with the help of God. Everyone's up to 'high-doh' now because of our company's *March Out Parade* tomorrow. None of us were let out any night for the past three or four days and we were kept busy scouring floors, cleaning windows, and applying black paint to the hearths and mantles. And that's not even half of we've to do either. We must've cleaned the guns and polished our uniforms and equipment more than twenty times already and you wouldn't believe how many kit inspections we've had in the last week alone.

Lieutenant-Colonel Collins-Powell is doing the inspection of kit and rooms after the parade tomorrow and I'd say he'll show no mercy if he finds anything out of place or anything that he's not happy with. Sergeant Sullivan is like a hen on the griddle the last while; one minute he's giving out to us, the next he's encouraging us and driving onto do better. If we can just get over tomorrow without any mistakes, we'll be grand. I was so nervous that I failed to answer nearly every question he asked me a short while ago, even though I've answered the same questions no problem loads of times before. I think he understood that it was just nerves though, because he wished me the best of luck in the *Céad Chath* when he was saying goodbye. He's a fine, manly sort of fellow, a man you couldn't help but have the height of respect for.

\* \* \*

We got through today without any major mishaps, thank God – the parade, the kit inspection and everything. Once it was all over, you were asking yourself what all the fuss was about and why we were so stressed about it all! It reminded me of the visits of the inspector to the National School long ago. We spent ages getting ready for it, preparing and learning everything we'd to do and say, and the schoolmaster (like Sergeant Red here) threatening us and cajoling us in equal measure. Afterwards, he would tell the schoolmaster to give us a half-day after he'd finished his inspection and we'd be left wondering what all the worry and stress had been for in the first place.

The parade was really something to behold. It was an incredible sight out on the big square with the sun shining down on a hundred unsheathed daggers and bright brass uniforms. The ordered crunch of boots marching in rhythm over and back across the square and the mathematical perfection as all ranks marched in unison. The officers calling out and repeating the orders from one company to the next, and the powerful band music filling our hearts with courage and pride. It was an occasion that will live with me forever. If this parade was the sole reward we had at the end of all the hardship and training here, it'd have been worth it.

We also had a presentation at tea-time in the canteen today. We'd organised a collection last week and each platoon presented their non-commissioned officers with a big box of cigarettes. In the case of our Irish-speaking platoon, it was Sergeant Red we made the presentation to. Each sergeant then made a brief speech to their platoon. The first sergeant to speak told us that he'd spent a good many years in the General Training Section and had put many different army companies through his hands, but that ours – Company One – was the best of the lot! Everyone clapped and cheered at this – except Rattigan, needless to say! He couldn't let it go …

'The same old shite every time,' he mouthed from the corner of his mouth. 'They say this to every company that's leaving! It's an old fib at this stage and you shouldn't believe a word of it! They'll spout the same rubbish to the next crowd who're released from here, I can guarantee you!' We were all on such a high that we paid him no heed, though. Seeing as tomorrow's Saint Patrick's Day, we received our pay today, and myself and '06 headed out to Brownstown to have a few drinks. I invited Maitias to come out with us if he wanted, but he said that he was happy enough to stay in and relax. He seems much happier in himself now though, as if some great weight has been lifted from him somehow. Who was in Williams' pub in Brownstown when we got there only Sergeant Sullivan and he gave us a great welcome as soon as he spotted us. He was a different man completely this evening – full of chat and the best of crack, and we spent the rest of the evening in his company. On our return, we said goodbye to him on the periphery of the Camp as the rules say that non-commissioned officers and regular soldiers aren't supposed to socialise with one another after hours of duty.

Well, that's us finished with the Curragh anyway. We'll be going to Galway the day after tomorrow, with the help of God. A thousand farewells to the frosty mornings out there on the square and the regular tongue-lashings of the red-haired fellow; and the sheep that'd almost come into the room to you, they came so close to the barracks; and the old woman selling sweets down at the corner on pay-day. We've waited a long time for this day and now it's finally here. There's a shiver of anticipation going up and down my spine.

\* \* \*

We reached Galway today around 3 p.m. on the train and there was a lorry waiting outside the station to transport us to Renmore. I was over the moon when we were finally let in through the barracks gates. My wish has finally come true and I'm now a soldier of the Irish-speaking *An Chéad Chath*!

I was on a total high. It was as if I was in Heaven, God forgive me! The minute we were off the lorry, we were ordered over to one of the rooms in Block 'B' to make our beds. It'll be a bit chaotic here for the next few days as they reorganise the Battalion, they tell us. We're not sure yet what Company each of us will be assigned to either – whether it'll be Company A, B, C, or D – the titles of the companies as they currently stand. This evening, we were told that we'll be training now again as hard as ever and that it'll be as if we did nothing at all down in Kildare! This barracks is very nicely laid out. Inside the front gate, on your left, is the guard-room and the battalion room and the Officer's Canteen to the right. Opposite the canteen is a fine grass park that edges the Parade Square. On one side of the square are Blocks A and B, two fine two-storey buildings, where infantry and non-commissioned officers sleep and opposite this again are the two canteens – one for the regular soldiers and one for the sergeants. The buildings here are all limestone and they look much better than the red brick they have up in the Curragh. The soldiers' quarters have high, narrow windows which really add to the look of the barracks.

I really wanted to call back to Knocknacarra so that all my relations could see me in uniform. I was reluctant to leave '06 and '90 Murphy by themselves in a town they're not familiar with though and so I brought them 'downtown' to show them around Galway city instead. Because I'm so proud of everything to do with Galway, I thought that they'd be too, but I was wrong

They haven't stopped giving out about the canteen here in Renmore since we arrived and they showed very little interest in the city either. I kept thinking I'd spot Margaret any minute as we made our way around town but no such luck. I can't understand why the lads are so critical of the place because Galway's a lovely city by any standards. The air here is soft and fresh, and the smell of the sea is really healthy. Galwegians are a relaxed and soft-spoken crowd of people too. And there's nothing nicer than to stand quietly for a while on the bridge in the centre of town and listen to the musical murmur of the water below as the peace and silence embraces you. Galway has many other fine aspects to it too that you won't find in any another city in Ireland, in my opinion. It's the only city in Ireland where you'll hear working-class people speaking Irish in the pubs or on the street-corners and you'll come across all types of people in this city. You see the Aran Islanders in their fine traditional costumes or the people in from Connemara in their white bawneen and the black Spanish-style hats, especially on fair-days and market-days. And there are the old people in from the other side of the county too who wear clothes that hark back to the nineteenth century and who still speak the Irish dialect of east Galway. In summer, the city is always very crowded with brightly dressed visitors and there's always a fiddler or an accordion-player belting out a tune on the streets. Everyone has heard of the Galway Races, and it would be difficult to find a more Gaelic crowd of people anywhere than the crowds who gather for the Races that week each summer.

As for the people of Galway town itself, they're very devout and always given to the 'poor mouth'; they're always bemoaning something that's happened and they tend to have a fatalistic outlook on life. And if anyone knows this, it's the likes of me, seeing as I was born just a few miles west of the city myself and some of my relations are exactly like this.

We walked the length of the town a few times before heading in for a pint. At one stage, I spotted Maitias and a few other soldiers down from me on the bridge chatting to a group of girls from back west, and I would've given anything to have joined them, but I couldn't abandon my two pals seeing as they're new to the town. What harm! My friends here will get used to the place fairly quickly and I'll be free to do whatever I want then.

We have this weekend to ourselves and we're free to do whatever we wish, other than that we've to be back in barracks before midnight each night, and we've the Mass Parade[20] tomorrow morning. You can apply for a a 'weekend pass', but you have to be in quick with your request. The way it works is that you write out your request and hand it to whoever is in charge of your room; normally, these requests aren't refused without good reason – unless you're down for guard-duty or something, say. None of our small platoon have been on guard-duty yet, but I'd say we will be soon.

The food here is nowhere near as good as it was in the Curragh; there's a fine big canteen here that's nice to go into though, and the kitchen is right next door. Some of the finest and strongest men that I've ever seen are in this barracks, many of whom are from the Aran Islands and Connemara. Still, the most numerous group of all here is from Donegal. I'm surprised at the amount of Irish that's spoken here, I have to say. I'd say only about a third of the men here actually speak Irish every day, but most men can speak Irish if they had to. As far as I can make out, it's only the native Irish speakers who use the language regularly, unless it's parade time or some other official occasion. Worse than this still, is the fact that this latter group use English only when speaking to people from the Gaeltacht. All the native speakers here use Irish only amongst themselves, and there are a number of them who've very little English.

There are no 'language enthusiasts' here, unless they're amongst the officers and the only reason that Irish is still the main language here is down to the native speakers really. Any lad who wanted to learn Irish couldn't find a better opportunity anywhere than by coming here. In fact, there are lads here who'd very little Irish when they first enlisted and who are now quite fluent, and who've picked up their Irish just by listening to others or by the way almost. How much better could someone's Irish be if they came in here with the deliberate intention of learning the language though? That's the real question.

'06 and the others had no interest in going out today and so I headed over to Knocknacarra to visit my relations. They were delighted to see me, especially my grandfather, and they asked me loads of questions about army life – the pay, the conditions and the discipline here and all the rest of it. I felt really proud of myself sitting there at the kitchen table as they questioned me about the military life! They were fairly busy with work down in Joe's house when I got there, so I didn't spend as long in that house as in the other place. I think that my cousin Pete may have been a bit jealous when I called in wearing my Army uniform.

'Pity that I didn't enlist with you that time and I'd be as good as you now,' he says.

'Musha, pity you didn't,' says Meaig, safe in the knowledge that he'll never enlist now, 'Pity you didn't; for all the good it's doing you here now, you'd be as well off over in Renmore.'

'Musha, shut up now Meaig, and put down a drop of tea for us there,' said Joe then; he doesn't like anyone else taking a swipe at Pete except himself that is.

They too asked me a lot of questions about the army while we were having tea, but I didn't mind that one bit. I enjoyed it really.

Poor Grandad is gone a bit doddery and confused. He's a good age now. He tried to stir himself once or twice and join in the conversation, but as far as I could make out, he didn't know that I was there at all. He just thought that the others were talking about me, that's all. 'That lad was mad to join the Army,' he says at one stage, 'mad, I swear!' But then again, where would he leave it? Didn't he see old Peter Condon running mad across the fields a few years ago, the same as a child would? He jumped the wall of the Goff and next thing he was running east like the wind!' Grandad seems to have forgotten that his own daughter is married to one of Peter Condon's sons; or maybe he doesn't care at this stage! The Galway Golf Club has been right next to us for the past twenty-one years, but my grandfather has only ever referred to it as the 'Goff'. He's over seventy now, but my grandfather still looks as fit as a fiddle; if he had to, he could still get up and sprint off as fast as a hare

I'd say. Who should I meet leaving Joe's house but Michaeleen South. 'Oh, hell's bells, but what brought you into the army?' he says. 'Oh shur, I've been in the soldiers for more than a year and a half now,' I told him, exaggerating a bit.

'By God, but if that's so, it's a life that suits you well, sonny,' he says. He was as nosey as the rest of them though – asking me how much I earned a week and whether they were very hard on us in the army and a thousand other things. They're all very curious about it when you meet them, and they're never satisfied with whatever answer you give them. They always want you to give them more, and there's no solicitor as able as them when it comes to asking questions and getting information out of you. And worse still, when you tell them what they want to know, they don't make much of it. They might as well have just asked you the time of day for all the interest they show. I told Michaeleen a fair few lies before I headed back into Galway again, then spent the rest of the evening wandering around the town. There were many nice women from Aran and Connemara knocking around, but I didn't see any sign of Margaret and I didn't meet any girl who knows her either. There's a good chance that she's gone off to England with the rest of them, I'd say. I have to ask Maitias whether Juleen has any news about her. Juleen herself is back west in her home-place in Connemara these days, and God knows when she'll be coming back to Galway town next. They've a very nice church in Renmore. It has lovely stained-glass windows and two big marble plinths on which the names of the Connaught Rangers killed in the First World War are inscribed. The sermon was given in Irish, of course. We had a nice, small breakfast after Mass and though I could've eaten twice that amount of food, if I'd got the chance. Renmore is a place that'd give you a very good appetite, similar to the Curragh, but you'd still be hungry there too. The canteen isn't very good, with only biscuits and thin slices of bread available and you can't get those nice small cakes that they have in other barracks either. Poor '06 is suffering badly with the hunger these days and can't stop praising the Curragh now. 'Not by bread alone …' I said to him a while ago, trying to cheer him up, but all he did was throw me a sorrowful look and repeat how hungry he felt.

There are some fine men in this Battalion, Cuirín Mór from Cornamona, Pádraig Ó Flaitheata from Inisheer, Beartla Ó Maoilchiaráin from Carna and many others whom I don't know yet. The best men are in D Company, young fellows who've been here just a few years and who've trained as gunners. Almost every man in D Company is from Connemara and it's the most Gaelic of all the companies. You'd never hear a word of English spoken there. We are in B Company, temporarily at least, and there are a good few older soldiers in our group. One younger lad here is from Ring in County Waterford, and he has very sweet Irish indeed; I could listen to his Irish all day. Three other men here have transferred down from Sixth Battalion in Athlone, two of whom have very little Irish. I met the third lad previously – that night in Athlone just before Maitias and I enlisted – but he didn't let on to recognise any of us this time though. He's from Turbot Island, back west from Clifden, and he's a kind of a leader over the other two men. Neither of the three mix much with the other lads here at all, and I'd say that they were sent down here against their wishes really. One of them is a small block of a man from Carlow and he's a very handy boxer apparently. He's won a lot of prizes for his sport, they say. His pal from Tralee is a fiery, wild-looking fellow they call 'Ciarraí' (Kerry). The Inis Turbot[21] fellow is the only one of them who has any Irish and even if he's not that fluent, he speaks it very correctly. His name is Patrick Ward by the way. He's a great man for sleep, and just loves to spend the day in bed snoring his head off. Mind you, he's out late most nights. He did me a favour there the other night anyway, fair play to him. I'd been asleep for a few hours or so when someone shook

me awake and I saw a big block of a fellow standing over me, someone
I'd never seen before. He'd a nasty look about him, and I could tell he'd
been drinking. 'I hate recruits' he says, pushing me around. 'I'd prefer to
see the devil himself here waiting for me when I get in at night instead
of you bloody recruits. D'you hear what I'm saying to you?'

I was still half-asleep and was a bit slow taking in what he was saying
though because he got even thicker then, for some reason. 'Wake up
you hoor! Wake up and pay attention when you're speaking to a three-
star soldier!'

Ward must have woken up then because next thing he says to your
man, nice and calm – in a voice that completely veiled the threat it
contained:

'Well, do you know what fella? If you don't leave that man there
alone and go to sleep for yourself I'll hammer your head so far down
between your shoulders that the Sergeant-Major will think he has a
tortoise on parade tomorrow!'

'Ok Wardy boy,' says your man suddenly changing his tune
completely as if it was all just a bit of innocent fun. He left me alone
after that.

Training again today. Lay down and retrieve weapons, the issuing
of orders that are a bit vaguer than usual, the estimation of distances –
and so on. There are a good number of older soldiers out training with
us these days – they're on a sort of refresher course as they call it in
English. They're a fine manly lot too, I swear, all of them with pipes
jammed between their teeth rather than cigarettes; they all smoke when
given permission and their conversation is eloquent and interesting too.

Joeen Beag[22] is one of them and he's a funny son of a gun. His cousin
('*Milseáin*') or 'Sweets' Hynes is here too (they call him 'Sweets' because
of how sugary he is in his dealings with everyone, always telling people
how great they are and that …). Joeen never tires of teasing 'Sweets' and
playing pranks on him. Old Peadar Gordún from Lettermore is here

and his sidekick Mac Ruairí from Donegal. They're another two who look as if butter wouldn't melt in their mouths. But you wouldn't be up with them when it comes to playing pranks on people and trying to make them look stupid. They're awful messers altogether.

The Sergeant who's training us is from Lettermullan, if I'm not mistaken, and it'd be difficult to better him as an instructor. Mac Donnacha (McDonagh) is his name, but everyone calls him Sonaí Neidí.

Another speaker of Irish is in our room now, a man they call (*Colm an tSeaimpín*)[23] Colm the Champion. He's a powerfully built man who's constantly chewing plug-tobacco and has no respect for anyone who's small or weedy. I heard him telling a bit of one of the old stories there the other day and I couldn't understand for the life of me how he could remember all the long extracts and discourses – the likes of: '*D'ardaíodar na seolta móra bocóideacha bacáideacha … go ndeachadar … ag treabhadh na farraige falcánta fíordhomhain nár treabhadh riamh cheana is nach dtreabhfar arís go lá deireadh an tsaoil.*'[24] ('They raised their billowing sails and ploughed waves never ploughed before and never more ploughed again till the end of the world.')

He knows some of the Gaelic folktales also in addition to many of the ancient proverbs and folklore that the older people once had.

It's odd but I can't help noticing the strange way that Irish and English words are mixed together in everyday speech here as a sort of a creole – sometimes with very funny results. It's not unusual to hear someone say the likes of this, for example:

'Do you have any *buicsí* (buckshee) knife Maidhc?'

'No, brother, I'm *síos* (down) one.

'Was that picture any good last night Seán?'

'Well, the picture was very good but the *actáil* (acting) was brilliant altogether; having said that it was *ag stickeáil amach* (standing out) from the very beginning who committed the murder.'

I heard one young lad from Camus say: '*Cén áit 'na numberáileann siad* na *gym shoes?*' (Where do they number the gym shoes?) and instead of '*tabhair dom an maide cnaipe sin*', they normally say 'tabhair dom an *button-shtick*'. I suppose that this kind of mixing of words and phrases is inevitable given that the two languages are competing with one another here every day of the week. Still, I think it'd be as easy for the lads to use the correct (i.e. Irish-language) terms for the words rather than using these bastardized terms all the time. They say that this kind of creolization of language is as common in those parts of Wales where Welsh is the native language also, so much so that they don't even bother inventing new Welsh terms for certain words at all.

Some of the lads here look fierce 'gildy' in their army uniforms and they also take advantage of small opportunities to make their uniforms more fancy-looking. Some of them place a tiny piece of mirror inside the double 'F' of their cap-badges to make it stand out better and their insignias and badges are very well-marked. They also make circular lead shapes to put inside the bottom of their trousers so that the trouser-cloth will drape perfectly down to the toes. They cover two small pieces of lead with circular strips of cloth, but when you think how heavy a pair of hobnail boots is anyway, this doesn't make their feet much heavier than they are already. All of these tricks are technically against army rules of course, but they let people get away with them a bit if they add to the overall neatness of the soldier. Other soldiers have the habit of shortening the peaks of their caps while raising the top of the cap even higher – (by placing three slivers of wire inside it) – so's it looks like a German soldier's. Officially, this isn't allowed either, but it's amazing how many fellows are let out the front gate of the barracks at night with their caps like this. Nothing looks worse in my opinion. They look like an image of Henry VIIIth in my opinion!

Slam Féir ('Bunch of Hay') grabbed a hold of me as I was leaving the canteen after dinner today. He was standing in the doorway and pulled me by the sleeve as I was passing:

'Listen here, little brother, I don't recognise you at all. Are you from back west, do you mind me asking?' I knew well what he wanted, but I also knew that I couldn't get rid of him too easily either without telling him to shag off.

'Well, I'm not too far from here,' I said. 'I'm from back the other end of Salthill.'

'Exactly sonny, a nice little town.'

'And tell me this – who're you related to?'

'I'm related to the Condons. McCauley is my surname and my dad's from Clare. He's a Quartermaster who's stationed down in Spike Island.'

'Orah, you devil, you're Jim McCauley's son, are you? You couldn't be!'

'By God, but put it there old stock,' he said shaking my hand. 'Ah shur, there were never two lads as close as me and Jim McCauley back in the day!'

I did hear my old fellow mention your man sometimes, but they were never that friendly, from what I heard. 'Ah shur, no one'd be thirsty for long if Jim McCauley was still here,' says your man motioning me towards the wet canteen, almost pushing me in the door. Damn it – but I'd no choice then except to buy him a pint, and one for myself as well. The wet canteen was mobbed and you could barely see yourself with all the tobacco-smoke coming from all the old 'sweats'.

The company there were a really, manly crowd no doubt about it; every man with a great big frothy pint propped in front of him and everyone speaking sweet Connemara or Aran Island Irish all the while. The Little Tailor from Donegal himself was in there and I tried to speak to him in Irish for a short while; I couldn't understand much of his dialect, however. The next time I looked around, Slám Féir had emptied his glass and was singing my father's praises again. I knocked back the rest of my pint and called for two more drinks.

*Holy Thursday Mass this morning.* Aren't the altars laid out really nicely this day every year? I don't think that the country people pay as much attention to the rituals of Holy Week as the townspeople do. Most of the men in this barracks are from the country originally and the Easter ceremonies aren't as important a thing for the men here as they are in the city, I think. It's very different in Kilkenny on a day like today. Back there, everyone goes from church to church today and compares the decorations between one and the next. Which church is laid out more nicely? Which has the most flowers?

I took a trip back to Seán Ó Néill's house today. It was well past time for me. Herself and himself had a great welcome for me and when I was leaving they asked me whether I'd be happy to work Race Week for them if I could get off from the army then, and I told them I'd be delighted to. I could do with an extra few bob then because I'll have to buy a new suit and various other bits and pieces then. I was back in Galway town soon afterwards and ran into '06 Reaney on the street. We went into Myles Lee's pub and drank four or five pints each at our leisure. Myles has a very nice daughter, a very bright and educated girl, by my soul, and she's not a bit stand-offish when it comes to chatting to us soldiers – not like some of the other dippy types you get around town. She's a lovely-looking girl too, and she's the first girl I've met in a while that I loved having the chat with. We went down to Maggie Ann's after this and later again, we went onto Delia Lydon's where we stayed until after closing time. There's a fish-and-chip shop just next door to Delia Lydon's and we went over there before we went home. We were hungry by then needless to say. This shop belongs to one of the non-commissioned officers from *An Chéad Chath* and because they sell boiled *crúbeens*, Cuirín Mór has christened the fellow who owns it 'Pig-foot Pat'. We got *crúbeens* and a paper filled with chips in Pig-foot's place and by God was it tasty too!

We're in Renmore a week today. Good Friday is always a lonely day, it seems to me. I always feel bad now that Lent's drawing to a close and I know that I haven't kept it as well as I should have. Today was a holiday in the army, of course, although we had a Church Parade twice.

Myself and the lad from Turbot Island had a great chat today. He was telling me all about their lives on the island – fighting and collecting seaweed, and the rest of it – and all of this without so much as a *púcán* or sailing boat in sight. They travel very far out to sea in their currachs, and they look down on the people of the mainland because the latter are reliant on whatever they can make from the shore. In fact, the Turbot Island people refer to the people of the mainland as 'Gobáin'.[25] Your man's grandfather is 'King' of the island. (They have a 'King' here also, down in the Claddagh; his name is Eoin Ó Conceanainn (John Concannon).) Your man from Turbot says that we here should be humble in his presence seeing as he's got 'royal' blood in his veins and that we shouldn't refuse him money or anything else that he asks for! When the fellow who's called Mac a' tSeaimpín[26] heard this, he let a roar of laughter out of him and said:

'Well, if you're the son of a King, then I'm the son of a Champion! And doesn't the whole world know that you have to give pride of place to a Champion always? One of us has to be the "King" of the room here anyway, whatever happens.' The two lads laughed, but I wouldn't be a bit surprised if they take one another on later to see who's the strongest.

The lads here are really interested in trials of strength and no wonder too, seeing as some of the strongest men in Ireland are right here in this barracks, and it's *An Chéad Chath* who normally win the summer tug-of-war competitions. Cuirín Mór has a lot of Irish and he knows a lot of folklore too, but there's another lad from the same place who's got very little Irish. His surname is Stuffles and he has a really strange accent. He's looks more like a Kerryman than a Connemara-man in my opinion, but now that I think of it, his accent is the same as the people have around Erris and those parts. I'm lucky that I live within an ass' roar of the old place here, unlike many of the other lads here who've no connection whatsoever with the land. I went back to Knocknacarra to Joe's house on Easter Monday and had dinner there – bacon, cabbage and some lovely potatoes. After dinner, Joe winked at me and nodded towards the door. He got up from the table, grabbed his hat and made as if to leave. 'Where are you off to now, if you don't mind me asking?' says Meaig, removing the cover of the baking tin with the tongs.

'I don't mind at all. I don't mind one bit. I'm heading over to check on the red cow. Every day's the same for me when it comes to my responsibilities, you know.'

'Yeah sure! Back to Francis' pub in Barna is where you're off to, I'll bet. Or maybe that's where your cow is grazing too, is it!' says Meaig laughing. Joe and I slipped out the door before she changed her mind. Peadar was waiting outside with the small mare hitched to the cart, and we set off at a good trot up the tarred road. Meaig's voice came to us on the wind, warning the lads to be home on time to milk the cows. The two of them let a roar of laughter out of them and gave the mare a skelp so she'd go faster. The beer wasn't great in Barna, but I enjoyed our trip to the pub all the same; sitting up on a barrel, nice and relaxed, listening to the locals speaking Irish. My head was full of memories heading back on the road. It was the alcohol that set my mind racing needless to say. I thought of that day long ago when myself and our Caoimhín Beag (Little Kevin) went out on the tide in the old currach full of holes, our single oar a big old stick that we found in the ditch down from Hackett's house. We were really lucky then we weren't all drowned as many older and wiser men than us perished in that same spot, never mind small, innocent kids like ourselves.

Joe and Peadar had to milk the cows and bring the milk over to Salthill to their customers afterwards. I went with them even if I couldn't help them with the deliveries seeing as I was in my army uniform. It wouldn't look good for a soldier to be seen bringing a canteen of milk to the door of a guesthouse, not that the other lads could understand this – but anyway. After milking, they were keen to go for another drink and so we headed down to Donnellan's. Donnellan's is the pub where all the country lads go anytime they're in Salthill. I remember being in there years ago during Race Week when I was just a small boy. I sat up on a barrel of porter swinging my legs while I drank lemonade and ate a currant bun.

There was a good crowd in Donnellan's – Barna people and people from Furbo and Rahoon – and most of them had Irish. There were a good few *Claddagh* people in there too, all of them in their blue suits, blue jerseys and check caps. One of them told a good story about a day he'd been in some pub drinking in the company of an Englishman. They were having a great chat by all accounts and the Englishman was getting fonder and fonder of Ireland and the Irish the more porter they sank. Eventually he says to the Claddagh man anyway:

'Blimey, Pat, I like your country and the people. Everyone's so friendly. There's only one thing, though: I can't understand this 'ere Irish language of yours.'

'Arah, you needn't worry about that, Sir,' says your man, 'sure I haven't a word of it meself.'

'You ain't?' says the Englishman with a look of surprise. 'Then what's this you been talking to me all day!'

When middle-aged and older men from our area meet in the pub like this, they speak Irish amongst one another. They always speak English with the younger crowd though, and more's the pity. It was well after 10 p.m. when I got back to town, but there were still a good few soldiers ambling around. They prefer just to ramble around town like this than go to the Pictures, and the majority of the Connemara girls working in Galway town are the same. This is their favourite pastime – just wandering up and down town until it's time to go home. They all normally keep to the one side of the street when they're walking – 'the haepenny side' as it's known – and many's the boy and girl who've met each other in this way and begun courting down through the years.

'A thousand farewells to you Margaret. You were always a lovely person.'

Many of the lads are gone home for their first weekend off and the rest are inside in the barracks having a sleep. Some of the lads like the bed so much that they don't even get up for their meals and have good friends of theirs organised to bring back mugs of tea and slices of bread to them from the canteen. Officially, you're not allowed to bring any food into the bedrooms here, but this is another minor army regulation that's regularly ignored.

*An Capall* (The Horse) is a funny character, no doubt about it. He spent a good deal of time over in America, they say and returned home during the Great Depression before enlisting in the army here. When he has a few drinks in, he likes to buy a big cigar and put on a Yank accent. They say that he lived in the Bronx when he was in America, and I'd say he learned a trick or two over there. He's very fond of gambling if he can get someone to play a game of cards with him that is. I think the older crowd are all 'onto him' by now however, and so they don't play with him as much as before. Although himself and the cook Slam Féir are good friends, he's always slagging him off all the same. In fact, he's the worst for berating Slam Féir and yet it's nothing more than a harmless mock 'civil war' and a bit of fun really. In other army barracks, it's the custom that they collect small amounts of money from everyone for the canteen attendant once a week, but this isn't the tradition here. Anyway, the Horse placed a small wooden box down on the head of the table one afternoon with 'Help the Horse' written on it. When he went to shake the box later to see was there anything in it, he was disappointed not to hear any rattle coming from it.

'Bad enough, my braves,' he says, 'you must all have empty pockets.' The Horse will never use a simple word when he can use a few complicated ones instead. 'Braves' or 'Heroes' is the term he uses to refer to the other soldiers. The 'Food Residence' is what he calls the canteen and he always puts the abbreviation '*An tUasal*' (Sir) before the soldiers' surnames, irrespective of who he's talking to. He's easily riled however, and everyone steers clear of him when's he's angry or annoyed about something.

I switched my bed upstairs last night because I thought it would be nicer to be up at the top of the house, but it didn't work out unfortunately. About 2 a.m. I was woken up by two fellows who were fighting about something that happened downtown a good while ago. No sooner was I asleep again but I was awoken a second time by a big block of a fellow pulling the bedclothes off me. I could tell straight away that he'd a drop in and I big wide grin on him that went from ear to ear.

'Get up out of that, little brother,' he says, 'get up out of that there so that I have a sleep for myself.'

'Have you not made your own bed down below?' I says.

'Arah, I never make my bed, not if I've recruits around who can do it for me,' he says laughing. Then: 'You're no good to me now sonny though. Get out of the bed now quick for me, good lad. I'm a kind of a cuckoo, do you understand and I throw the smaller birds out of the nest!'

He burst his arse laughing at this and so for an easy life, I climbed out of my nice warm bed and dressed your man's bed below for myself. I slept fine for the rest of the night, but, even so, I'm going back downstairs to the other room tonight. At least I'll have some peace down there. Sonaí Mhichil Sala is the name of the lad who kicked me out of bed last night and when he got up this morning I says: '*Dia dhuit, a chuach*' ('God with you, cuckoo') to him. He laughed nice and innocent. I'd say he's a fellow who's no business here in the army at all. He probably hasn't the slightest interest in it as a way of living really.

I slept very well last night, and I'm really glad that I switched back down here again. There are lots of 'characters' in this room even if they're not as good a bunch of soldiers as the crowd in D Company above. (What I mean by that is that they're not as neat or as obsessive about everything military-related as the lads upstairs.) The lads down here are more interesting as people in my opinion. Take Cuirín Mór, for example. He's as strong and as brave a person as you'd meet anywhere, but he's also clever and wise beyond his years, as well as being great company. Mac an tSeaimpín is a big, powerfully built fellow too but also a great storyteller to boot. The Platoon Leader Mícheál Ó Sé has his bed up there at the top of the room, and he's forever scratching his head and complaining about how difficult it is to get any sense out of the lads here in the mornings when he's trying to root them out of bed. He's always up before the rest of us, even if he's as fond of sleep as anyone else. He goes around the room to all the beds then trying to wake everyone up with 'Get up Ward, get up I say, or you'll have a charge against you later on.' (I wouldn't mind but the same man is a decent 'old skin' who wouldn't ever bring a charge against anyone.)

'Out of the bed now Colm or you won't see town or Lydon's tonight; 'Ó Tuathail, out I say, or what are you thinking at all? You'd swear that you were all up in Butlins on your holidays the way you're going on. Oh, God help us but here comes the Sergeant-Major! You've me hanged now! Out now the lot of you or you'll all have C.B. until Christmas!'

Ciarraí is always very cranky in the mornings, just after he gets up. It's not even safe to look at him then, never mind talk to him. He got into trouble this morning though. Cuirín Mór asked for a bit of 'four-by-two' so that he could clean his gun and your man started cursing and telling him to go to the store if he needed 'four-by-two' or anything else either. I wouldn't mind but Ciarraí actually had plenty of the stuff to spare himself; he was just cranky because he was out drinking last night and had a sore head. 'Don't be cranky now Ciarraí' says Cuirín Mór to him then in English. Oh little brother, but that's when Ciarraí went ballistic altogether! He grabbed hold of the oil bottle and flung it full-force at Cuirín Mór. If he'd hit the Turbot Island man, he'd have had one really sore head for himself, I can tell you!

'All right Kerry boy,' he said, 'this is going to hurt you more than it hurts me,' he says and grabs hold of Ciarraí, lifting him straight off the ground, then drags him out to the wash-house, kicking and screaming. The Kerry lad is no softie though and he fought hard, twisting and turning like a salmon trapped in a net. It was no good though. He couldn't escape Cuirín Mór no matter what he did. Next thing, Cuirín Mór has the tap on and your man's head shoved under it. He let him go eventually and returned to the room. Ciarraí followed him a few minutes later, cursing like the devil, the water dripping from him all over the floor. Most of the lads burst out laughing when they saw the state of him, but me and a few other lads who aren't as physically big as the rest of them kept quiet. Not that all the lads in this room are 'hard-chaws' – far from it! There's a very nice lad here from the Aran Islands, a lad by the name of Tomás Ó Conceanainn who's an absolute gentleman. He's tall and thin but he's a grand, friendly look about him. He has perfect English and Irish and he reads a lot, and I can tell by him that he doesn't like too much bad language or drunkenness. Another strong lad who's as nice as you'd meet anywhere is Ó Tuathail from Cleggan. I've never heard even one swear-word from his mouth since I first came here.

They say that the Battalion is due to be reorganised shortly and that a good few men will be picked out of Companies A and B, and transferred to Company D. But I hope that most of us in this company stay here – apart from the one or two whom we'd be better off without!

* * *

# Working in the Canteen

Well, we have the trials for one-star and two-stars over with now and we've been getting an increase of fourteen shillings a week in our pay for the past while. Also, we're allowed to sew the two-star badge onto our sleeves now and this means a lot, especially seeing as we'd done nothing but training and marching for so long down on the Curragh in Kildare that we were beginning to ask ourselves – what was it all for? Myself and '06 Reaney were left in B Company while Maitias and '90 Ó Murchú were transferred to the Gunners' Company. Most of us are now 'employed' – that's to say that we've been put to work in the various canteens and stores around the barracks. Some of the lads don't mind this but then there are others, myself included, who prefer to be left idle – either that or to be out training. Neither Cuirín Mór nor Colm a' tSeaimpín are ever given 'employment' as they're both as clever as the devil and can disappear or 'go hiding' as quick as a flash – especially the minute they're required for duties. The world knows but the pair of them are like grand lords of the manor, the way they stay stretched out on their beds relaxing half o' the time. And then there's myself and the others who're always washing plates or cleaning for the Quartermaster.

I'm in the O.N.C.'s Canteen these days and it's not the worst place in the world to work either as they only have one supper each day and you're finished fairly early come evening. Another advantage of working here is that the food is better than in the only other canteen here – or when it isn't better, at least you get more of it. I'm waiting on the tables here because I mentioned to the Recruitment Officer that this was what I was working at before I enlisted and this was duly noted on my file.

There are two cooks on duty here – Seán Ó Conghaile from the Aran Islands, a quiet and easy-going man and Cóilín Ó Maoilchiaráin from Maighinis. Another man works here sometimes too. Peadar Jack they call him and he's from Waterford. Seán Ó Conghaile is very easy to get on with, but the devil himself would find it difficult to make sense of Cóilín sometimes. Cóilín Morgan is the name by which he's known in here by the way. I suppose that this must be what he's called back home. Cóilín's a powerfully built man with two fierce-looking eyes in his head. When he's in good form, you couldn't meet a nicer fellow, but when he's angry or upset about something, you'd be best steering clear of him altogether. Most of the waiters don't last too long in the canteen here because Cóilín's so moody, they say. I get on fairly well with him most of the time, however. He is one of the cleanest men I've ever come across and hates any kind of dirt or mess.

He gave me a tongue-lashing this afternoon – not that I blame him really. What happened was that he sent me into town after dinner to buy eighteen herrings for the tea. He gave me his own bicycle and I set off happy to have a break from the barracks. I bought the herrings down in the Fish Market anyway and placed them in a small box on the bicycle carrier. Everything was fine until I reached Eyre Square and ran into '06 who was just returning from the hospital where he'd just donated a pint of blood, something he does fairly regularly. (Everyone who donates a pint of blood gets paid one guinea in addition to a few bottles of porter.) Well '06, generous soul that he is, invited me into the Corner House bar and seeing as I still had a small bit of time to spare, I eagerly took him up on this. We didn't notice the time slipping by though, and when I finally remembered that I'd better be going, it was already nearly tea-time.

'Oh Lord, I have to hurry back to the barracks with the herrings or Morgan will kill me,' I says to '06. I cycled out along the small path that skirts the railway line as fast as I could go and I was completely out of breath by the time I got back. Oh my God! It was only then that I realised the cover was missing from the box on the back of the bicycle and half of the herrings were missing too! I turned around straight away and went back until I reached the far end of the railway line again, but only found three of the herrings. I wouldn't mind if I'd still had enough money left to buy another batch of them, but I didn't. All I had left on me was four pence! I had to come back with the few fish I still had left and face the music. Sheepishly, I walked into the canteen where Morgan was waiting. He was actually holding the big frying pan in his hand and had it over the stove ready to roast the fish.

'You came back Dónall,' he says, his voice nice and calm. This wasn't a good sign at all, I thought to myself.

'I did Colm.'

'Have you the herrings with you Dónall?' he asks.

'Well, I have and I haven't,' I says, praying quietly that he wouldn't explode when he heard the rest of it.

'You have and you haven't?' says Morgan, imitating me. 'How do you mean – you have and you haven't?'

'Well, I lost some of them on the way back Colm,' I says. Oh, my son, but that's when he went crazy altogether!

'You lost six of them! You lost them, is it? Where did you lose them you fool? May the good Son of God save us. How's it we can't even send you out on a simple little job like this without you making an idiot of yourself!'

'I spent the afternoon looking for them along the "line" and halfway down the town,' I says feebly. I didn't mention anything about the Corner house of course because he'd have eaten me alive on the spot if I did. I escaped the kitchen as soon as I got the chance and began setting the table for tea. Cóilín had to make a rissole[27] for the O.N.C.'s that there were no fish available for, and it goes without saying that he wasn't one bit happy about it. On returning to the room later on, Cuirín Mór was waiting for me. I steal a few little bits and pieces from the kitchen for him sometimes when I get the chance – sausages or sweet-cakes or stuff. Given what'd happened that evening however, I'd been too afraid to ask for my own tea, never mind stealing anything extra for someone else!

'Did you bring any spoils back with you Núibín?' asks Cuirín Mór. (He's christened me Núib ('Stub') or Núibín for some reason.) 'Musha, devil a bit, little brother,' I says and explained what'd happened. He wasn't happy to hear this at all though. 'You'll have to do better anymore Núibín. I can't be serving as your protector free of charge, you know.' Cuirín Mór maintains that he protects me from others, but the truth is that no one says anything to me, so I never need his protection. He's always at the same crack whenever we have boxty for dinner in the canteen too. 'Half of that for *An Bodach* ('The Churl')' he announces, and I have to give him half my dinner. This doesn't bother me much however as, in the main, he's a good comrade to have – that's for sure. I've never seen anyone to go through money as quickly as him, though. As soon as he's paid on the Wednesday, he heads off to play cards and he often hasn't a halfpenny to his name by the time the night's over. Either that or he heads down and drinks whatever money he hasn't spent on the cards. He relies on the '*séaclaí*' (shrimp) as he calls me, and Ciarraí to buy him tea and bread down in the canteen and to loan him a few pence every now and then.

We're a much tighter outfit here now and we've great fun in the room some nights. Tuesday night is my favourite night as nearly everyone stays in and we've great crack telling stories and jokes. Colm a' tSeaimpín and Mac an Bháird are always knocking sparks off one another and slagging, and they're always very witty. It's just as well because if they weren't letting off steam like this, they'd be fighting amongst themselves as they often have physical fights with one another too. The man who's our Company Captain at the moment, Captain Cusack, is very nice and so too are the O.N.C.'s. Mícheál Ó Sé, who is in charge of our room, wouldn't hurt a fly or cause trouble for any man here.

Gerry Gavanly came down from the Curragh here a while ago and he's in with us in B Company now. Like me, he was delighted to say goodbye to the Curragh, and he's as well-known to everyone in Galway town and back Cois Fharraige way now that you'd swear he was born and bred there. Between attending Gaelic League meetings and meeting Irish speakers around Galway town, he's always on the go, and you'd hardly see him around the barracks after duty-hours at all. He's the big hero of the Irish-language community in the barracks here and if there were others like him, every last word of English would be rooted out of Renmore in no time at all. Mac an Bháird is always busy annoying Gerry, any chance he gets, and often it's when Gerry is rushing off to an Irish-language event in Galway town somewhere that he tries to delay him. 'Wait, wait, hero,' the Turbot man might say to him: 'I put you under a magic ordinance not to eat the same meal at any table or to sleep twice in the same bed unless you give me enough change to get into the Corner House.' Gerry doesn't believe that you've to show any deference to An Bodach, however, even if he's the grandson of a King, and Mac an Bháird always has to let him go free in the end, without getting any 'tribute' from him.

Another man that you wouldn't see around the place either, once duty-hours are over, is '07 Ó Donncha. He's always very quiet during the day and any night that he stays in, but when he has a drop on board, you couldn't quieten him. He's from somewhere down in Limerick originally and has a very sweet voice. He'd sing a stave from an opera for you that's as good as anything you've ever heard although the following morning, he hates it if anyone even mentions that he was singing at all. He rarely joins in the banter and the storytelling in the room here and it's usually just when you're not expecting it, that he'll say a line or two of a poem, or even a full verse. He'll declaim it aloud and then go quiet again and you won't hear a gig out of him for the rest of the evening.

He gave me a fright one day, before I got to know him properly. I was sitting on my bed cleaning my gun and your man was lying on his own bed across from me. He had his cap pulled down over his eyes as if he was asleep. Then, all of a sudden, he jumps up in the bed and calls out loudly:

*'Shall we expose to vulgar sight the raptures of the bridal night?'*

He took his towel and soap from his kit-box and went out to the wash-house.

I was returning from the toilets – or the piss-house as it's called here – that same day, when I spotted him standing in front of the mirror preening himself. He was dressed to go out on the town, his uniform polished and gleaming and a fold in his trousers so sharp you could shave yourself with it. When he was finished admiring himself in the mirror, he curtsied artfully to his reflection and said:

*'Full many a flower is born to blush unseen, and waste its sweetness on the desert air.'*

I'm not sure whether he was referring to himself with this comment or what he meant exactly. '06 Reaney was telling me that your man knows an unbelievable amount of poetry off by heart, although you'd never see him reading a book of poetry. He's someone who's quite deep and hard to fathom really I'd say, but he's a good soldier too; he minds his own business and doesn't annoy anyone here one way or the other.

I was given a few days 'confined to barracks' yesterday and I was also made to pay for a pair of gym shoes. What happened was that we have kit inspections very regularly these days and when one was announced the other day, I'd no bit of white *blanco* to apply to the gym shoes. They were too dirty for me to leave them out and no one else in the room had any *blanco* left either. Then, just as the kit inspection began, I came up with a quick solution. There was a bucket of whitewash left outside the toilets by one of the workmen who was painting the walls so I dipped the gym shoes in the whitewash and left them out on the windowsill to dry. They were soon as white as any of the other shoes. I got through the kit inspection then no bother and wrapped the gym shoes in newspaper to keep them clean. That was all fine until another inspection was announced suddenly yesterday and when I removed the runners from the newspaper, hadn't the whitewash eaten through all the canvas in the shoes! They'd holes in them and looked as if they were about to fall apart. Cuirín Mór and Colm an tSeaimpín burst out laughing at the sight of them and says Cuirín Mór:

'They're the nearest thing to two old rotten currachs that haven't seen tar for fifty years!'

'Yes, you should caulk them with tar Núibín,' says Mac an tSeaimpín chewing on a piece of plug.

'Do you think it might strengthen the canvas?' I says hopefully.

'Sure,' says Mac a' tSeaimpín, 'it'll make them as stiff as leather. There's a tar barrel back there at the back of the canteen but you'd want to get a move on.'

'Yes, and once the tar's dried, you can apply the white *blanco* to them and you'd never know that whitewash was applied to them at all,' says Cuirín Mór.

I headed over to the tar barrel, my canvas shoes tucked beneath my arm and rubbed them with tar using a small piece of wood until they were completely black and went back to the room. 'That's it little brother,' says Mac an tSeaimpín, trying suppress a laugh, 'Leave them out there on the window now so they can dry and you can lash a bit of *blanco* onto them then later.'

Alas, I didn't even get the chance to do this because two minutes later, in walks the Company Quartermaster and Lieutenant Dunne alongside him.

'Room, room-attention,' says the Quartermaster. We all jump to attention and the Lieutenant says: 'At ease.'

'Every man next to his own bed,' he says and the kit inspection began. It wasn't long before they reached me and they were quick to notice that the canvas gym shoes were missing.

'Have you no gym shoes Private McCauley?' says the Lieutenant. I was in a right mess now and I wasn't sure what to do. When he got no response from me, the Lieutenant lost his patience. 'Well, do you have any gym shoes man? "Yes" or "no"?'

'I have Sir,' I says, unsure of what else to say.

'Where are they then?'

'On the windowsill, drying out,' I says.

'Oh, so you're after applying *blanco* to them then?' he says, with a face that said he'd lost all hope in the world. 'I barely know you yet, but I've noticed this much about – that you can never give a straight answer to a straight question. Your mind is some sort of a strange and complicated labyrinth where you find it easier to spout a load of rubbish than to give a simple "yes" or "no" to anything. Now show me your gym shoes if you have them.' I'd no choice then so I went over to the window and took the canvas shoes in from outside the window. A snigger went through the room and the Company Quartermaster's face grew darker. 'Silence!' he said angrily. The Lieutenant's eyes widened as he stared first at the canvas shoes and then at me. He couldn't believe what his own eyes were telling him. You could've have heard a pin drop in the room in that moment, everyone's lips sealed for fear that they might burst out laughing despite themselves. Finally, the Lieutenant clears his throat and says to the Quartermaster: 'There's no new rule in the forces that says you should've a black colour on your gym shoes, is there Quartermaster?'

'If there is Sir, I didn't hear anything about it,' says your man. 'I thought as much,' says the Lieutenant turning to me. 'I'm not even going to ask you McCauley how this messing happened. I'm too frightened to ask and God knows what weird and wonderful excuse will emerge from that bizarre mind of yours. It's a crime against the army to destroy any of its equipment however, so you'll be charged with this misdemeanour and you'll have to pay for a new pair of canvas shoes.' The Quartermaster made a note of this and they moved onto the next man. The minute the inspection was over and the pair had left the room, the other lads gathered around me taking the piss about my poor canvas shoes. Cuirín Mór and Mac an tSeaimpín were the worst of the lot, even if it was their bad advice that'd got me into trouble in the first place! 'God knows but someone should compose a new song about that pair of gyms,' says Colm a' tSeaimpín gobbing tobacco out the window. 'A song?' says Ceannaire Ó Sé[28] laughing; 'a song is it? Someone should write a book about them, never mind a song! What in the world would possess any intelligent man to try the likes of that? By dad, I don't know what it is but the younger generation today are going to pot. There was no crazy stuff like that with the old soldiers long ago. Doing too much reading McCauley is what has you the way you are ... By dad, black canvas shoes no less!' Cuirín Mór always says that Ceannaire Ó Sé looks a bit like the dog that delivers the post in *Curly Wee and Gussie Goose* and now that I think of it, there is a strange similarity between them alright, especially when Ó Sé laughs.

'06 Reaney was worse than me today, he was short so much stuff. 'These Connachts have me ruined, old boy,' he says, replacing his kit in the box. A huge amount of kit gets nicked from this room, no doubt about it; and yet the person who's cleaned out doesn't hold it against those who've cleaned him out for some reason. No sooner does one fellow find out that he has a brush or a button-stick missing, but he's waiting his chance to swipe it back again, and his eyes are peeled for anyone who's gone out and left their kit-box open by mistake. Then he swoops quickly and grabs whatever he needs – and often something extra into the bargain! No one here would ever complain to the Quartermaster about something being stolen from them and if someone did, no one in the Company'd have any respect for them either. Of course, if you've a good lock on your kit-box and you keep it secured at all times, you're grand. You have to be on constant alert though because if you let down your guard for even a second, you'll pay dearly for it!

When I first arrived here, a trick was played on me that was as cute a one as you'd see anywhere. I'd no lock on my kit-box in the first few weeks and one old soldier noticed this.

'Have you no lock for your kit-box, little brother?' he says to me one day, letting on to be all concerned about it.

'Not until I buy one. You can't get them over in the canteen, can you?'

'Well you can, I suppose, but the old yokes they sell there are fairly useless to be honest. Shur, you could unlock them with a pin. You'd be better off leaving your box open altogether, they're that useless. Tell you what though. I've a fine strong lock here that I'm not using at the moment. Look how strong it is,' he says, taking this huge padlock out of his kit-box to show me.

'It's a good one alright,' I says.

'Here, I'll sell it to you if you want. You can have it for a shilling.'

He gave me the lock and the key and took my shilling. Everything was grand anyway and I put the lock on the kit-box. Later on that day I went back to get something from the kit-box but, to my horror, the lock was gone! Strangely enough though – an exact replica of the lock your man sold me earlier was securing his kit-box. I examined his lock carefully and I was sure that it was the exact same as the one he'd sold me earlier that morning.

He must've had another key and he must've taken the lock from my kit-box the minute he saw me gone. Who came into the room the next minute but your man and so I went up to him and accused him of playing a trick on me. But he just looked at me as if I'd just accused him of murdering his own mother or something, then grabbed me tightly by the arm and says: 'Take it easy, sonny,' as if calming a crazy person down. 'You don't know what you're talking about now. And shur, you can't be going around accusing people of taking stuff without any proof. Suppose now that I was a really bad dog; couldn't I go and make a complaint about you – about you accusing me of stealing? Blast it sonny but you're crazy if you think you can go around slandering people like this. Now just cop on to yourself now, will you?' I realised immediately that I was only wasting my time arguing the point any further. He'd my lock now and there was nothing that I could do about it, especially seeing as he was a big strong block of a man who looked at you as much as to say – 'Don't mess with me.'

'Touché,' I says, in imitation of the French people I've read about in books. But on my way out again, what does he do but calls me back:

'Listen here, sonny. You don't have any use for that key of yours anymore do you, now that you've no lock to go with it?'

'Touché again' I muttered under my breath and handed him the key as well!

Army uniforms are the most commonly stolen items here because they can be sold downtown and there's great demand for them amongst fishermen and farmers. You can get up to twelve-and-sixpence for one of these shirts sometimes. Every soldier has three shirts – one that he wears, one that's in his kit-box and one in the wash. The one that's currently in the wash is always the safest one as it can't be stolen from there – or if it was stolen, you'd be given another one instead. Even the one you're wearing isn't totally safe though as some of the lads here are such clever thieves that they'd nearly swipe it off your back unknownst to you! As for the shirt that's kept in your kit-box, you can never be too sure whether it'll still be there or not when you go looking for it. In a way, the soldiers here would remind you of the stories about the Red Indians long ago. They say that it was once a badge of pride for the Indians to fleece their enemies of their possessions while the latter were asleep – the more silently and cleverly they did this, the better. Well, it's the same here! If you manage to swipe another man's shirt when it's not so easy to do – your victim nearly has more respect for you in a way really! For example, Cuirín Mór would prefer to swipe one shirt from

Colm a' tSeaimpín than steal two from the likes of me, or anyone else
like me – i.e. the type who isn't as cute about guarding his stuff. You'd
often hear the likes of this here:

'Did you steal anything from my box Packie, little brother?'

'Did I steal anything from your box Colm? Are you joking me, are
you? Of course, I didn't I'd never steal anything from you Coilmín! A
good comrade me!'

'I know all that Packie, but I heard that you were drinking big frothy
pints down in Delia Lydon's last night and you know in your heart inside
that you left the barracks here without a penny in your pocket yesterday.
Maybe you lifted my fine new shirt to sell it to that dealer downtown
did you? Or maybe you gave it straight to the boatmen down the docks?
The same boatmen love getting the 'greybacks' as you well know Packie!'

'Oh, come on now Coilmín, son; give up that bad-mindedness now
and don't be so suspicious of your old friend like this. You're the last
man in this room here that I'd ever steal something from and well you
know it.'

'I know that Packie brother, but how do I know that you haven't
fleeced every other man in this room already?'

A half an hour later maybe, and Packie goes looking for something
from his kit-box, and what do you know – a shirt or a trousers belonging
to him has been swiped, and Seaimpín has disappeared downtown!
You'd hear the roar of anger Packie let out of him down in
Ballyloughane!

'Oh, thieving Seaimpín, you dirty thief; as sure as I'm alive, it's you
who stole my shirt! May you go and rot you dirty waster; what a pity
that I didn't swipe two shirts off you last night when I'd the chance
instead of one!'

Poor Ciarraí's the man who's stolen from the most here, mainly
because he finds it so difficult to protect his kit-box I think. He leaves
it open half the time and he has no skill in stealing, no more than poor

'06 Reaney does. He came back to the room the other day only to discover that he hadn't a pair of socks left to his name – everything gone! What does he do then but empty out whatever small bits of stuff he'd left in the kit-box onto the floor, and invite everyone to take whatever they wanted from him right there and then!

'Here, here, c'mon you lot. Don't be shy about taking anything now. You wouldn't be one bit shy, if I wasn't here, I'm sure,' he says.

Seaimpín came over to see what was left in the small pile and promptly spat on the ground to show his disrespect for it.

'Musha definitely, sonny, I wouldn't take any of that shite there – even if someone paid me to take it. I never saw any soldier with a pile of rubbish the likes of that before, and I've a lot of service under my belt at this stage.'

Ciarraí got really mad at this and flung the stuff back into the box again. 'The next man that I see coming within a half-mile of my box, I'll break every bone in his body,' he says in a ferocious voice. Cuirín Mór opened his mouth in mock-fright and pulled the collar of his great-coat down over his face – making out that he was petrified – while everyone else just burst out laughing. It is mostly to the boatmen (the Aran Islanders and the foreign fishermen, in particular) that they sell the Army shirts and trousers stolen here to, but many of these clothes are brought to *An Mangaire* ('The Dealer') also. He works as a barman as his main job, but he buys a lot of shirts and trousers from us 'on-the-side' and sells them at a profit to the boatmen. The big advantage of this from our point of view is that it's much easier to find An Mangaire down the pub where he works and we don't need to go wandering around the docks looking for a buyer for our stuff. As he's the middle-man, you can't really blame him if he doesn't give us as good a price for the shirts and trousers as the boatmen give him. An Mangaire is one cute operator and no one ever gets the better of him too easily in a negotiation. He's from Cois Fharraige somewhere and he's such a smooth talker that he could charm the birds down from the trees! When you call into him, in the pub, your parcel beneath your arm, he gives you the greatest welcome ever, pulls you a pint straight away whether you want one or not, and chats to you about the weather and the ways of the world outside for a while, anything rather than the real reason you're there to meet him. He might give the odd sideways glance at the parcel you've placed on the counter, but that'll be it. Finally, after a good deal of small talk, you'll tell him what business has brought you there to see him – all of this palaver even if he benefits a lot more from the entire transaction than you ever will. The minute you mention why you've come to see him, he gives this haunted look and he's dead serious and all the hail-fellow-well-met stuff goes out the window straight away. Next thing, he's acting like a man who finds the whole business of buying and selling to be completely beneath him, a sordid thing that has the potential to destroy the friendship he's built up with you. 'Ah well … I don't know sonny … I'm not sure … I've bought way too many of those shirts recently and there isn't the same demand for them now as there was a while back – you know yourself. And I get bugger-all out of the deal anyway. It's difficult to make any profit when you're dealing with the boatmen, you know,' he'll say.

If you've any cop-on then, you'll pretend that you're not interested in what price he's offering and you'll say something about a farmer from Claregalway who offered you fifteen or twelve-and-sixpence for the same shirt the other day; or maybe something about a boatman who told you to keep a few shirts for him. Then make as if you're about to leave and the chances are that he'll tell you to hang on. 'Show it to me so sonny,' he'll say in a put-upon voice. 'Oh … still, I don't know – it looks a bit worn doesn't it? These shirts don't take much wear, do they? – especially after they've been washed a few times.'

'What do you want for it so?' is his next tactic and it doesn't matter how low a price you quote him, he'll look horrified and start whining:

'Oh. May God grant you luck you innocent sonny-boy you. You don't seriously think that I could give you that much for it? God bless you, but will you have a bit of sense for yourself good man! Here, put it there (i.e. 'shake hands on it'); I'll give you a seven-and-six pence for it, and another pint of porter free of charge – for good luck. Now, what would you say to that?'

You're as well off accepting his offer – that's unless you've a bit of the huckster in you or you're more stubborn than most because An Mangaire is the ultimate wheeler-dealer and he always gets the best of any bargain. That said, Cuirín Mór and An Seaimpín always get a better price for their stuff than the rest of us – I think. An Mangaire's more afraid of them than he is of others. By the way, many of the other soldiers here don't like it at all that the young recruits here are 'ruining the market' on them. An Seaimpín came in the other night and he was really disgusted because An Mangaire told him that he was looking for too much money for the shirts he was flogging and that the younger recruits were selling them to him for just one shilling each! 'Damn those latchicoes anyway,' he said, removing his shoes, 'wouldn't you think they'd have the decency to steer clear of the market altogether when that thieving Mangaire is making a fool of them all and they don't even realise it. Everyone knows that it won't be worth the trouble soon stealing anything, the way things are going.

Myself and Cóilín Morgan finally said goodbye to one another – not that it made a whole lot of difference to my life as I'm working up in the Officer's Canteen now a lot of the time. I got sick of Cóilín giving out to me all the time (not that he didn't often have good reason to) and put in a request to the Company Captain asking for a transfer to some other duty. For a while then, I was back to a nicer regime of training and being part of the work-groups that do various odd-jobs around the barracks. That's until the Sergeant who's in charge of the

Officers' Canteen came up to me the last day and told me to replace one of the waiters there who's out sick at the moment. That Sergeant's a funny one I can tell you; he's the closest thing I've seen to a leader of one of those press-gangs long ago. Whenever he needs anyone for work, he just marches straight into the bedroom or anywhere else the lads are gathered and just orders as many bodies as he needs out to do whatever it is. He's clever too about who he selects for work and there's no fear that he'd tell the likes of Cuirín Mór or Colm a' tSeaimpín to go up and work in the canteen, waiting on tables or washing dishes. More than anything else in the world, he hates to see any younger recruits sleeping in on a Sunday morning or on a holy day and it's those days that he's always going around looking for helpers.

'Tut, tut, young men stretched out asleep in the middle of the day. Soldiers – supposedly! Don't you get enough time for snoring at night not to be doing a Rip Van Winkle on it? You'd swear that you all had sleeping pins shoved in your arses the way you men go on!'

He'll let out a sarcastic laugh and make a charge at one of the lads, ordering him up out of the bed and telling him to dress himself immediately. He has a strange habit too when he's talking to you of translating everything he says from Irish into English – simultaneously – so that he begins to sound like one of those bilingual government notices you hear on the radio every now and then.

He made a beeline for our room this afternoon and, after he'd spent a while mooching around, like an old banshee surveying the dead of the battlefield, he made his way over to me. I'd my blanket pulled up over my face quietly praying that he'd just go away. I let on to be asleep but to no avail. My fate was sealed on this occasion. You can't fool the Mess Sergeant that easily. He gave a snort of derision, scratched his chin momentarily. '*Bhfuil tuirse ort a Mhic Amhlaigh?*' ('Are you tired McCauley?') he says.

'Damn it, but I am, Sergeant. I was out late last night.'

'You were, were you? Out late, you say?'

He laughed again and sucked some air in through his teeth (another unusual habit of his), and says:

'Well, if you're tired because you were out late at night, you can't blame anyone else but yourself – you can't blame anyone else now, can you? Here, here, wake up now like a good man – get up now like a good man and come with me over to the canteen. You won't have much interest in staying out late by the time I'm finished with you, I can guarantee you that. Not after you've got through a few jobs up in the mess.

'You too Ciarraí. Get up out of that sonny; I've a little job for you too – I'll find some work for you too boy!' He gave a doubtful glance in Cuirín Mór's direction as if unsure whether to bother with him or not, but Packie gave him such a venomous look that he decided against it. Myself and Ciarraí had to go with him while those other chancers got to stay on snoring. Whatever about anything else, there's no doubt that the person who's resilient and strong has more respect here and is deemed higher in the pecking order than poor old shrimp here.

'Don't forget to bring back my share of the spoils with you Núibín,' Packie calls over to me quietly as I was leaving.

'Aha!' What's this? What did he say?' the Sergeant says.

'Oh, nothing at all, Sergeant,' I says.

'Keep away from that buck; he's no good' – He's bad news, the Sergeant says.

The canteen that's the Officer's Mess is the last place to find yourself working in, I think, even if some other lads here see it differently. Some of the officers here are the nicest people you could meet and they're reluctant to ask you for anything at the best of times. Still, it's difficult to feel entirely comfortable around them and their conversation is fairly boring too in my opinion, especially compared to the lively discussions we have back in our room. I find this strange because you need to have a fairly good level of education to be an officer. The younger and most newly qualified officers are definitely the nicest ones, the ones who're just out of Military College. They are much friendlier than the older officers and more inclined to make conversation with you. The friendliest of all are Pádraig Ó Siochfhradha from Kerry, and Pádraig Ó Cearbhaill, from Dublin. My mistake, I forgot to mention Antoine Ó Murchú, also from Dublin, a man who is very highly respected by all the men in his Company (D Company). Of all the other officers, Captain Uinsionn Bastion, the hurler, is the other man whom the infantry soldiers here have great respect for. In the canteen, I was given a big vat full of cutlery to wash. I was lucky enough though that I was right next door to the kitchen, and in compensation for the fact that I'd been one of the few people chosen to work there, I planned on swiping as much food as possible once I got the opportunity. I washed and dried all the cutlery first and tiptoed out to the kitchen to see what I might swipe. The Mess Sergeant was sitting quietly in the corner of the kitchen as if he knew what I'd in mind all along! 'Good lad, McCauley, you weren't long finishing that job – that job didn't keep you long. Here, follow me now like a good man, I have a small job out here for you,' he says. I followed him out trying to hide my displeasure. He stopped then outside the house and pointed over in the direction of a big can of floor polish that he'd ready for me, 'D'ye see that floor polish now? Get a piece of old cloth and give the floor a good polish. You'll get the cloths in the utility room over there and give it a good shine – Make sure you give it a good shine, now mind! And report back to me out in the kitchen when you've that much done,' he says. I took my time finishing this job but eventually I'd it done. In fact, I was just taking a break for a minute when out comes the good Sergeant again. 'You're finally finished? Finished at last? It took you long enough man. Right – right-oh! Come over here now till I show you what's to be done out in the yard,' he says, sucking air through his teeth again in that strange way of his – like a cow drinking water or something. I was on a right downer by then as I thought he'd have let me go after all the work I'd already done for him. Next thing, he gives me a pile of work to do out in the yard – chopping wood, and sweeping, and enough general cleaning that even if I took it handy, I'd have been there for the rest of the day! It was nearly ten o'clock that night before I was finished and slipped back into the kitchen on a quick food-raid. By the luck of God, there was no one in there, and I managed to swipe a nice big piece of sweet-cake and two thick slices of beef. On top of that, I filled both my pockets with apples, before I heard the heavy steps of the Sergeant coming down the passageway outside. I closed the food cupboard again, stood out in the middle of the kitchen and adopted as innocent a look as I could. 'I've everything done now Sergeant,' I says, the minute he comes in, but he sensed that I'd been up to something I'd say because he gave me a suspicious stare for a minute. 'You've finished then?' he says sucking more air in between his teeth and gives his chin a scratch, as if trying to think of something else. 'What's the foolish look on your dial for, Mac? You look like Simple Simon there, by God! See here now – be here again tomorrow morning. I'll need you up here for a few days till '08 Costelloe comes back off leave. You can go now – dismissed!' I didn't hang around a second longer I can guarantee you! He probably has enough to do minding the bar but I was really on-edge for a while afterwards in case he noticed that there was any food missing. This Sergeant is from Cashel in Connemara and he's as fluent in English as he is in Irish – hence his strange habit of simultaneously translating everything he says from one language to another. It's just a habit of his though. It's not that he's showing off or anything. He speaks 'bilingually' like this almost unknown to himself at this stage. And he's not as big a stickler as some others here either, when all's said and done. He's relaxed enough in his ways too. For example – suppose he told you to be up in the canteen for eight o'clock in the morning – you wouldn't have to be there at that time if you really didn't feel like it, the reason being that he'd quickly forget that he'd told you this at all. But then, if you happened to pass by him at some point during the day – even if you're on urgent business – there's every chance that he'll nab you, shove a brush or a cloth into your hands, and put you to work on some job or other. Only recently, I'd to go up to the canteen to find the Day Officer because I needed him to sign my pass. I was only in the door when your man was over to me in a flash, brush in hand.

'Here, here – the very man! Grab a hold of this and brush out the basement boy, and put down a fire in there – and do a good job now, mind,' he tells me.

'But I'm just about to go downtown on urgent business for the Sergeant,' I says.

'Don't mind that. What's more important than doing your duty – duty first Mac!'

'Here you go now. Do as I tell you, and when you're finished with that, I've another small job for you.' I knew it was useless protesting so I took the brush off him and let on that I was going off to do what he'd told me. The minute he was gone however, I found the Day Officer, got my pass signed and disappeared out the gate as quickly as possible. And next day, when I ran into the Sergeant, he'd clean forgotten that I'd neglected to follow his instructions.

I thought Ciarraí would probably be there when I got back to the room, but there was no sign of him. He'd been sent cleaning bedrooms and it was a long time before he was done. Cuirín Mór was waiting for me though and I divided out my 'spoils' with him. 'You did well Núibín,' he says. 'I commend you on your efforts. I think I'll have to tell that fool above to keep you working there from now on. I wonder will Ciarraí bring any stuff back with him too – what d'you think? If you can't supply me with enough of the spoils, then I can always put more patronage his way.'

Myself and Ciarraí had a row this morning. It was strange how it kicked off too. Ciarraí's hot-headed enough at the best of times, but he was more irritable than normal this morning. He was out last night and told me to stop whistling a few times.

'You're worse than a bloody canary,' he says.

I knew that I'd to stand my ground this time, however. No one in the Company'd have any respect left for me otherwise – so I kept on whistling as if oblivious to Ciarraí's comments. Next thing, he throws down whatever bit of kit he's cleaning and walks over.

'Didn't I tell you to stop whistling?' he says.

'Maybe you did,' I says, 'but shur what about it anyway?'

Next thing he punches me in the mouth as hard as he can. I was lucky that none of my teeth broke, he hit me that hard! Next thing it's war and the two of us are out on the floor punching the hell out of one another. One minute, I had him and the next, he was clobbering me and on it went. For a while it looked like he might get the better of me but I wasn't doing too bad as long as I kept his arms pinned down. Whenever he got one of his arms free he lashed out and punched me mercilessly. I got a few hard punches in once or twice, but I'd few chances to really nail him that I should have taken but didn't. Then, just as both of us were starting to tire, the others pulled us apart. Funnily enough, Ciarraí's mood improved after that. It was as if he'd worked some of that bad temper out of his system. Once the fight was over we entwined our little fingers one against the other for a second – as a sign that we held no grudges or bad feeling towards one another. I thought I'd fought really well, especially when you consider that Ciarraí is a strong and wiry sort of a fellow, but all Colm a' tSeaimpín did was spit contemptuously into the hearth and say:

'That's the nearest thing I've ever seen to two young puppy dogs scrabbling around with one another on the road. God forbid that either of you'd ever marry one of my sisters. I'd need a big power of a man, sixteen stone at least, a man who'd have my back when I'd be fighting.'

'What would your old lad[29] say if he saw Núibín arriving home with your sister, Colm?' says Cuirín Mór.

'Oh Musha, little brother, don't you know what he'd say! He'd cry his fill first and then he'd drive the two of them back across the Daingean bridge with a hay-fork. It'd be the same with my old lad,' says Packie; 'it'd kill him altogether, I'd say. He'd probably head out to Carraig an Bhalbháin[30] and refuse to come home again until they agreed to build a bridge for him – something that'd never happen.' I enjoyed listening to this banter, but Ciarraí didn't think it was that funny at all.

'I hope you're not including me along with Núib in that category,' he says proudly, but Packie just burst out laughing.

'"Category" is it? I'll give you bloody "category" from now on, so I will, you thieving Ciarraí you, especially if you return from the canteen here with nothing – like you did last night!' Ciarraí got mad then and begin f-in' and blindin'.

'Watch yourself now you billy-goat or I might have to christen you again,' says Cuirín Mór .

Of the three who arrived from the Sixth Battalion in Athlone together, only Cuirín Mór and Ciarraí are left now as the other man managed to transfer back to his old battalion again. You'd think that most soldiers would really prefer to stay here in Galway given the great advantages of being based here, but that's not always the case. I suppose your man was lonely and missing his old friends back in Athlone.

Cuirín Mór[31] came out of the guard-room today. He'd been confined there for fourteen days as punishment for hitting another man. I was standing outside Block B when he was released from guard-duty and he stood at the door of the guard-room for a second then threw back his shoulders, and gave us the 'thumbs-up' sign. Then he crossed the parade square, walking as straight as a man who'd challenge the world – a big smile on his face. Easy for him to laugh, mind you. He's one of the biggest, strongest and bravest men in Connemara, and that'd be a source of great pride for any man.

My seven days 'confined to barracks' finished today and I'll have to take part in the Leader's Parade every day now for the next week. I was lucky that I didn't get a worse punishment really because this is what happened:

When I went out on the Leader's Parade, last Saturday, everything I was wearing was borrowed from others. I'd been out late on Friday night drinking and had no preparation done for parade the next morning and so I ran around then on Saturday morning borrowing stuff. I borrowed a pair of shoes from one man, some other equipment from another man and a musket, and a uniform from someone else. I've often done this trick before and I thought I'd get away with it again. But, unluckily for me, Company Sergeant Ó hIceadha[32] was suspicious at how polished and nicely turned out I looked and questioned me on all my stuff. So he makes a note of everything I was wearing and says sarcastically; 'Are you sure you don't have anything on you belonging to me?' – then charges me and I'm punished as described.

I was on sentry-duty last night with my old 'reliables' – Mac Ruaidhrí, Joeen Beag, and 'Milseáin' Ó hEidhin. My uncle, Captain Peadar Ó Condúin[33] was Guard Captain. We're assigned to guard-duty quite often these days, but I don't mind this too much, especially when the company is good. The first two sentries are supposed to go out once darkness falls, but sometimes this can be a little later depending on things. We alternate then, two men inside and two men outside – and the pair who're on duty outside have to circle the barrack walls, one inside and one outside, and meet one another again at the back-gate. If you need to, you can call the Guard Captain by blowing a whistle, but needless to say, this happens very rarely. The sentry carries a loaded gun of course, with about fifty bullets in it altogether. The Duty Officer comes around about twice a night, or more frequently if he's a '*Gildy File.*' And if he happens to catch you unawares, he gives you a right bollocking. If the Officer's a '*Cushy File,*' he probably doesn't bother you much – so the sentries are much happier to see certain officers coming than they are others.

It's grand walking around on sentry-duty up until about midnight. You hear all the different sounds on the air at this time of the night – the echo of boots crunching across the square or the odd bar of a song as sung by someone who's had a few drinks, or the like. After midnight, however, it's as quiet as death out there and you'd get a bit nervous sometimes, passing the dark corners when your buried childhood fears resurface. Then, when your two hours are done, you give a whistle to the man who's to replace you and make eagerly for the heat and the comfort of the guard-room for a while where you can have a nice strong cup of tea next to the fire. I really enjoy guard-duty though because you get to hear the old-timers tell you about life in the army in years gone by. The older soldiers have very little respect for the young lads and the newest arrivals here. I suppose that this is the way of the world everywhere you go. According to themselves anyway, when they were in the pride of their youth, they were a cut way above the younger lads today. Then again, the new recruits today will probably say the same thing about the next batch that come in after them – say in twenty years' time. The majority of the older soldiers, the ones who are married anyway – live in Galway town, but seeing as he lives in Clarinbridge, Joeen Beag sleeps in the barracks here during the week and goes home at the weekends. Joeen Beag and his cousin, 'Milseáin' Ó hEidhin are in the same company as me, but Mac Ruaidhrí and my uncle Captain Ó Condúin are in the Quartermaster's Company. Mac Ruaidhrí's a funny fellow at the best of times, but he's even wittier still when the older lads are 'sparring' with him as Joeen Beag and Mac Uí Eidhin were the other night. Mac Ruaidhrí is the 'Great Prophet of Doom' and you'll never hear any good news from him. He's always on the ball with the latest 'bad news' for everyone and he has a long hangdog face too which only adds to his aura of misery or despair! The bad news he had for us tonight was that this barracks is to be closed down and we're all going to be transferred to Athlone, or, worse still, to Mullingar maybe.

'Ah well – they can do whatever they want,' he says; 'as far as I'm concerned, I haven't long to go now before I've my time done anyway, and they can transfer out to Hong Kong then for all I care!'

'You're planning on going out when your time is up?' says 'Milseáin' Ó hEidhin to him then, as if only half-interested in his latest prognostications of doom!

'Absolutely! Shur what else would I do? Stay here in this place, is it? I've spent too long in the army as it is! Pity, I didn't take my ticket when I had my first stint in the army over, shur I'd have been way better off.' Joeen Beag butts in then and says:

'I thought you'd some small bit of sense Milseáin? Don't you know well that you wouldn't get Mac Ruaidhrí to leave the army even if you were to drive him out with a pitchfork? Shur, where else would he go, you bollocks? He wouldn't be able to do a normal day's work now anymore as a civilian – shur he's too institutionalized at this stage. Mac Ruaidhrí will stay where he is, believe you me. At the end of the day, he knows what side his bread is buttered on! Sure, you'd leave here sooner than Mac Ruaidhrí ever would. And doesn't the world and it's mother know that you won't leave *An Chéad Chath* until you've a beard reaching down to your knees!' 'Milseáin' Ó hEidhin admitted that he might have been a bit naïve in his thinking, but Mac Ruaidhrí explodes rightly then:

'Ho ho, would you listen to who's talking? You're one to talk Joeen Beag, that's for sure! You're the least inclined to go out of anyone here. Mac Ruaidhrí will go out this time. Wait'll you see. You all think that I'm just waiting for the useless pension from here, but that's where you're wrong! You'll think I'm talking rubbish when I tell you that I'm going to have my own shop there downtown, come this time next year – but I will – mark my words!'

'Ha, ha!' he says then, as if he'd just wiped the floor with them in the argument. (Needless to say, he hadn't knocked a stir out of them – they couldn't give a shite at all this 'blather', one way or the other.)

'Milseáin' Ó hEidhin took a good drag on that battered old tobacco pipe of his and says:

'You probably won't be too hard on anyone who needs a bit of credit every now and then so Mac Ruaidhrí, I'd say?' I don't know whether Mac Ruaidhrí really copped it that Milseáin was taking the piss out of him though – because next thing he says all serious and solemn:

'One thing that there won't be is "credit",' he says. 'Money up-front, money up-front! How long do you think my shop would last if everyone in the barracks here came in looking for credit?'

The conversation came to an abrupt end because the Captain came in just then and ordered myself and Joeen Beag out on guard-duty. It was a beautiful night outside, a full moon in the sky. The time went by really quickly too, and two hours seemed like just two minutes. Myself and Joeen Beag were out at the sentry-post as dawn broke and it was an amazing sight. The magnificence of the sky would have lifted the darkest of hearts, the first rays of light peeping through the eastern horizon and moving slowly across the sky, driving the darkness westwards across Ballyloughane, Ardfry, Tamhain, and Mutton Island. The light extended westwards then across Galway Bay until the Aran Islands revealed themselves on the tip of the horizon. It was a radiant and beautiful morning, thank God, and there wasn't a whisper of a breeze in the sky, the surface of the bay so still that it looked like a magic, exotic ocean far away. My heart swelled with pride at the beauty of the place, the ancient and majestic grey of Renmore Barracks and all the fine Gaeltacht men who live within its walls. God knows, I was sorry to go in again this morning once guard-duty was over and leave behind the magnificence of that world outside. Cuirín Mór was Room Attendant today and I got little sleep. Anytime I was about to nod off, that f——r would make noise and wake me up again. In the end, I gave up trying to sleep and decided to have the chat with him. 'Oh, Núibín, haven't you very little respect for your patron that you'd prefer snoring away in bed there instead of making conversation with him? By God – how do you expect me to get through the whole day here without anyone to talk to? You're a strange b——ks all the same Núibín, aren't you?'

I have my C.B. over with, but I'm worried that I might get more of it again soon – that, or a worse punishment still. I was absent from guard-duty last night and that's one of the biggest crimes a soldier can commit.

What happened was that I went out to the library in the afternoon to get a few books – to keep me going for the week. I was determined to be back in plenty of time to go on guard-duty, but temptation came my way and I was powerless to resist, I'm afraid. I was walking down *Shop Street* on my way back from the library when I met Ciarraí, who'd just been to the pawnshop or the 'pan', as we call it here. He'd left a uniform in on behalf of Captain Larkin who'd told him that if he hurried back to the barracks straight away, he'd give him a loan of one crown for his troubles. Once Ciarraí felt the weight of the five 'twenties' the pawnbroker gave him in his pocket however, he lost all interest in the barracks, in Captain Larkin, and in everything else but the sight of a big frothy pint. Still, he might've better avoided the temptation to go in for a few pints if he didn't happen to run into me just then. He'd a good excuse to go to the pub then, or so he said anyway.

'Come on Núib, and we'll go in for one,' he says.

'I don't mind. I can't delay long though, as I'm on guard-duty tonight,' I says, and the two of us go into Larry Hynes' pub. We'd a few pints in Larry Hynes' and went on to Maggie Ann's for a few more. We got nice and happy in ourselves and then moved from there down to Delia Lydon's. A few more pints there and neither of us were making much sense. 'Larkin can go to hell,' says Ciarraí, paying for two more pints. 'The same goes for the guard who's on tonight,' I says.

It was dark by then and we headed down to the Brooklyn Bar in Woodquay where we might run into some other lads from the barracks. The woman who owns this pub is from Annaghdown and she only recently returned from America with her two sons. Her husband's still working over there, but she says he's returning to Ireland himself soon too. The Brooklyn's one of the most popular bars with the soldiers here in Galway and no wonder too, seeing as the woman who owns it is always very nice and welcoming to us all. The Claregalway and the Annaghdown people all congregate there and the Menlo people especially. Who was there already when we come in but Cuirín Mór, staring at the dregs of porter at the bottom of his glass. He perked up the minute he spotted us though and downed his last drop of porter in one go.

'Well, you're very welcome little brothers,' he says, making room at the counter for us. ''Course we're welcome,' says Ciarraí, sarcastically and orders three pints for us, all the same. I hadn't a penny left at this stage and there was a big dent in Captain Larkin's five twenties by then too. Ciarraí went out to the toilet and the minute he was gone Cuirín Mór says:

'Drink plenty now Núibín because his generosity mightn't last long. Larkin'll be on his way down I'm sure, and Ciarraí won't be long turning cranky, I'd say.'

The crowd in from Annaghdown were in flying form by then and began singing like the old piper of long ago. But they'd only the one tune for some reason – 'The Valley of Knockanure'. They sang this over and over again so that we were all so sick of it in the end that Cuirín Mór finally calls loudly: 'The Daltons are dying with monotonous regularity for the past half an hour now.' The music stopped suddenly and an angry look came over the singers. Next thing, the strongest-built man amongst them arrives over and asks whether we wanted trouble! Neither I nor Ciarraí wanted any hassle, but Cuirín Mór didn't give a damn and said as much straight up to your man's face. Unsurprisingly, your man didn't like this, and I think there'd have been a ruckus straight away, if the barwoman of the Brook (Bean a' Brook, as we call her) hadn't ordered us all out of the pub. 'Damn you lot, I've never seen you in here that you're not arguing and fighting,' she says to the singers. This bothered them more than us even if Cuirín Mór stormed out the door all disgusted and offended-looking. 'It'll be a long time before you'll ever see any of us in here again, my good woman,' says one of the singers as a parting shot, but she couldn't have cared less. 'All the better,' she says, closing the door behind them. That was all the satisfaction they got from her. I felt sorry for them really being thrown out like that, but it was just as well for us because myself and Packie would have had the worst of it, if they'd stayed much longer. Packie got a hiding from the same crowd previously when he tried to defend a fellow soldier who'd five or six of them laying into him during a fight one night down at a dance in the Commercial. Ciarraí was delighted that we got out of there this evening unscathed, because while he might be fiery, he wouldn't have been able for them. He called for three more drinks. The drinks had only just settled when Captain Larkin arrives, his jaw set and a poisonous look in his eyes. 'Where's my money you thieving muckbird?' he says to Ciarraí.

Ciarraí was 'well-on-it' and burst out laughing at this – as much as to say that Captain Larkin was hilarious altogether! 'Is one crown any good to you?' he says, slipping off his high stool. 'One crown,' roars Larkin, 'one crown, is it! How much did you get for my old uniform?'

'I can't remember now,' says Ciarraí all jokey-like.

'How much have you left?' retorts Larkin trying his best not to explode with temper.

'I only have seven and sixpence – I'll give you one crown now and you'll get the rest on pay-day,' says Ciarraí.

'Give me that crown right now you rotten latchico,' says the Captain who was fit to be tied at this stage. He took the two half-crowns from Ciarraí, gave the three of us a filthy look then stormed back out the door again. 'I hope you've more than a half-a-crown left Ciarraí boy,' says Packie the minute he was gone, his voice slightly slurred. Your man got annoyed at this. 'Of course, I've got more than half-a-crown left. Do you think I'm an idiot or what? I don't see why yourself and Núibín are here drinking with me and the pair of you without a penny to your name, by the way. You'd think you'd have your own money on you and not always be skiving off others. Go to hell now, the two of you. You're not getting another damn thing off me!' I could tell that Ciarraí's attitude really got on Packie's goat, but he was cute enough to play the diplomatic game. 'But Ciarraí, little brother, didn't I just save your ass from that gang that just left there, and I thought you'd be only too glad to share whatever you have with me in gratitude for this? Maybe it'll be me who'll have money the next night we're out and you know well that I wouldn't ever see you thirsty then, would I?' To quote the Horse, however, Ciarraí 'had made flint of his heart' and nothing would move him. 'That crowd who left were all bluster. They were no threat to anyone – if you were listening to them at all,' he says, 'and what you have, you hold – as they say. I'm off now to find someplace quiet for myself – somewhere I can drink my pint in peace.'

Packie Mór didn't like this one bit and I knew by him that he couldn't wait to give Ciarraí a hiding once we got back to barracks. 'Right so you miserly puck-goat, you,' he says, under his breath. 'Just bugger off now after ruining the night for us, why don't you! God help you though when we get back to the barracks and I get my hands on you. I'll batter you so bad that every bone in your miserly body will ache, mark my words.' Packie issued this threat in whisper but it was enough to stop Ciarraí in his tracks. He adopted an innocent grin then even if I think he was closer to crying than anything else.

Next thing, he's back to the bar again and ordering three pints. We'd got our way in the end. What couldn't be got through soft talk had been secured by threat and intimidation!

Myself and the other two were put under open arrest on our return to barracks as punishment for being absent when we were supposed to be on guard-duty. I was very well-on-it by then and couldn't have cared less about this charge really, but when I got back to the room, Captain Ó Sé went crazy. He rises from the kit-box he's sitting on like the poet of old 'meditating on the vicissitudes of life' and says in a tormented voice: 'You're finally fecked McCauley! With all the messing and stupidity you've been at in the army, you've been nailed at last. Absent when you're supposed to be on guard-duty – the biggest offence any soldier can commit. You'll be charged soon boy, and your punishment will be so heavy that you won't leave the guard-room again until you've grown a beard a foot-long!' To be fair to him, Captain Ó Sé's a decent old skin who's worried that I'll get myself into right trouble – more than anything else. Luckily for us, the 'woman of the house' down the Brook gave us credit this evening so's we weren't totally broke by the time we got back to barracks. I uncorked a small *Baby Powers* I'd brought back from the pub and gave Captain Ó Sé a slug of it and that calmed him down a lot.

Despite the Captain's dire predictions, I got off fairly lightly in the end. All I got was a ten-shilling fine and the loss of a day's pay. This is a heavy enough punishment I know, but it could have been a lot worse. It was the Captain himself who tried me, as it happens. I was brought into the Company Captain first, and I knew exactly what he'd say – 'Down to the (Platoon) Leader with you.' I went in to see the Leader then, certain that I'd get two weeks in the guard-room but thank God, I got off more lightly than this. I better watch it from now on though as this kind of messing isn't me at all.

We've had a Mission here for the past week and heard a lot of fine sermons in Irish as part of it, even if they don't mention Hell as much as they used to years ago, it seems to me. Still and all, what we heard from the Missioners would set you thinking, that's for sure. The majority of the lads here went to Confession at the end of the week, me and Cuirín Mór included. There's not as much cursing and swearing around the place since.

\* \* \*

## A Visit to Carna

I received a letter this morning from my old friend Mícheál Ó Cualáin inviting me back west to Carna for a few days at the end of next week. I first got to know Mícheál up in Kilkenny when he was working on the fairground there stacking turf for a contractor from Roscommon. When that job came to an end, he got a job in the same woollen mills I was in, and from then on, we were the best of friends. Mícheál is due to move to Pittsburgh in America soon and this is why he's back home at the moment. I was never in Carna before this (the furthest west I was prior to this was Carraroe) and please God, I won't miss out on this opportunity. I've to be careful that I don't do anything wrong or act out of turn over the next few days, otherwise, I won't get my pass.

The weekend in Carna was one of the nicest weekends I've ever had. I travelled back west on the five o'clock bus, on Saturday evening and that trip alone was as good as any part of the holidays this summer. The bus was heaving with people and everyone was in great form, the laughter and the wit flying back and forth. There was a little bit of English spoken until we reached Oughterard but from there on, you heard nothing but Irish. I was in a bit of a daze trying to take in the landscape we passed through – a landscape as beautiful and remote as you'll get anywhere in the world – doing my best to eavesdrop on the conversations around me at the same time. I was standing as it was so crowded with goods and people. A woman standing next to me was a Yank – probably of Connemara stock – and it was obvious that she found the journey difficult. She was suffering, the poor creature. The journey wouldn't have been so rough on her if she'd been standing at the front or the back of the bus, but she was right in the very middle and it was very bumpy. She was surrounded by women except for one fellow who was squashed up right next to her; the same man had a drop on board as he sang non-stop from the minute we left Galway. Strangely enough, his songs weren't the ones we were used to at all – 'Goodbye Dolly, I must leave you,' 'It's a long way to Tipperary' and other songs that the English soldiers used to sing in the First World War. But then, when he spoke to anyone, he had the sweetest Irish you've ever heard. He seemed a nice, friendly fellow, but I thought it was very selfish of him not to offer his seat to this woman standing next to him and eventually, I plucked up the courage and whispered to him:

'You should give your seat to that woman beside you as she's being thrown all over the place on the bus.'

'Oh, certainly, certainly, little brother,' he says, standing up, 'pity you didn't tell me earlier – I'm blind you see, since the war.' We'd a good chat then, the two of us. He told me that he'd a lot of respect for the British even if he still felt loyal to Ireland too. He pulled a watch from his pocket and handed it to me to hold. It was a watch for the blind – that's to say that you could feel the figures and the two hands on the watch-face with the tips of your fingers and tell the time that way. I was mortified, needless to say, that I'd said anything to this old fellow at all, seeing as he was so nice; at least I'd the satisfaction of knowing that I'd helped out that visitor who looked much less stressed in herself now. We'd a bit of a delay at Maam Cross so I went into Peacocks for a drink.

I got my pint and stood out in the doorway of the pub looking over the wild, fierce landscape and the mountains around about. The air's so fresh here that it makes you feel healthier and more energetic straight away. Connemara has something indefinable and mysterious about it, there's no doubt about it, and I've never been there that I haven't felt its strange magic. The small villages we went through after this were really beautiful – (even their names were lovely) – Scríb, An Gort Mór, Doire Iorrais, Cill Chiaráin, An Aird Mhór, Róisín na Maithniach, and my destination – the small village of Carna. My friend was waiting for me at the bus-stop and he had a great welcome for me. We went into Maidhcí Uí Mhóráin's pub for some of the black stuff. We'd a good chat before going back to An Más where the Ó Cualáin family live. We both had bikes. Mícheál had got the loan of one for me. It was four miles back to his house. To the north of us stood the Twelve Pins, so high and blue – the most noble-looking mountains I've ever seen. The lonely whistle of the snipe came across the bog to us, while to the south lay the shoreline and the vast expanse of ocean stretching away to the horizon. Overlooking this great vista were the two giant hills *Na Sceirde* and *Cruaich na Caoille*, like two eternal sentinels of the Irish coast.

We reached Mícheál's house, and yours truly got a great welcome from his brother and his mother. We stayed up late talking until one by one, Eddie, Seán and Pádraig went off to bed. We chatted for a good while about our times working in the Woollen Mills back in Kilkenny and when we eventually checked the time, it was one o'clock in the morning. 'We'll go to bed now, in God's name,' says Mícheál, 'because I think we'll go to 9 o'clock Mass tomorrow morning with God's help.' I slept like a log and woke early next morning, then went outside to take in the amazing sight. 'How could anyone leave this place and go to live in the smog and filth of the big city?' I thought to myself. Sadly, you can't make a living by admiring the amazing view every day though, as the old woman said long ago. For most families here, there isn't enough work here for the eldest son to subsist on when he gets married, never mind anyone else in the family staying at home. Emigration is a normal part of life here in Connemara for generations and it doesn't look like this will change anytime soon. These grim thoughts disappeared from my mind the minute I heard Mícheál calling me in for breakfast. 'Come in for your food here Dónall,' he says, 'you're worse than a bloody tourist standing out there, you idiot you.'

'I was just looking at the mountains,' I says – 'the way that they change colour.'

'You must be well-used to mountains by now, between the Clare mountains across the bay there from you in Renmore and shur, can't you see the Blackstairs and Sliabh na mBan from Callan there, up in Kilkenny.'

'I know Mícheál,' I says, 'but they're nothing compared to the mountains here.'

We cycled into Carna to Mass, at a nice steady pace, everyone who passed us on the road, hailing us warmly. I was amazed at the amount of cars that were outside the church and when I mentioned this to Mícheál, he said that many of the older people now take a taxi to go to Sunday Mass. Connemara's changing, the same as everywhere else. It's the same with the clothes that people wear at Mass. You don't see as many of the older crowd wearing the 'báinín' anymore. And some of the young people had the most modern fashions – even if the city slickers think that everyone who lives west of Barna is a redneck and looks like one too! Some of the men in Connemara are the tallest and strongest-looking men you'll see anywhere in Ireland today and that's no exaggeration. I thought that the lads in Renmore were strong looking, but they aren't a patch on some of the lads you'd see gathered outside the church after Mass in Carna. Goldsmith's words came to mind – 'But a bold peasantry, their country's pride, when once destroyed can never be supplied'– and my heart filled with hatred for the government that allows the finest of men and women to emigrate across the water, because they can't make a living here – in their own country! The same sad thoughts came to me when we were at the céilí the other night. The place was packed to the rafters and everyone having a whale of time. Still, you knew by the majority of them that their minds were somewhere else and that they'd mentally cut their ties with home already. All they talked about was the big cities of England and America. And at least half of the young people there had already left anyway. They were home on holidays and the other half will be leaving soon. Thinking about this really bothered me and it came between me and my enjoyment of the night, if I'm honest about it.

I'd to come back on the morning bus and although my visit to *Iorras Aithneach* was too short, I was still very sorry to leave. My pal accompanied me as far as the bus and when we said goodbye, we both knew in our hearts and souls that we mightn't see one another again until after we are dead. Pittsburgh of the dark fog is a long way from here.

Cuirín Mór was Room Orderly when I got back. He put down the brush he was holding and shook my hand in welcome, then insisted that I join him in *Damhsa na Péiste*. This is a dance that Cuirín Mór invented himself apparently, and he dances it whenever he's in good form to tell everyone that life is wonderful. As part of this dance, you've to twist and turn yourself like a snake or an eel and it includes a lot of strange moves and unusual steps. 'Aha, a hundred welcomes back Núibín,' says Cuirín Mór then, 'tell me all about it now; who the big bruisers you fought were and which fine girls you charmed, and how many gallons of poteen you drank back in Tearmann'[34]. (He always calls the Connemara Gaeltacht 'An Tearmann' implying that a separate and distinctive race of people live out there.) I was about to say something but Cuirín Mór got in first. 'But tell us this now Núibín, of the big heart; have you much money left after your hols?'

'Very little,' I says. 'How'd I have much coming back when I'd very little going out west in the first place?'

'All the same, Núibín, you've enough left to buy us both a mug of tea and a handful of biscuits, surely?' he says plaintively. I told him that I had just about – and next thing we're hopping and jumping the room doing *Damhsa na nGabhar* ('The Goat Dance') – another one of his strange dances! A minute later and I'm still hopping around like a puck-goat and whooping and shouting when my friend comes to an abrupt stop. He's grabbed hold of the sweeping brush again and he's back to sweeping the floor again, his head bowed like a monk. Lieutenant Dunne's standing in the doorway, his eyes wide with surprise. And this is when Cuirín Mór really sells me out, the fecker! First, he lets on that he hasn't seen the Lieutenant at all, then suddenly stands to attention as if he's only just suddenly spotted him and gives the order – 'Room – attention!' I stood to attention and the Lieutenant walked in, an angry scowl on his face. He walked straight over and stood in front of me for what seemed like an age, saying nothing, then gave the order – 'At ease'.

'Is it a habit of yours to give exhibitions of this type on a regular basis, McCauley, do you mind me asking?'

I was still in a state of shock and couldn't get a word out. Worse still, I felt a sudden urge to laugh for some strange reason! Cuirín Mór butted in with his tuppence-worth.

'Oh, he gets these fits regularly sir,' he says. 'I often thought he had it in him to be one of those dervishes …'

To give the Lieutenant his due though, he cut Cuirín Mór off right at the quick – before my erstwhile comrade made a right 'holy show' of me altogether.

'I wasn't asking you Cuirín Mór. I think that Private McCauley is probably able to explain himself to me just fine. He's no problem talking or explaining his actions on other occasions anyway.' I had to say something in my defence – and quickly. There was nothing worse than standing there like a fool, saying nothing. 'Well Sir,' I says, 'I was so happy to be back here in the barracks with all my comrades again that I started dancing around the place. I was on weekend leave, y'see, and I've only just got back.' The Lieutenant gives a thin smile at this and says:

'Well – at least – I'm glad to hear that you're so happy with this place. It's better to have one soldier than ten conscripts – or at least, that's what they say anyway. Get your work uniform on now McCauley and go over to the Battalion Quartermaster's Stores – because he needs one or two men for some work there. You too, Cuirín Mór. Don't let me see you hanging around here any longer.'

Lieutenant Dunne left the room again. Cuirín Mór's in no mood for dancing now that his stint as room orderly's been cut short like this, you can be sure. And needless to say, he blamed me for the fact that he was caught!

'Curse you anyway, Núibín, you're nothing but bad luck. Why the hell didn't you stay over in An Tearmann for another while and you wouldn't have drawn that bollocks on me,' he complains, setting his brush aside for a moment.

'Wasn't it you who brought him down on us with your bloody *Damhsa na Péiste*?' I says. 'If we'd stayed quiet, he wouldn't have known there was anyone in the room here even.'

We'd no choice but to go where we'd been told, though and once I'd put on my work-clothes, it was across to the square to the Stores. If we'd been sent over to the Food Stores, that'd have been something; we'd have had some kind of recompense for our troubles then; but there was nothing in these stores we'd been sent to except guns, gas masks and shelves full of similar equipment.

The Battalion Quartermaster is from Corr na Móna – Ó Treasaigh is his surname – and he is well-respected as a very fluent speaker of both Irish and English. He has a lot of time for Cuirín Mór, but he doesn't think very much for me, particularly since he knew my father long ago and had a great respect for him. 'Your soul from the devil McCauley,' he says to me anytime that my kit is messy or I've an untidy look about me. 'Your soul from the devil, but you're not your father's son at all! You're one right messy little idiot, by God!'

I tried to pull a fast one on him one day a while back but it didn't work. What happened was that my walking stick had broken in two and I'd cobbled both halves of it together with a piece of twine. I'd the stick half-concealed beneath my leather belt in an effort to keep the damage hidden, but the Battalion Quartermaster spotted it straight away during room inspection. He took the stick off me and held it aloft so that the whole room could see. 'Aha, what do we have here?' he says, 'one of those big sticks that St. Patrick used to hunt the snakes out of Ireland, is it.'

Ó Treasaigh's face dropped when he saw me appear through the door for work today, but he brightened up again when Packie followed me in. 'Where were you for the past few days, McCauley?' he says. He knew well where I was, but he was trying to get a rise out of me. 'I was back in Carna visiting friends Quartermaster,' I tells him. 'Up on Cnoc Meá visiting your relatives and all the fairies as well, I'll bet,' he says. Myself and Cuirín Mór laughed at this and the Quartermaster got a good kick out of it too. We were sent out to clean some Bren guns and this kept us busy until tea-time. '07 Ó Donncha, the poetry and opera man left us for Athlone today. He's doing a course in the Military Police. I don't know who recommended him for it or what possessed him to apply for it, but I'm sure of one thing – he hasn't got the makings of a Military Policeman in him. For one thing, he's far too nice for that kind of a job; secondly, he's too fond of going out for his few pints. He'll be back here before long, I've no doubt, and it won't be as a member of the Military Police either.

One man who's due to be transferred to Dublin soon is my old friend, '06 Reaney, and I suspect that he won't be there too long before he'll leave the army altogether. His family are going to 'buy him out of the army' as they say, and it's probably just as well. He had very little interest in soldiering from day one and he's even less interested in it now. It's nearly nine months now since I first got to know him that day up in the Curragh when he was polishing the buttons on his uniform. When he leaves, that'll be another link gone with the time I spent up there. There are only four or five men left now from that original company – Maitias (in D Company), Máirtín Cúc, Ó Murchú, myself, and '06 Reaney. I don't have as much contact with Maitias these days, not that we fell out with one another at all or anything. Maitias's going out with a girl from back home for a while now – (both Juleen and Margaret have been over in England a good while now) – and I wouldn't be a bit surprised if he gets married soon. Myself and Cuirín Mór went walking by the shore this evening, over as far as Ballyloughane. On our return, we walked back along the 'line', walking on the timber ballast that separates the wooden cross-beams. The moon – or at least a good chunk of it – was high in the sky by then and it formed a big pathway of light, a giant road reaching across the surface of the sea. The walls of the barracks and the Tower stood out as dark reflections against the moonlit sky and we stopped for a good while to take in the view, it was such an incredible sight. On nights like this, you'd give anything to be able to remain outdoors. The sky looks so fresh and pure that you'd swear we lived in a perfect and faultless world. That was how I felt tonight anyway and Packie echoed my sentiments. Cuirín Mór is a strange creature in this regard. Certainly, he enjoys the usual pleasures – drinking, betting and courting girls – but he's also very deep in his own way and has a strong appreciation of beauty and nature. He gets as much pleasure from a spectacular sunset or from the morning music of the lark as any poet ever did.

A year from today is when Cuirín Mór will go out on his ticket –

the same as most of the other young men here who enlisted in 1946. The cream of *An Chéad Chath* will be finished then and in the words of Tomás Ó Criomhthain – '*ní bheidh ár leithéidí arís ann*' (our like won't be seen again) – especially given that the young Gaeltacht generation are all leaving for England. There's only the odd few lads enlisting in the army anymore these days and already, you can sense that a good few of them are unsatisfied and impatient with their lives here in Renmore. Many of them can't wait for when they'll be free to go back amongst the civilian population again and head for England. That's where the 'big money' is these days. Every letter sent home by relatives over in England just whets the younger generation's appetite for emigration even more. In fact, many lads here don't even bother looking for work at home anymore, once they've their training done. They just leave here and head straight over to England.

Almost everyone in the room here's asleep now tonight and the only illumination is that small 'pilot light' that's left on all night. When I glance around the room and everyone asleep in their beds here – Colm a' tSeaimpín, Ciarraí, '06 Reaney, Ó Conceanainn from Aran, Ó Tuathail from Clifden, my 'patron' Packie, Cuirín Mór, and everyone else – I feel a special solidarity with them – yes – and a special pride because I'm one of them. It's long past time for me to close my eyes and sleep.

Most of the Battalion went to Athlone today to act as a guard of honour there next Monday, Easter Monday. General Mac Eoin will take charge of the guard of honour and most of the captains and commanders from the west – between F.C.A. and others – will be on parade. We'd a nice trip up to Athlone in the lorries, everyone having the crack. We were all billeted in an old Artillery building, even if it's not the best place in the world – the whole lot of us crowded in on top of one another, like trout in a fish-basket. Some of the older married soldiers are glad to get away from home for a couple of days, but there are others, like Joeen Beag who hate any discomfort and any changes to the regular routine back in Galway. Once we'd our beds taken out of the stores and our tea drank, Packie went off to find some lads from the Sixth Battalion whom he knew had money and who could buy him drink. He was broke as usual – it goes without saying. He must've done fairly well on the skiving-drink front because he was well-tipsy by the time he got back about eleven o'clock tonight. Larry Woods, his old buddy from Thomastown[35] was with him and Woods came precariously close to drawing the Horse on himself. The Horse was making his bed and just getting ready to go to sleep and he'd a good drop of drink on board himself. As he was making his way out the door again, Woods tapped the Horse on the arse and says:

'Good night, old horse!'

I wouldn't mind but he could just as easily have said this to any of the rest of us as Woods didn't know which of us had this nickname. Normally, the Horse doesn't mind us using this nickname for him, but he took exception on this occasion, seeing as this was an outsider to our group taking liberties … 'Whazzat?' he roars at Larry, straightening himself, 'why you lowdown son of a gun, ef I git my hands on you I'll sure 'nuff give you "old horse". I'll you show you some reg'lar Brooklyn rough stuff you Goddam punk!'

By the luck of God, Larry's deaf in one ear and so he didn't even hear the Horse roaring at him. Otherwise, there's every chance that he'd have come over and started a row with him. The Horse followed him as far as the door of the room, and only that he didn't have his night-shirt on, he'd have followed Larry outside, I'm sure.

I hadn't a penny to spend tonight and so I just spent the evening hanging around town. I recalled that evening long ago when myself and Maitias first enlisted in the army here, and how lonely the pair of us were after saying goodbye to the two girls in Galway city. A fairly long period of 'exile' lay ahead of us at that point, but thank God, we won't be gone longer than two days this time – and we'll be back down in

Galway again. I met Flash Farrell, Salty O'Rourke and a couple of other lads from the Sixth Battalion down on the bridge where they were chatting up three girls. One of these girls was stunning and very well brought-up, and after a while, I was bold enough to ask her out on a date. I asked her half-jokingly if she'd like to meet up with me tomorrow night and I was sure that she'd say no – but to my surprise she said she would. We arranged to meet after the Rosary in the Cathedral tomorrow night. Mary Mulhall is her name. I told Cuirín Mór about her there a while ago but regretted it almost immediately I'd said it. He says that he wants to come with us so that he can check out her genealogy for me! I think you're probably better off sometimes not having a 'patron' at all! Larry Woods and his other older army comrades will all be broke by tomorrow night, and chances are, Cuirín Mór plans on bumming money off me instead then!

We put on a powerful turn-out and display for General Mac Eoin – *An Chéad Chath*, the Sixth Battalion, the Artillery, the F.C.A. – from both east and west – and I'm not sure how many other groups. Your heart couldn't but swell with pride as you watched the lines of well-drilled men marching to and fro, and all their polished brass and gear shining brightly in the sunlight. As soon as the parade was over, we were set free for the remainder of the day. We have the rest of today and all day tomorrow to ourselves and are free to do whatever we wish until it's time for the return journey to Renmore.

The town was black with soldiers for the past few days and wouldn't you know it – weren't there a few fights between our lads and the members of the Artillery section. The Artillery and our Irish-speaking Battalion have never got on well and there's usually a row when either group runs into the other. I didn't see the dust-up at all, but they said it was a fight worth seeing. Cuirín Mór clocked five or six of his attackers they say, before they managed to knock him to the ground; Flaherty from the Aran Islands fought a great fight too apparently. There's a big, wide lump of a man in Artillery who goes by the nickname of 'Concrete Block', and he's so tough and difficult to beat in a fight. They say that he gave some of the best of the Irish-speaking lads as good as he got until Colm a' tSeaimpín nailed him. 'Concrete Block's' sidekick Big Domigan from Mullingar also proved quite a handful for some of our lads apparently. Our Battalion are on a high since though, as our lads believe that we were clear winners of the fight. Mind you, you can be sure that the fellows up in Artillery think the same thing! In fact, they're probably up there right now boasting about how they put the 'Tá sé's'[36] in their place.

As evening drew in today, I was worried that I wouldn't be able to sneak out to meet Mary unknown to Packie, but things worked out fine in the end. When it was time for me to go, Packie was 'out-for-the-count' – snoring loudly in his bed. He likes his sleep, the same as many of the others here. I met Mary outside the church and we spent the evening walking around town. Both of us were quite shy in the beginning, but the conversation came more easily to us as the evening wore on. If I was staying on here in Athlone, I think that Mary would keep going out with me but seeing as I'm not, we both have no business going out together anymore. All the same, I really regretted it when I'd to say goodbye to her last night outside the house she's lodging in. She won't be able to get permission to go out this evening and we'll have left here by tomorrow afternoon.

We were frozen with the cold by the time we reached Renmore today after two hours or more in the open-topped lorries from Athlone. No one said much on the way back and we all breathed a big sigh of relief on spotting the sea near Oranmore. We've a few days holiday now as compensation for being on duty during Easter, but what good is that to us seeing as none of us have any money – not until we get paid until tomorrow anyway.

Nearly every man in the room here is asleep (the only person who's awake still, I think, is Gerry Gavanly who's disappeared into some Irish-speaking den downtown somewhere like *Áras an Chonartha* or the like). If we manage to avoid the Sergeant up in the Canteen above, we'll be fine to go out this evening. I know that he won't bother Packie or Colm at all, but if he comes around looking for people to work for him, myself or poor Ciarraí won't be safe, that's for sure. Máirtín Cúc was down here on visit a while ago from his own Company and the two of us had great crack. We've invented a 'language' of our own that we use sometimes for the hell of it – it's a kind of a funny imitation of some of the 'school Irish' as used by certain public officials these days. We go overboard with this crazy 'lingo' sometimes and we'd be nearly cracking up. When we're playing this game, we refer to one another as '*Oide*' (i.e. teacher, tutor) and the barracks is the '*Ollsoil*' (university). The reason is that there are a couple of 'honours' lads here who are always trying to impress the girls they meet down in the city dance halls with the fact that they're University students – instead of what they really are – infantry soldiers.

'Oh, Teacher de Núib, how art thou this morning?' says Máirtín to me when he arrives into the room.

'Excellent, Teacher, excellent altogether,' says I.

'I was trying to enhance my mastery of the *Modh Coinníollach*[37] there a while ago as it happens. You know what I am referring to – "I would hit, you would hit, he/she/they would hit" etc. Unfortunately, I seem to get it confused with the Past Habitual tense. Do you find that you have the same problem, Teacher de Núib?'

'Yes, I find the same thing is an issue for me also.'

'And since we are speaking of the word '*buail*' (hit, strike), I heard that there was – oh, how shall I put it – a bit of a ruckus, or a fight between the students of our Institute here and the students of the Artillery University the other night.'

'I didn't witness it myself Teacher, but it is true that such a ruckus took place.'

'Did your colleague, Dr. Cuirín Mór play any part in the ruckus?'

'He didn't, as it happens. He was out making 'sweet talk' with some unidentified and innocent girl when the two groups of heroes went to battle. Either that, or he was – oh, how shall I put it – "extorting drink"? – well, scrounging drink might be more accurate, to use the *patois* of such individuals.'

'Interesting point, Teacher! Are you one of those people who considers the students of this University to speak a form of *patois*?'

'Oh, there is absolutely no doubt in my mind that what they speak is a *patois*, Teacher. Take for example such corrupted forms as the following – "*Fuair sé an-reamhar*" (He got very fat); "*snakeáil sé amach*" (he snaked out) and "*Tá mise Giolla Seomra*" (I is Room Attendant) – you couldn't say that these commonly used forms are a good form of Irish by any means?'

'I suppose you are right, Teacher. Maybe this is a natural evolution of the language, however, and that such forms will be accepted at some stage in the future.'

It was Captain Ó Sé waking up who put an end to this discussion. He scratched his head and began fostering around in search of his cigarettes. No sooner had he a cigarette lit but he says:

'God Almighty, but you're the most talkative individual I have ever come across in my life McCauley. God knows but you're the next best thing to a talking machine. This must be why you're so thin – your tongue just working non-stop. Take it easy, fellow or you'll wear away to nothing with all the blather you go on with and all we'll be able to see of you in the end is your glasses.'[38]

He choked with laughter at this example of his own wit, and the noise he made was enough to wake up Mac a' tSeaimpín.

'Well, do you know how it is now Captain? The likes of him should be put into a big room by himself and they should be left there blathering away to themselves until the soul has left their body. Honest to God, they're worse than a pack of geese, so they are.' Cuirín Mór woke up just then and let a roar of laughter out of him. 'Well, that's a good analogy alright there Colm,' he says, 'our Núibín has to be the nearest thing to a goose I've ever seen anyway. The way he begins to honk and stutter when you ask him for the price of a few pints is a prime example of it!'

'Orah, bad cess to you man, aren't I bailing you out every day of the week?' I says, 'Shur who always gives you the entry price when you haven't a red cent to your name? Who buys milk and biscuits for you over in the canteen – just in case you aren't well-fed enough already as it is? Who—?'

I didn't get any further with my list as Cuirín Mór jumps up out of the bed and says quietly:

'An Insult to the Master, oh Núib! An insult to the Royal Blood! You'll have to pay for that Núibín, you sure will.' Cuirín Mór was on his way out to the toilet but decided to kill two birds with the one stone. He dragged me out of the bed and across the room, just the same as he'd done with Ciarraí previously, then he shoved me under the tap and gave me a good 'baptism'. I'd just my night-shirt on and between the chill of getting soaked and the freezing floor, I began to sneeze. I gave my patron a sharp belt on the nose and before he could register his surprise at my fighting back against him – I ran back to the room to dry my head, sneezing and shivering all the while.

'Oh, musha, damn that softie of a young lad!' says Colm a' tSeaimpín, 'any young lad who starts sneezing after having a few drops of water thrown over him – shur he's on his last legs already!' In comes Packie then, holding his nose where I belted hit him. 'Guess what Núibín of the Fleas did to me Coilmín?' he says. 'I don't know. What'd he do?' says Colm. 'He gave me a clout on the nose,' says Packie in a voice so astonished that you'd swear a beggar had just offered the bishop a cigarette.

'And is that how little respect you demonstrate for the King's stepson?' says Colm. 'Lucky for you that you didn't clout Mac a' tSeaimpín, I can tell you, or you'd get a full dip in the water, never mind a brief baptism!'

'No, it isn't revenge that I seek, despite his exhibition of rebellious pride. No. He just won't have me as a patron anymore, that's all. From now on, he'll finally have to learn how to defend himself.'

'Hang on a minute, hang on a minute,' I says. 'You can be my bloody patron still if you want to be, but let's leave the boxing out of it this time, will we.' 'Alright,' says Cuirín Mór, 'I forgive you your offences then Núibín, but you should know now that I will extract great title from you for the next while, until you've compensated me in full for what's happened.'

Everything's back to normal now again, although my bones feel sore after the crack that went on.

I went out after dinner today and rented a rowing boat (at a shilling per hour) from the Dolan family in Woodquay and rowed up the Corrib as far as Menlo village. It's a little bit early in the year still for boating but, I still really enjoyed the afternoon. Lord knows, I spent many an afternoon rowing out on the lake last summer too. There's no nicer pastime than this, in my opinion and if I owned my own boat, I'd be out on the Corrib every day of the week. The sleepy 'lip-lop' of the waves as they touch the boat, the smell of new-mown grass on the whispering wind and then, to cap it all, the most beautiful of sights anywhere in the world – the golden sun melting along the backs of the Maumturk mountains. When the sun sets there, something magical happens and the peaks are transformed into the mountains from the Land of Wonder. Next thing, you guide the boat in next to the murmuring weir beneath the trees. The odd stroke of the oar is all that's needed because the current carries the boat along to its resting place beneath the trees. Back on land, you feel energised and full of life again after being out in the fresh air for so long and to top it all off, you head off to the Brooklyn Bar to quench your thirst with a nice cool pint that herself[39] serves up to you. This is my idea of pure happiness and there isn't a day that I don't get out of bed that I don't thank God for bringing me to such a lovely part of the world as this.

'Lord, but there's no comparison at all between my life here and the life I had when working in the Woollen Mills. Back then, there was the awful heat and the smell, the ceaseless racket of the weaving machines and the looms; that and the dead heat and congestion of the Woollen Stores, all of us frozen with the cold in the winter or perspiring profusely in the summer; and the beautiful new-green landscape of the world outside, a constant source of torment to us. You hear many people telling you that the army is a dog's life – that the soldier has no freedom whatsoever, and this, that and the other – but I say that the soldier has plenty of freedom; as long as he fulfils his duties and these are not overly onerous. Even if we'd only half the freedom we have at the moment, I'd still prefer this to living alone in a big, ugly industrial city somewhere – somewhere where you'd never even get a glimpse of lake or sea, or the last of the sun's rays fading on the hills.

I've saved a pound of my pay and put it aside during the last few weeks because I'll need some money shortly to buy some 'civilian' clothes for myself. For a while now, we've been given 'permanent permission' to wear shop clothes after duty-hours and many of the lads in D Company take advantage of this privilege. You wouldn't see any of the lads from our Company going out in civilian clothing however, as they just don't have the money to buy them. And even if they had such clothes, they'd have to keep a constant watch over them for fear that someone else might swipe them and flog them down at the 'pawn'!

Brown (or 'yellow' as Connemara people say) and blue suits are the most popular civilian clothes amongst the lads above in D Company. A white shirt, a *fairisle* jersey and a tightly knotted tie is the most common outfit of theirs. Their trouser pants are usually fairly wide at the bottom, although this style's gone out of fashion now in many places today. Fashionable or not, it makes for a very neat 'rig-out' and I'll need to make sure that I get something similar when I've the money together to get a suit made myself.

It's a pity though that the majority of the lads are no longer as keen on wearing their army uniforms when they go out as they once were – especially seeing as most of them look very neat and tidy when they're 'in uniform'. It's the dances downtown that are the cause of this I think, because many of the local girls don't like the sight of an army uniform and they often refuse to dance with a lad who's in uniform. Instead of trying to challenge this false snobbery and get rid of it however, many of the lads have just accepted the fact that is the way things are and have left their measurements for civilian clothing in with the tailor. I suppose that if the lads in our company were more interested in women than in drinking, they'd probably all do the same; the lads in our Company have no interest in the women, at least not until their pockets are empty that is.

Recently, since I've started saving and spending my money more sparingly, I go up to visit the lads in D Company in the evening and we've a great night's chat and socialising there sometimes. A good few of the lads up there are trying to save money too the same as me so's they have something to live on when they're out on 'their tickets' in about six months or so. There's always a good crowd that stay in these evenings instead of going out on the town. One lad in this group is another Connemara lad named Micheál Ó Cadhain, a lad I get on very well with even if he doesn't get on with all his colleagues up there. He's a tall wiry fellow who's as fit as a greyhound and who has a huge interest in boxing, similar to his close neighbour from home, Cuirín Mór. The two of them often box a few rounds against one another and although Cuirín Mór's heavier and stronger than Ó Cadhain, there's never much between them, for as long as it lasts. Ó Cadhain is so stubborn and headstrong that he'll never give in, not unless Cuirín Mór says that it's time to stop. Micheál has a reputation for being a very tough individual, but I can say that in any dealings I've ever had with him, he's always proven very kind and helpful. They say that he only ever spends four shillings of his pay, and that he leaves the remaining 2 pounds untouched. Still and all, he never asks anyone else for the loan of anything, and there aren't too many men in this Battalion who can say that! About six of the lads in D Company are from the 'the northern side' as the area around Cornamona and Joyce Country is called here. Cuirín Mór is from this area as are Micheál Ó Cadhain, Peadar (Tamsy) Seoighe, Frank and Breandán Ó Cadhain and Seán Ó hUigín. I love listening to them speak Irish as their dialect is quite different from the lads from south Connemara. They don't elongate the words as much when they pronounce them and the way they pronounce their vowels is completely different. Say a man from south Connemara says the word 'ceann'[40] for example; it sounds very similar to the word 'Seán' except that it's closer to the English 'Q' sound in terms of pronunciation rather than the 'C' that comes at the beginning of the word. But the lads from up north would always pronounce that same word 'ceann' more like this – 'khan'. They also say 'Eilí' instead of 'eile'[41] and 'cat'[42] instead of 'cut'. The Connemara and the Aran Islands lads usually say 'mí' instead of 'mo'[43] – for example, 'mo dheartháir' (my brother) or 'mo rothar' (my bicycle) or the like is pronounced as 'mí dheartháir' etc. But I think the northern lads pronounce this word as 'mo', that is unless I am very mistaken. Another example is the word 'leithéide'.[44] The people from Joyce Country pronounce every syllable of this word whereas those from south Connemara say 'lae-dí'. But damn this for a question anyway, I'm after dwelling in too much detail on something that I know very little about to be honest.

The two uppermost rooms in this block are held by D Company and I usually go to the room on the highest level of all just beneath the roof when I visit in the evenings, because it's these lads that I know best. I don't think the Gaels have ever gathered anywhere that they didn't divide up into different factions and it's the same even in D Company where you have competition between the different 'tribes' – the lads from south Connemara and the 'northern crowd'. On top of this there are other further smaller divisions within the larger groupings. For example, the people from Lettermore and the surrounding areas consider the people from Carna too 'anglicized' in their ways whereas the Carna people consider themselves to have the finest and most powerful men anywhere in Connemara, the most beautiful women, the best musicians, and the most fluent speakers of Irish etc! Another group again are the Rosmuc people who consider themselves the finest boat-men, a community who are strong and tough and who look down on the Cois Fharraige people as a breed of 'dealers' and hawkers who're constantly running over and back to the markets in Galway to sell the produce of their labours. For their part, the Cois Fharraige crowd – and this attitude stretches back as far as An Cnoc, I think – consider the Connemara people further west as a wild and uncivilised crowd. Whatever the reason, the different villages all look down on the one another, and you'd hear the lads reciting this rhyme and others similar to it fairly often around here:

*Is deas an baile an baile seo, is deas an baile Maighinis,*
*Is deas an baile 'chuile bhaile ach Cladhnach glas na bhfaochan!*
('This village is a nice village, the village of Maighinis is nice,
Every village is nice, every one except for grey Cladhnach of the periwinkles.')

The first three lads from Cornamona that I mentioned there – Cuirín Mór, Micheál Ó Cadhain and Tamsy speak only Irish to one another, but they can also speak English well if they have to. Both Breandán and Frank Ó Catháin have Irish from the cradle, but you'd know from their speech that they spoke more English at home than Irish. They're from Cleggan and I don't think that this is a very Irish-speaking area at all. Ó hUigín's Irish isn't good at all and his English is probably better than his Irish really. He's from Recess and I'm surprised that his Irish isn't more fluent because I've met other people from there whose Irish was as good as anyone's. And speaking of Carna, some of the finest men in D Company are from there originally – the likes of Stiofán Ó Conghaile from Dubh-ithir, or Stiofán Mhaidhc, as they call him. Tall, handsome and powerfully built he's one of those lads the women are always after down in the dance halls in Galway town. He has six brothers also, each of whom are more handsome than the next. One of them named Maidhc won the Army Boxing Championship a few years ago, (Cuirín Mór won it this year, by the way) and although Stiofán has no great interest in boxing, you'd be hard-pressed to find a fitter man in *An Chéad Chath*. Stiofán can't listen to anyone tell a story without trying to better it with a story of his own – one that's more amazing still. That's what happened tonight. We were all sitting around the fire chatting and telling yarns about fishing and hunting the smaller wild animals of the Irish countryside when Micheál Ó Cadhain started telling us about stoats and their habits. I could tell by Stiofán's face that he couldn't wait for Ó Cadhain to finish so that he could try and top it with one of his own. And the minute he got his chance, he launched right into it:

'By God, boys,' says he, 'there was a man back our way and he caught a stoat one day – and what did he do but skin the stoat with his penknife, while the animal was still alive!' (Legend has it that if you skin a live stoat and make a purse of its hide, then you'll never be poor.) 'He made a purse out of the stoat's skin and the holy day knows that he had tons of money afterwards.'

Cuirín Mór gave a look of incredulity that annoyed the hell out of Stiofán, I could tell! 'God knows but you're fairly thick at the best of times Ó Cuirín,' he said defensively staring at him and the other man roared, like a wild bear. 'Yeah, I'd want to be fairly thick alright to believe a story like the one you've just told Ó Conghaile,' he says. 'For God's sake, no man in Ireland could hold a live stoat and skin it at the same time.'

'We've lads who can do that back in our place alright,' said Stiofán firmly.

'You've some right wonders back there alright – well, according to yourselves anyway. God knows, I've never met any man from Carna yet that wasn't boasting about something or other!'

Ó Cadhain rubbed the palms of his hands together in malicious glee at this, because similar to most of the lads in this Company, he isn't overawed by Stiofán. No one said anything for a minute, but then Ó Cadhain rekindled the fuse once more.

'Oh, I remember now what I was thinking … There was a fellow in our place and he ate the two hindlegs of a live pig one day.'

'Sure, he feckin' did,' said Ó Cuirín, exploding with laughter, 'but I think that man's people were originally from Carna, now that you mention it.'

'I seriously doubt it,' says Stiofán trying to seize the initiative again, 'I doubt if they were from Carna because there's no way that they'd have gone to live out in the wilderness you people have out there.'

'By God,' says Ó Cuirín into the breach again, 'but they loved the place.'

'"Arah, isn't this a fine piece of level ground out here" is what they said the minute they hit the crossroads at Maam Cross.'

Stiofán was fit to be tied by now, but he contained himself and began whistling instead, as much as to say that he'd lost all interest in this conversation. The main reason the lads are jealous of Stiofán is because the women always make a beeline for him out in the dance halls like the Astaire Ballroom[45] and the Commercial.[46] He's a very talented dancer and he has a very nice way with people when he wants to. As soon as 'Women's Choice' is announced, there's a rush from the girls in Stiofán's direction from every corner of the hall. Another ('bodach') 'boyo' has joined us recently and he wasn't long learning how to imitate the other two bucks either – Mac an Bháird and Colm a' tSeaimpín. This is Sonaí Mhichíl Sala or 'Aon Déag'[47] Ó Cualáin as he's also known – the same fellow who dragged me out of bed one night last year. He was made a captain there a while ago, but he was too easy-going to have any real control over the men he was responsible for and he wasn't long being moved to another section. He asked to be moved to another Company and ended up in with us. He's a very decent person really, I have to say even if he can get a bit obstreperous when he's a few too many pints on-board. Although he's only of average height, he's very broad-shouldered and strong. He's a strange class of a soldier really though because when he's out on parade, for example, he's far from the neatest man in the Battalion. Another fine recruit has joined us from the Curragh recently who was added to our company too within the last fortnight. He's another big block of a man and quite similar in appearance except that his colouring's darker and he has high cheekbones that would put you in mind of one of the nobility from India. He also walks in a very stately manner, holding himself erect like one of the nobility, and when he speaks his tone is measured and refined. A few of the other lads noticed this regal air about him also because they've already nicknamed him 'the Maharajah'. His surname is McMahon, by the way, and he's from County Clare. I don't know why on earth he was sent to *An Chéad Chath* because he has very little Irish and would prefer to be stationed in Dublin. He's a very quiet lad and doesn't say a whole lot and the other lads in the room here are intrigued by him seeing as he doesn't drink or smoke. Also, he goes to the Pictures nearly every night of the week and says that he'd go to the dances more often if he had a new suit of clothes. Rather than throw a bit of water on his hair and pass a comb through it when he's going out for the night, the same as the rest of us here, the Maharajah spends a good half-hour applying hair-oil to his scalp and then another half-hour combing his hair. Still, Mac an Bháird was only saying there a while ago that he thinks the Maharajah is made of good stuff and will turn out a good solider yet. Mac an Bháird said that he may even decide to become his patron yet! I'm not so sure that this is what the Maharajah wants – but anyway...!

The number of men in this company has remained constant over the last while, even with the odd new recruit joining every now and then. My old friend '06 Reaney's gone up to Dublin now and '07 Ó Donnchú's down in Athlone. I was sorry to see '06 Reaney leave after all the times we went out for pints together. I hope things work out for him anyway whatever happens.

# Chapter 9

A group of us were sent over to Carna this morning to put up a wooden prefab for the FCA and I was part of the work-gang thankfully. The prefab was broken up into different bits and there were four lorry-fulls of them altogether. The soldiers were brought over on the fifth lorry and seeing as we've some of the most hilarious lads in our Battalion here – we'd a mighty crack on the journey over. Cuirín Mór and myself were there as were the Maharajah from B Company; Cuirín Mór, Micheál Ó Cadhain, Stiofán Mhaidhc, Ó Flaithearta from Aran and Shouter Ó Tuathail from D Company. The Sailor Burke and Mac Fhloinn from Donegal from A Company were there with us also. We comprised five lorries altogether and had three motorbikes travelling alongside with Captain Stapleton from the Transport Corps in charge.

When we reached the crossroads in Maam Cross, we'd to wind our way through the huge crowd of people and livestock gathered there for the fair and Quartermaster Ó Treasaigh wasn't long telling us a good one about it. This fair used to be a big place for fighting in the old days and they didn't fight with their fists either but with ash-staves and blackthorn sticks. As soon as the buying and selling was over for the day and once they'd a good drop on-board, the fighting would start. It'd be one faction against another and they'd do terrible violence to one another once they began the stick-fighting. Anyway, there was a fair there one day many years ago and was no sign of the fighting starting for whatever reason. It was gone 3 o'clock and no one had stirred when a small little man came out of one of the drinking tents. He was the master of one of the factions and pulled out his watch. 'It's gone 3 o'clock at the fair of Maam Cross,' he says 'and not a blow struck yet. We're shamed in front of the whole world!' Then he jumped onto the back of one of the peelers on duty there and hit him across the head with his blackthorn stick. The fight kicked off straight away and it was chaos. And everyone kept their pride intact. There's nothing like this here anymore, and not for a long time either but, that said, there were men at the fair today who were as big and as wild looking as I've seen anywhere. They were there from every part of Joyce Country[48]; big strong powerful-looking men who'd knock a bullock over with a belt of their fists. Some of them were clean-shaven and more of them had unruly beards, and the majority of them had a wild look about them. You couldn't but note the ruddy, healthy look of them. In fact, we army lads looked a bit puny really next to them even if there are plenty of powerful men amongst us as well. But anyway, soldiers always look a lot paler than others because they spend so much time on duty indoors, and anyway they don't get the same good feeding that the country people get. We travelled straight on until we'd passed Recess and then turned across in the direction of Cashel. We took a slightly roundabout route here so that we wouldn't have to cross the bridge at *Coill Sáile*[49] seeing as it's so narrow. Even the public bus has to take it very easy when it's passing over that bridge and you can feel a bit dizzy when you look down into the river from it. If the bus was to keel over into the water there, I don't think anyone would come out of it alive. Myself and the Maharajah really enjoyed the journey and the beautiful landscape around us today, but as for Flaherty from Aran, he was just stretched out on the floor of the lorry fast asleep. It was his first time in Connemara and yet he wasn't that bothered what the countryside looked like. He woke up, just as we arrived into Carna, had a quick look around him and said: 'Bloody hell lads, I thought Aran was bad, but I've never seen anywhere like this before!' This jibe was directed at Stiofán Mhaidhc (Connolly Bán) because they're always picking at each other. Stiofán gave Flaherty a filthy look, but he said nothing. The first concern we had once we arrived to our destination was getting a cup of tea and so we went into the Garda Barracks in Carna where we got water – and permission to boil it for ourselves. The Gardaí welcomed us and Sergeant Calhoun told us to make ourselves at home. We drank the tea and ate some eggs out at the gable-end of the house and it was a lovely meal, that's for sure.

The Garda Barracks in Carna has a strange design and some people claim that it was built from the wrong plans. The plans for a military barracks in north-west India and the barracks in Carna got mixed up when they were building it years ago – or so they say anyway – not that I give any credence to this myself. There are far too many stories like this doing the rounds for even half of them to be true; either that or the British authorities who erected these buildings in times past were all incompetent and I don't believe this was so.

Our meal over, we began work. We took the various sections of the cabin from off the lorries and placed them in the small field opposite the Garda Barracks. When we'd that done, the Captain told us to relax for a while and we stretched out on the grass smoking and chatting. Of course, I couldn't sit still and so myself and Sailor and 'Shouter' Ó Tuathail headed over to Carna village to have a drink in *Tigh Mhóráin* there. Shouter's mother is from Carna and so he wanted to see if there was anyone around that he knew. We didn't meet anyone we recognised however, and after we'd drunk three pints at our ease, we headed back to join the other soldiers. But, oh my God, when we got back to the lorries, hadn't the other lads already left! We'd missed them by just a few minutes, Johnny Shéamais, a former soldier who'd been in *An Chéad Chath* at a stage of his life informed us. They'd headed off out the Cashel road, he said. There was nothing we could do then except start walking back along the road and pray that they'd notice we'd been left behind and come back for us.

'Oh, feckin' hell lads! We're in a right mess now,' says Sailor. 'Ara, we'll be *alright*,' says the Shouter. 'Captain Stapleton's a sound fellow, he'll come back for us yet. Pity we didn't stay for a few more drinks instead of quenching the candle,[50] when we did.' The sun was beating down hard now and we didn't know how long we'd have to walk before the lorries might return. Next thing, we heard the sound of a motorbike coming along the road. It was Captain Stapleton himself. He pulled up beside us, propped his goggles on his forehead, and stared at us out of it. 'Absent from duty without permission,' he says in a deadpan voice. Then, focussing on me, he added:

'This is all your fault McCauley, I'd swear on it! The three of you are under open arrest until you return to the barracks where you'll be charged.'

We'd to stand to attention, and then he ordered us to jog along the road in the direction the lorries had taken. This was worse than any punishment that I might've got back in Renmore because if any of my friends from Carna spotted us running along the road and the Captain behind us on the motorbike, herding us like sheep, we'd be mortified! Bloody typical … we'd barely gone 200 yards up the road when someone spotted us! It was Bridie Shéamais, the sister of the Johnny who'd told us about the lorries already leaving. Bridie's a big woman who loves slagging and teasing. And she wasn't going to let this opportunity pass, by my soul! No way! A huge smile lit up her face when she saw us running.

'By God, but aren't you the fit bunch of lads, out running on a day as warm as this? Come back on sports day and I'll put money on it that you won't leave a cup or a trophy after you against the local lads here!'

I didn't care what else happened now. I knew that everyone'd be talking about this back in Carna soon and the embarrassment would be something else. The lorries were about a mile-and-a-half away and we were very relieved when we finally reached them. Cuirín Mór was in the lorry nearest to us and he reached out his hand to pull me aboard. The minute I climbed in though, I knew I'd made a mistake. 'Hey, I get a smell of porter off you Núibín,' he says. 'So you went off drinking pints and you didn't even think of inviting me, your comrade along with you? Did it not occur to you that I might be thirsty too, you dirty little redneck you? What goes around comes around though, doesn't it Núibín – you feckin' traitor you?'

The lorries started up and the next moment we were off. Cuirín Mór jumped on me and began to batter me, but I fought him off as best I could. I had to give in in the end, though, and by then, every bone in my body was aching!

I enjoyed the trip back to the barracks even if some of the lads couldn't wait to get it over with – the reason being that today's pay-day. The lads can't wait to get paid and head out on the town. The Shouter was right about Captain Stapleton being a decent old skin because no sooner were we back at the barracks than he called the three of us aside and warned us not to go absent without leave ever again – (me, especially!) 'We'll forget about it now this one time,' he said, and let us go.

Cóilín Morgan sent word that he wanted me for work this afternoon and although I was loathe to respond to his request, I knew that he'd catch up with me sooner or later. I'd no option but to go down to him. Morgan doesn't normally send for someone unless he wants to give out to them about something and I have a fair idea that this tongue-lashing is a well-deserved one. I wrote a bit of a song the other day about an old sailing boat that Cóilín was working on for the past few months. He's been doing it up for some of the Battalion's non-commissioned officers. They bought it in Athlone – there must have been extra money in the kitty, I'd say – then brought it down the Shannon and transferred it by sea onto Galway. It looks like a right ugly tub in my opinion, not that I know much about boats. The prow and the stern are the same shape and size. For a while, Cóilín was working on the boat every single afternoon and you'd hear the sound of his hammer coming from the stony sliver of shore where the boat was beached. Eventually, he had the *Dulci Belle* seaworthy anyway – (I kid you not! That's what he named the boat!) or at least he claimed it was seaworthy! One fine sunny afternoon some of the O.N.C.'s went out sailing in it and wouldn't you know – they were barely fifty feet out from shore when the boat went down and its passengers had to scramble and swim their way back to shore as best they could. Those involved tried their best to cover up what'd happened out of embarrassment, but it wasn't long before everyone knew about it inside the barracks and out. I just couldn't let an opportunity as good as that go a-begging and that's when I came up with seven or eight verses of a poem about it. I had to compose these verses in English as unfortunately, I have no skill at writing poetry in Irish. Someone could've written a really great and witty song in Irish about this or not, if they'd had that particular talent. I brought all the older O.N.C.'s into this ballad too and mentioned lads who wouldn't even have ventured out of the canteen and gone down to the shore to look at the *Dulci Belle*, never mind gone out sailing in her! This is what I wrote:

## THE VOYAGE OF THE DULCI BELLE

*'And now my task is nearly done,' cried gallant Cóilín Morgan,*
*'My ship she glitters in the sun, and truth she was a bargain!*
*I can't discern, from stem to stern, the slightest imperfection,*
*While standing there so proud and fair for Treacy's keen inspection'*

*Her bows were neat, her decks a treat, her engines were a treasure,*
*A noble ship, and built for speed, despite colossal measure.*
*Her masts so tall exceeded all, in nautical endeavour*
*With ropes and sails and shining rails she was a joy for ever.*

*And down below the crew did stow the things that would be needed,*
*The packs and racks and iron beds, a score or more exceeded.*
*While bed cards gay, in neat array, and heaps of respirators,*
*Comprised a precious cargo for those hardy navigators.*

*And in the crew was Tom McHugh, our awesome Sergeant-Major,*
*And Treacy brave to rule the wave, no better man I'll wager;*
*And sure enough there's bold McNuff and Quartermaster Cotter*
*While Phil Mac Andrew stands on deck with paper, pen, and blotter.*

*She left the land by breezes fanned, through monstrous billows*
*cleaving,*
*Her nautical manoeuvres, they were well-nigh past believing!*
*The Claddagh men turned out to see our schooner's stately sailing*
*While Peadar Ryan was seasick lying, across the fore-deck railing.*

*So on and on, proud as a swan, her charted course pursuing,*
*Till all the crew came up to view a storm to westward brewing.*
*The clouds so dark, the lightning's spark, the west wind's wild elation,*
*Bestowed upon our mariners a sense of trepidation.*

*'All hands on deck,' the Skipper cried, 'I fear the pumps need mannin',*
*If all goes well, we'll ride the swell and beach in Errislannon!'*
*'Twas hope in vain, for too much strain, brought sails and mast down-*
*crashing*
*And left the crew with loud hulloo through tangled wreckage thrashing.*

*'Abandon ship,' the C.Q. cried, 'I feel she'll turn over,'*
*'Then that being so we needs must go,' says Jer, the Dingle Rover.*
*But none can say up to this day, if safe they came, or foundered,*
*Or if all being well, the Dulci Belle, to calmer waters floundered.*

*But in Renmore for evermore, an anxious watch we'll keep*
*And hope and pray, they'll come some day, safe from the boundless deep.*
*So until then, enlisted men, enjoying routine's cessation,*
*Are glad the Céad Chath Gaelach has become a 'cushy station'!*

When I'd it finished, I made a few copies of the poem and passed them around amongst the lads. Soon, nearly all the men in the barracks had read it. It was then that I was told Cóilín wanted to see me though and rather than annoying him any more than I'd already done, I decided to go up and get it over with quick. I was nervous as I made my way over as I didn't know how he might react to the song. I knew that I was in trouble the minute I walked in the door of the canteen however, because he was there waiting for me, a big tasty dinner laid out for me. (Cóilín has the strange habit of laying out a dinner for whoever he's about to tear strips off, then while they're eating, he gives them hell!)

'Oh sit down there now for yourself Dónall, sit down there son,' he says and I sat down without a word.

'Here, eat up there son,' he says, shoving the mug of tea and the plate of meat closer. He took out his penknife then – it was closer to a scythe than a penknife, and that's the truth, but anyway – and began to pare a big plug of tobacco for his pipe. He kneaded and shaped the tobacco the way he wanted it, then tamped it carefully in his pipe. There was no hurry on him. It was as if he was building up the tension – so that he reminded me of a big cat playing with a mouse before it goes in for the kill.

'I heard that you've composed a song, Dónall,' he says.

'Oh, I don't know that I'd class it as a song really, Cóilín,' I says, respectfully, sensing the explosion that was coming.

'All the same, it isn't every man who can put pen to paper as good as you can, Dónall,' he says.

My unease increased. I knew I was really in for it now.

'I was described in the song, by all accounts, Dónall?'

I was finding it difficult to swallow any of the food at this stage, I was so anxious, but I managed to take a slug of the tea and Cóilín came to the point:

'It's a bad show for you to be going around composing songs about people like that, Dónall. There's nothing gallant in this song composition trade of yours at all; in fact, there's something downright ignorant about it really – and it doesn't suit you one bit either. Now Dónall, as you know yourself, the people back west aren't well off by any means, but even so – they're the nicest and most generous people anywhere in the world when it comes down to it. They work hard and they earn their bit the hard way. But they have their pride, Dónall, and they don't like anyone else making fun of them! Maybe the Connemara people aren't as well off as the people who are always running into Galway every time they've a handful of potatoes or a dozen eggs to sell,' (that's a dirty dig at the people of our place (Knocknacarra) and I reddened from ear to ear) 'but even if we aren't, we've our own ways of making a living. We go out to sea fishing and we make whatever money we can from our smallholdings, and we do all this without any of the advantages that the crowd who run the hotels and who live on the outskirts of Connemara have! Now Dónall, I'm telling you all this so's you'll know what's best for you, from now on, y'know? Here, do you want another drop of tea there? You won't? But the next time the mood for composition comes over you, don't bring my name into your poems please, alright?'

I'd wolfed down the food by now but what good it did me, I don't know. All I wanted now was to get out of there as quickly as possible. I thanked Cóilín for the food and made as it to leave. I wasn't going to get away that easily though.

'Hang on a minute there, Dónall,' said Cóilín. 'Hand me that piece of paper there with the ditty written on it, please, like a good man.'

I handed him the short song and he walked over to the fire and burned the page in the embers, then gave me the sign that I was dismissed, and I raced out and back upstairs as fast as my legs could carry me. It was a pity about the song being burned like that, I thought to myself, but I comforted myself with the thought that most of the lads had it off by heart by now anyway.

The mackerel are very plentiful in Galway Bay these days. All you have to do is walk into the water anywhere around here, dip your cap in and pull them out, that's how plentiful they are. The water's teeming with them. The lads are always down on the rocks these nights fishing, although it's a pointless activity for them in a way, seeing as they've nowhere to roast the fish afterwards.

Cuirín Mór caught three big mackerel there earlier this evening. He gave them to Ciarraí to roast for him down in the kitchen of the Officer's Canteen. Ciarraí's been working there for the last while. He wasn't too thrilled about this request from Cuirín Mór and made his feelings plain to him.

'Damn you man, yourself and your bloody fish, don't you know well what the Sergeant will say to me if he catches me down here cooking for you?' he said in a beaten voice that indicated he'd no choice other than to do what Cuirín Mór told him. I could tell by Packie that he was sorely tempted to give Ciarraí another dip in the taps so's to put manners on him. He restrained himself though and just repeated his request nice and polite:

'Good man yourself, Ciarraí; it won't take you more than two ticks. Remember how hungry you always were yourself before you went up there to work amongst the meat-pots of the rich! You'll roast these for me now like a good man and I'll call down to the canteen window in about a quarter of an hour to collect them.'

A disgusted Ciarraí took the mackerel from him – as if to say that he was being handed something rotten – cursing under his breath.

'Aha, Ciarraí, you ungrateful little pupil you, I'll redden your arse for you once I've eaten my mackerel,' said Cuirín Mór, and himself and myself started a bout of wrestling to pass the time. I was as keen on a piece of fish as Cuirín Mór was and so I made sure to tag along with him up to the canteen a little while later. The window was open and we spotted Ciarraí taking the frying pan from the flame sure enough. There was a mouth-watering smell in the air.

The minute he spotted us at the window, he laid the fish out on a plate, and brought them over. Disaster! He'd bloody roasted the fish without filleting them first. He'd roasted them head, tails, innards and all – the exact same as they were handed to him!' Cuirín Mór went ballistic and tried to grab Ciarraí by the collar and pull him out through the window.

'Look what you've done, you cannibal you!' he screams. 'You didn't clean them at all. You didn't even take the heads off them! What sort of an idiot are you, you dirty puck-goat you – you stupid shithead! What kind of a gobshite are you at all?'

Ciarraí was stunned. The poor fellow'd been expecting the exact opposite – judging by his shocked look. He'd been expecting high praise from Packie for his work and not this at all!

'Ara, why didn't you bring your mankey old herrings somewhere else then, instead of to me?' he says, disgruntled. But Packie lets a roar out of him:

'Herrings! Herrings by God! Do you not know the difference between a mackerel and a herring you dirty old fool you?' he says.

'I was a farmer at home, not a bloody fisherman,' Ciarraí retorted proudly. This was the final straw for Packie; he couldn't take it anymore.

'A bloody goat-farmer!' he roared, whacking Ciarraí in the face with the largest of the mackerel. The Canteen Sergeant appeared then suddenly before we realised it. He stuck his head into the kitchen and sniffed the air.

'Who burned the fish?' – 'Hey, who's the fish for?' he repeated in Irish but this time we didn't hang around to hear any more of his bilingual abilities. We were gone in a flash. Back in the room, Packie explained to Colm a' tSeaimpín what Ciarraí'd done. Colm had very little sympathy for him, though.

'You were a worse idiot to give him the mackerel in the first place. Shur, those people don't know jack-shit about seafood or fish or stuff,' he said.

\* \* \*

# The Galway Races

It's that time of the year again. The Galway Races are on. And I've received seven days C.B. for my bloody troubles! My punishment was one of those freak things too, I'm afraid. I was caught out on parade with a musket belonging to someone else, a musket that was only half-clean. And when Lieutenant Ó Duinn pulled me up out on the parade ground there was no one more surprised than me because I hadn't noticed I'd the wrong gun! Only the previous evening, I'd given my own musket a good clean. I thought of explaining to the Lieutenant what must've happened, but then thought better of it. Some other man must've had my gun and I'd only hang him if I said anything.

I was half-expecting the Lieutenant to ask me what the serial number was of my gun was – but he didn't. I would've been off the hook then when they realised that the dirty gun wasn't mine. I wasn't that lucky though, and was brought in before Captain Cusack to be charged. The charge against me was read out and the Captain looked at me enquiringly. I took this as my cue to explain myself, but the Captain raised his hand then to cut me short – 'Don't bother. Keep it for the next time McCauley,' he said, in a tired voice. Despite being confined to barracks, I managed to get out two evenings for the Races – and the two outings were well worth it as well. Myself and the other lads had the best time ever. There was me, Packie, Private Mac a' Leoin (Lyons)[51] that went out on the first night. Lyons is his real surname, but the Horse christened him Private Mac a' Leoin – the same as he christened two others in this Battalion. The latter are Lagar ('Weakness') Ó Loinsigh and Láidir ('Strong') Ó Dubhchónaigh. Lyons is married and he lives in the married quarter of the barracks on the other side of the O.N.C.'s Canteen. He's in the same company as us, but we rarely see him, as he normally helps the Company Quartermaster in the store during the week. He's become quite friendly with Cuirín Mór over the last while – they're like two peas in a pod – the way they get one another and have similar interests. They only differ as regards having a pint. Lyons loves his pint whereas for Packie, drinking is just a pastime he indulges in every now and then. Lyons is well-built and tough, but he's not a patch on Packie in terms of strength. He has very fluent Irish even if there's very little Irish spoken now where he comes from in Kinvara, on the border of counties Galway and Clare. Of course, he's been in *An Chéad Chath* for eleven years by now and has heard Irish spoken around him for most of that time. Similar to Cuirín Mór, he believes that it's the duty of the new recruits and the 'shrimps' to supply the older soldiers or the 'top dogs' with money and drink. This is his motto, and he often recites it:

°*Séard dúirt Naomh Peadar le Naomh Pól,*
*Na seansaighdiúirí bheith ag ól,*
*"Gus nuair nach mbíonn sé acu,*
*Na hearcaigh dhá thúirt dóibh."'*
('Saint Peter said to Saint Paul,
That the older soldiers ought to be drinking,
"And when they don't have beer-money
The recruits should give it to them."')

The Horse composed this verse originally, I believe, but Lyons adopted it as his own. Lyons is an excellent soldier by the way and he's always immaculately turned out on parade. If he wasn't so fond of the crack, he'd be a level or two higher in the Army by now, but he has no interest in that sort of thing. Singing and having a few pints and the crack are his favourite pastimes and when he's a good drop in, he dances a few steps of *Damhsa na Péiste* ('The Serpent's Dance') or *Damhsa na nGabhar* ('The Goat's Dance') as good as the next man.

The first night of the Races, himself and Packie went out dressed in their uniforms and indeed, they were a credit to the army, they were that well turned out.

'I'll leave it up to yourself, Núibín, how you manage to escape from the barracks and meet us below in the Brooklyn,' Packie says, as they were leaving. 'Yeah, and bring plenty of money with you,' Lyons added. It's alright for them to be talking; all they have to do is walk out the main gate and down the railway line. I'm going to have to escape out through the back-gate somehow and then make my way down the length of the train-line without being spotted and that's no easy feat, let me tell you! On top of everything else, I don't know if the bugle might sound out 'Stragglers' at some stage and I'd be in trouble then as I'd be well out of earshot by then. If they found out that I was gone AWOL again, there'd be another charge against me – this time for 'breaking barracks'. Still, any fear I had of being found out was overcome by the urge to go racing. The Races won't be on again for another year and by then Cuirín Mór and most of the other lads will have left by then. I've no choice other than 'to take my chances' – as the man says, and see can I get away with it. I polished my uniform buttons, shoved my cap into my pocket and made for the back-gate.

Luckily I made it as far as the back-gate without meeting anyone and I just walked straight out and made my way downtown. And as soon I reached Eyre Square, I knew that I'd done the right thing! The whole world seemed to be in Galway for the Races – Travellers of all types, Aran Islanders, country people, and every class and creed under the sun. From the Square came the music and mayhem of *Tofts Amusements* and the whole atmosphere was amazing. (*Tofts* have had their fairground in Eyre Square for the past fortnight.) I circuited the Square once quickly before heading downtown; part of me was wondering whether I might run into Meaig if she happened to be home on her holidays from England. I didn't meet her, needless to say, although there were a good number of people in from Connemara; it was easy to tell who they were by their clothes and also by the English they speak. The noise of the 'Bumpers' would deafen you, but the sound of the girls screeching as the Big Wheel reached its highest point was a happy one. The fairground has a thousand ways to part you from your money – all sorts of different *gimmicks*[52] and booths. You can throw your pennies on the game-board and see whether they land on the proper square or you can fling those small rubber rings at another booth in the hope of winning a small toy. You can throw darts at pieces of paper-money or at playing cards, and there are any number of lotteries and betting games that you can try your luck with. And in amongst all the confusion and noise, you hear the high-pitched entreaties of the small ragged tinker children. Their begging is a litany of sorts.

A good few of the new recruits from the Curragh were hanging around the Square, none of whom had the look of fellows who were heading off to drink porter. I notice that they aren't as well-built or as fine a bunch of men as the lads who enlisted in the army before this. The reason for this, of course, is that many of the strongest and most powerfully built men in Ireland now are heading straight over to England to work on the buildings rather than joining the army in Renmore. *An Chéad Chath* is going to be left in a bad way once the rest of the men who enlisted in 1946 are gone, there's no doubt about it.

I left the fairground and the Square and walked down to Woodquay where I was supposed to meet the other two lads. *Slam Féir* ('Bunch of Hay') was standing at the corner of Breatnach's pub and the minute he spotted me, he gave a big smile. I quickly disappeared into the crowd again though, and within the blink of an eye, I was down at Moons corner. Old-Rainey[53] from Tuam was playing the flute outside Fallers and I'd have stood there and listened to him for a while only that I knew Slam Féir would be down after me a few minutes later, and so I whipped off in the direction of the Brooklyn as quickly as I could. The Brook was overflowing with people. Even the crowd that herself threw out the other night were all in there again and I'd a hell of job getting up through the crowd to the counter. In the back-room, I found Cuirín Mór and Lyons and they were both really happy to see me – although Lyons pretended he wasn't. He has this idea that recruits like me get a bit cocky or 'up in themselves' if the older soldiers spend too much time socialising with them!

The pints weren't great in the Brooklyn (which happens very rarely) and the place was so crowded that we'd no comfort there either, so we said we'd go and see could we find somewhere quieter. I was secretly reluctant to leave the Brook as there was a small group of elderly people sitting next to us in from Menlo and they were telling stories about *Raiféirí an File* ('Raftery the Poet') – 'Filí' is the way the Menlo people pronounce that word.) My two comrades had very little interest in this conversation however, and so we threw back our pints and left. Then, when we got outside, Cuirín Mór came up with a different plan though. 'Do you know what we'll do now lads?' he says, 'We'll leave town altogether and go out to Salthill where we'll be amongst the nobility!'

'Ara, what would you be going out there for?' says Lyons. 'Shur, it'll take us half an hour to get out there. All the jaunts and buses up in the Square are too busy at the moment. Shur, we'd have two or three pints drunk in the time that we'd been going out as far as Salthill?'

'The night is plenty young yet for us to be drinking. Here, let's get out of here; the evening is too fine to be staying here in the middle of town,' countered Packie and we gave in to him anyway in the end. Lyons was right though – it took us exactly half an hour to get out to Salthill and although he was pissed-off that we'd lost valuable drinking time, he cheered up again the minute we got there. We got off the bus right outside the Bal and went in for a few pints there, after which we moved onto Keaveneys for a few more. From there, we went to the Rockland Hotel, whatever inclination for a fancy atmosphere had possessed us – and went into the lounge there. The only fault I could see with the place was that they weren't selling pints there and so we'd to be satisfied with bottles of beer. To be honest, if we weren't already fairly tipsy by the time we got there, we'd probably have felt a bit 'out of place' there as it's really a place where only the wealthier class of people drink.

We didn't give a damn who we might run into by that stage of the night though, and it wasn't long before Lyons struck up a song. It was the 'Bolshie Boy' but shur, no one paid him a blind bit of attention anyway. He'd just finished singing when three women walked into the bar, a mother and her two daughters by the looks of things and it was obvious that the women were Americans. The two daughters were really beautiful-looking and their mother was a fine, handsome woman too. They ordered drinks and then spent the next few minutes looking around them as strangers in a new place do. The eldest of the two girls was having a good stare at us and eventually Packie says:

'Damn it lads but she's a fine-looking woman and she's looking over this way too. Should we say "hello" do you think?'

'For God's sake, but would you just listen to them?' says Lyons – 'just listen to them and that's enough. We don't have to go talking to them as well. Shur, we don't need the night ruined on us, do we? Aren't we grand now the way we are drinking a few pints and singing a few songs – without drawing the women on us as well?'

Once Packie had spotted them, there was no stopping him though.

He had to go and chat them up. I was sure that they'd have no interest in us and would ignore us the same as many well-off Irish women would but – unbelievably – it turned out the exact opposite!

Two minutes later and they'd invited us to join them at their table and from then on, we'd had a great chat with them. You'd swear we'd known them all our lives.

They told us who they were, how long they were on holidays in Ireland for, what they did for a living over in the States, and a thousand other things. The two daughters both had nice blonde hair; their faces freckled, and their teeth and skin were really beautiful. I'd never seen city girls as good-looking as these two before, even if there are plenty of pretty girls in every Irish town. Whereas some girls might have nice skin, for example, then they might have something wrong with their teeth or their hair maybe. These girls were picture-perfect, however. Their complexions were so healthy and pretty and there was a simplicity and innocence about them too that was really attractive. They'd a touch of grandness about them too, because when we asked their mother what they'd like to drink, she said:

'Yes, we'll all have a drink, certainly, but let me pay for it please, boys. We're on our holidays here and it's only right that we should pay for them. Here now, we won't hear another word said about it, ok.' Then the mother pressed the little button that calls the waiter. We spent about an hour in their company and then they left for whatever hotel they were staying in. They'd a hectic day ahead of them the next day, they said. Cuirín Mór was a little bit quiet in himself on our way back to the barracks and I think he was probably pining after the eldest of the two daughters. He'd really fancied her. Lyons, on the other hand, was on a high and kept talking about the drinks that we'd got for free.

Who did we meet then up at the corner of Eyre Square, propped up on one of the jaunts, only Quartermaster Treacy. He hailed us over and offered us a lift back to the barracks. He was in flying form altogether and full of chat about the Galway Races. All the way back to the barracks, he switched fluently between Irish and English in a continuous flow of chat and conversation. As we came closer to the barracks, I became increasingly worried though. If the barracks orderly was to spot me getting off the jaunt just outside the barracks, then I'd be nabbed straight away for being absent without permission and I'd be in the shit. I needn't have worried however, because a few hundred yards from the barracks, the Quartermaster asked the man driving the jaunt to pull up. 'Now ghostie,' he says to me – 'I'd say you'll be keen to go back in the way you left, so we'll let you off here. Clear off now for yourself!'

He doesn't miss a trick, the same man. I thanked him and headed quickly for the back-gates. I spent a little while outside thinking of how best to get in before I decided to give it a go, climbing the barbed wire. I took off my cap, shoved it down into my pocket and began to negotiate the big rolls of barbed wire fencing there. I was doing alright at first and climbed to the highest point on the wire fairly easily. Next thing, my foot slipped however, and I fell down onto some of the barbs. Like those flies that get caught on the sticky papers I got stuck, and the more I tried to free myself the more I was bloody trapped. In the end, I was rocking back and forth, enmeshed in the wire and I'd probably be there still if one of the sentries hadn't noticed me and freed me. It was gone eleven o'clock by the time I finally got in. Cuirín Mór was worried and said he was just ready to go out looking for me.

Cuirín Mór, Mícheál Ó Cadhain, Tamsy and some of the other lads from D Company went out on their ticket today. God knows, I felt sorry watching them make their way over to the store for the last time to leave back their muskets and other gear. Sadly, it won't be long now either before Cuirín Mór, Colm a' tSeaimpín, Ciarraí and a good number of the other lads from our company go the same way. I don't know how I'll survive here when they're gone as there won't be anything like the same crack anymore. The numbers enlisting recently have increased again but even so, they're a different breed, a crowd that I wouldn't have the same time for. Most of them are 'Pioneers'[54] and as with many of those who're anti-drink, they're very careful with their money. They don't have the same sense of humour or the same love of witty talk either, and half of them aren't from the Gaeltacht either. A good few of them are from east Galway and they've no real interest in the Irish language either to be honest. I'm kind of sorry in a way that my stint in the army isn't up now too because I'd be able to leave here with the men that I've built up a good rapport with. I've another year to go though.

We were talking the other day about this side of things – the new breed of men enlisting and how they're all so small and weedy-looking these days when Colm a' tSeaimpín says:

'Orah, brother, any real man'll be embarrassed to stay in the army from now on given the number of shrimps that'll be here soon. God be with the days long ago when you wouldn't see any man who wasn't at least six-foot tall in *An Chéad Chath*. By God son, but there was nowhere we went then and no fight that took place, that we didn't always hold sway. Do you know how it is now boys, but if my "ould fellow"[55] was to see some of the recruits who're enlisting these days, he'd say that Ireland was finished.'

'True for you Colm,' says Packie, 'won't Núib here be the king of them all soon when we're gone!'

'Oh, but God help this country if any enemy attacks then,' says Colm, taking his musket down from the rack above his bed.

'Sure, they can always call on us, if that happens,' says Ciarraí, trying to be as good as the other two chancers.

'A musha, would you go off and jump for yourself you dirty old puck-goat you, who the hell would come looking for your help anyway? If you did the same as you did with my mackerel, you'd be feckin' useless to anyone. You're neither small or big, pretty or ugly. Núibín here knows his stuff even if he's a bit of a shrimp, but you – I wouldn't send you out to boil water,' says Packie. Ciarraí exploded then. He was already in bad form because he has no tobacco left and this exchange only made him worse again.

'I can tell you one thing for sure Cuirín Mór. I won't be sorry to see the back of you. You're worse than one of those landlords long ago, the way you swipe everything in this room. Who here has ever seen you with your own razor, soap, shoe polish or bottle of *brasso* since you enlisted? When did you ever have the price of a packet of cigarettes or the price of anything else either, for that matter? Of course, Núibín here, or whatever you bloody call him, should be delighted to see the back of you too!'

Packie's face clouded and he gave Ciarraí a filthy look. 'Do you know what it is now, Gobbo?' he says, 'only that I'm too lazy now to give you a hiding and only that you've just a few days left here anyway – I'd go over to you right now and put some manners on you!'

Ciarraí started pushing his luck then as he could tell Cuirín Mór wasn't going to do anything to him and started on with a long list of Packie's other annoying traits. The poor devil – he isn't going to be here for much longer anyway but of all the lads, Ciarraí is probably the one who's least prepared for life outside the army. He hasn't saved a red cent since he got here and neither has he bought any new clothes at all either. Bad as he is, at least Packie's made sure to buy a fine blue suit and he has six or seven pounds still coming to him – or 'on the books' as they say here. Packie has just one month left here and Ciarraí and Colm will be gone by then too. My heart feels heavy every time I think about Packie's departure, as there were no other two men in the army here as good friends as us; even if he often left me penniless! That's the way of the world these days though. You've no sooner built up a good friendship with someone but you've to say goodbye to them as quickly again.

Ciarraí went out on his ticket today – the first man from this company here to leave us – and God knows, we were all very sad to see him go, the poor man. He spent the last few days over in the wet canteen drinking with a bunch of lads he'd never hung around with before – and he didn't buy a drink for any us before he left either! He was always a tough one to work out, but the last few days really took the biscuit. He hadn't a thing leaving here, not even a pocket handkerchief to his name; the only clothes he had were the Martin Henry suit that each soldier is given (or the price of the suit, if you prefer that), a white-collared army shirt, a pair of army shoes and a cheque cap squashed flat on his head like a pancake. Ciarraí hadn't even a case or a bag when he left. All his worldly possessions were folded up in a small piece of brown paper that he carried beneath his arm. He went around and shook hands with each of us before he left and we – well, at least Packie and I definitely felt – that he wanted to say a lot more to us before he left, but he just couldn't get the words out, he was so emotional.

The exodus has begun now.

Myself and Packie went to the Pictures tonight. *Tarzan* was on and it was Colm a' tSeaimpín who recommended this film to us. He saw it himself last night. Colm rarely goes to the Pictures but when he does, he really analyses the film in detail afterwards, and his understanding of the themes and symbols in the films always amazes the rest of us. He comes out with stuff that we didn't know he had in him at all! The fact that he doesn't have that much Irish is probably the reason why he doesn't come across as very reflective or deep about cultural issues the rest of the time. He gave high praise to this film *Tarzan* though:

'It was a brilliant film, lads. This big wild churl of a man and he was running wild and buck-naked through the woods and living with the animals. He had no Irish; nor did he have much English either. Instead, he spoke in a kind of a growl, like one of those wild tigers.'

Needless to say, we had to go to the film ourselves, given this excellent recommendation.

He's a funny son of a gun, this same Colm – no doubt about it. For example, the other day I was reading a travel book about Ireland by H.V. Morton, a book that had a picture of a man and his donkey back in Connemara, a donkey and two creels of turf.

Normally, Mac a' tSeaimpín has no interest in books, but he was glancing over my shoulder this time. Next thing he says all-excited: 'Hey, that there's Seáinín Pheats Bheartla from our village in the photo!'

'It's hard to be sure about it Colm,' I said, as the photo was fuzzy enough and it was difficult to make out the man's face. 'I know, but I'd recognise that bucko anywhere. I'd recognise him quicker than I'd recognise Seáinín himself!' He meant that he recognised the donkey of course, not poor Seáinín!

I felt very lonely coming back from Mass today, remembering that today's Cuirín Mór's last Sunday here. I think he probably felt the same as he wasn't in good form today. And even when we got *boxty* for the breakfast this morning, he didn't say 'a half of that for the churl' to me like he normally does. We spent all today in the room, sleeping most of the time, or sitting around the fire chatting: Colm a' tSeaimpín went out on his ticket today and Packie will be leaving at the end of the week. I think even Captain Ó Sé felt a bit sad today about everyone leaving, even if he's seen people coming and going from the Battalion for thirty years and more at this stage.

Even the old-timers get a bit anxious or upset when they see a big crowd leaving on their ticket. I'd say it probably sets them thinking on the many long years they've spent in the army already and the many years that still lie ahead. Some of them probably get anxious when they think of the future when they'll have to go back to civilian life again, I'd say.

'God knows there's nothing wrong with the soldier's life, Núibín,' says Cuirín Mór, 'we've plenty of fun and crack here in the army that people out in civilian life don't have at all. What's in store for me now other than to sit into the currach with the old boy every day, the two of us without a word out of us and after all our hardship and toil, I'll be lucky to have more than a crown in my pocket at the end of the week. Speaking of fun and drinking, shur the older generation have no time for this sort of thing. If you were to pass the rest of your life like them, you'd have nothing but a hand-to-mouth existence for the rest of your days. No Núibín, there's nothing else for it but to buy a ticket and head over to John Bull's Island; at least you'll get well rewarded for your work over there. Something tells me Núibín that there's a nice little pub in Marble Arch, London – I can see it now as clear as day in my mind's eye – and with the help of God, you and me'll meet up again in this fine pub someday soon. It'll have a nice marble counter in it and a world of great big mirrors on the walls. Every drink you can think of will sit on the shelves inside that pub. There'll be a big clock there with a sweet, musical chime on it. And some fine day, Núibín, just when I'm starting to get sick of life and of staring up at that clock, the door of that bar will open and in you'll walk! And, Núibín, no sooner'll that happen, but I'll jump down off the high stool that's beneath my arse and I'll let a roar of joy out of me like the *Fianna* of long ago. And the two of us will do *Damhsa na Péiste* ('The Serpent's Dance') as a form of challenge to everyone else in the bar. And if that isn't enough for them, we'll do *Damhsa na nGabhar* ('The Goat Dance') as well just for good measure. We'll tear into it then and work our way through all the fine drinks lined up in the bottles there. And we'll let the world know that Núibín from Galway and his patron from Turbot Island'll never be fazed by anyone – not by all the English in the city of London!' Cuirín Mór went out on his ticket today and God knows, I found it hard enough to hold back the tears saying goodbye to him outside the barracks' gate.

He'd left all his equipment – his gun, his helmet and everything else – into the store since yesterday and all he'd left to do today was leave his Martin Henry suit over to the *Táilliúirín* ('Little Tailor') and get the legs of the trousers extended. We drank a few pints over in the wet canteen at dinner-time, not that we needed them really after all we drank last night down in the Brooklyn – myself, Packie and Lyons. Packie wouldn't let either of us put our hands in our pockets for drink. He paid for everything …

And when he was leaving, I stood outside the gate until my comrade was out of sight, then turned back in … Back in the room, Joeen Beag was there cleaning his shoes, before heading out on guard-duty.

'So, your old buddy is gone now, Dónall,' he says.

'He is,' I said.

'He was a great fellow altogether,' says Joeen, 'There was no harm in him at all, once you understood his ways.'

Mícheál Ó Sé stood up and stretched out his legs and yawned:

'Arah, he's really lucky, so he is. A fine, strong, young fellow in the first flush of his youth like him, and now he's heading out into the big world outside to better himself. Unlike us, who've to stay here until we're eventually thrown out and it'll be too late for us to go anywhere or do anything worthwhile by the time we get out. Pity that the world wasn't as good years back when we'd our first three years under our belts Joeen, and neither of us would be slow to say goodbye to the army then, I'm sure.'

\* \* \*

## Military Hospital Athlone

I went out sick today. I went out down to sick-bay even though I was hoping for a bit better than just 'medicine and duty'. To my surprise, I was ordered down here to Athlone Hospital. It must be because they're short of patients that I was sent down here – because I wasn't sick at all. I just wanted to go on the 'dodge' for a while. It's probably just as well that they sent me down here for these few days though, as I'd have been terribly lonely and missing my comrades who've recently left, if I'd stayed down in Renmore. This is a nice little hospital and you're allowed to stay awake as late as you like in the evenings so that you can get away with stuff here that you couldn't do back in Renmore. There are even a few from *An Chéad Chath* here including a man I wasn't expecting to see here at all – '07 Ó Donncha. He's not finished with his PA course yet apparently, but I get the feeling that he's already lost interest in it. He spends most of his day asleep by the looks of it, either that or reading books.

I had to leave my clothes into the store here, in the basement when I first arrived, and replace them with a blue uniform and a pair of slippers. I was also given a big mug, a knife, a fork, and two spoons to eat with, and told that if I lose them, or if they get stolen, I've to pay for them before I leave here again. That's what the Quartermaster told me, anyway. If I was to stay here for a month or so, I'd have a chance to put together a nice bit of money, seeing as I wouldn't have any way of spending it. Normally, any patient who's released from hospital gets a week or two's leave, (three weeks sometimes) and if I get that, I'll be able to go home with the help of God. And by then, we'll almost be into the New Year, and I won't feel the last year of my service going by so much. Little did I think when I was enlisting, that I'd be looking forward one day to being released from the army again. I haven't the same interest in it now since the other lads left.

The Doctor 'does his rounds' here once a day and there's always a nurse on duty here, a different nurse for each level or ward. The nurse on our level here, *an tSiúr* (Sister) Ní Fhearghail is from Galway, and you couldn't ask for a nicer person to have as a nurse. She's always happy and in good form and she says that she always feels a particular affinity with anyone else who's from Galway. She's a fine, pretty-looking woman also, a woman people'd easily fall in love with I'd say. Needless to say, she has the rank of Lieutenant, the same as all other army nurses, and so it'd be a waste of time for any private or O.N.C. itself to take a shine to her.

There are three rooms on this floor of the hospital and four or five patients to each room. Additionally, there is a nurse's station and a kitchen on this floor. The patient who's going to be let out of hospital next has to help the girl who works in the kitchen with bringing the meals out and other jobs. Sometimes the women working in the kitchens are cranky old battle-axes, but you can be lucky. There is a really beautiful-looking girl in the big kitchen down on the ground-floor and when she appears here, the boys all compete with one another to go and help her down in the kitchen.

There are four of us in this room here – myself, '07 Ó Donncha, a thrifty country fellow from Clare named Ó Ceallaigh, and a Company Quartermaster from Sixth Company whose surname is Fawl or Frawl. The Clare recruit is very frugal and he's always talking about how to save money. He's a nice singer as well though and he often sings a few songs for us here. The Quartermaster is mad about songs and music and in the evenings, he's always on at this young lad – and yours truly – to sing a few songs. He isn't like any other O.N.C. that I've met before at all because he never imposes his authority on anyone else here, even when he's well within his rights doing so.

I was stupid enough to sing an old ballad for him last night – 'She Lived Beside the Anner' – and he's been tormenting me to sing more songs since. Once I'd sung my song, he asked Ó Ceallaigh to sing one and he duly obliged. I could tell by the Quartermaster that he was on for a right old session and so's not to hurt him, I asked him to sing one himself. 'Oh feck it, I'm no good at that sort of thing,' he says, but no sooner had I stopped asking him for a song than he began humming a few tunes in a low voice. I'd a hunch that he was no blackbird, but I asked him again anyway, and this time he obliged. Over the years I've heard people who had no business singing, but this man beat all. He was woeful altogether! Not only did he sound worse than a donkey braying or a corncrake making a racket, but he had the oldest, the longest and the most ridiculous ballads you've ever heard. Some of these ballads were two hundred years old if they were a day, and you'd wonder whether the people who composed them originally were crazy or half-drunk – or both. One ballad he sang had a verse which finished like this every time:

'While fishes swim and small birds sing, young men do not prove true, my love, young men do not prove true.'

He sang each verse in a rough doleful voice, emitting a sort of tormented sigh at the end of each line. I had enough by the time he'd finished with his first song, but something crazy possessed me to ask him for another one. 'Well, gentlemen, I don't want to monopolize the evening,' he said, before launching into another melodramatic ballad all the same – something about some poor and misfortunate girl who'd been cuckolded and abandoned sometime in the eighteenth century. The poor creature's resolution to her problem came at the end of the song: 'I'll go into my father's cowshed when the cows are all in bed.'

I never did find out what brought the poor girl into the cowshed as I'd nearly drifted off to sleep by then. I was rudely awakened from my half-sleep by the Quartermaster though: 'Wake up Galway and don't be a wet blanket. We're only starting yet!' Needless to say, he was right and we really *were* only just started! I'd to sing a few more songs and then Ó Ceallaigh followed me, but the Quartermaster sang three songs for every one of ours! '07 Ó Donncha has the best voice of the lot of us but he was trying – unsuccessfully – to get some sleep over in the corner of the room. A half an hour later, when Ó Ceallaigh was nearly asleep and I was just drifting off, the Quartermaster was still droning quietly away to himself about betrayed women and treacherous landlords.

There are a good few lads from *An Chéad Chath* here at the moment but only '07 Ó Donnchú and I are in this room. Most of the others are up on the top level of the building, including Sergeant Ó Loideáin from Maighinis, Darach a' Búrca from Aran and Mac Ruaidhrí from Donegal. I went up to them this afternoon and Mac Ruaidhrí says that Renmore is like a morgue now seeing as so many lads have gone out on their ticket recently. Mac Ruaidhrí was sent down to us from the Curragh today and he was full of the joys of life – as usual! He's a glass-half-empty sort of fellow and he'd his usual round of bad news and depressing stories for us, one worse than the next!

'They're going to break up *An Chéad Chath* now soon,' he claimed at one stage, and the way he said it you'd have imagined that he was delighted about this latest development. 'Ah, shur, it's not worth keeping it going anymore seeing as there aren't enough recruits for it now. Some of us will be sent to Dublin and some of us to Mullingar. Wait'll you see lads – it'll be Mullingar for us!'

'Who was telling you that Mac Ruaidhrí?' says Sergeant Ó Loideáin, winking at the rest of us.

'I heard it down in the games room a while ago from a man who'd never tell a lie,' says Mac Ruaidhrí, as if what he said was gospel.

'They're all in a mad rush to leave the army so,' said Ó Loideáin, 'but, by God, if they knew what was ahead of them when they leave here, they mightn't be half as quick to go. Unless it's changed a lot since I was over there last, the place across the water isn't half as good as they make out.'

Sergeant Ó Loideáin went out previously on serving his time here and spent a while working over in London before re-enlisting again.

'God knows, many's the morning I was rushing out to catch the work-wagon and I says to myself – Orah, Seán my son, you'd have stayed back in Renmore now if you'd had any "cop-on"!'

Jim Bullstrom from Baile na hAbhann came down from Renmore today. He'll be finished up in the army in a fortnight's time or so, but he's not even thinking about that now; he just wants to get better first as he's had poor health for a while. You've never seen as a lad as devout as Bullstrom. I've never heard a curse-word or a vulgar phrase from him. He's always praying and the others in *An Chéad Chath* have great respect for him. There's not many lads would ever try and make fun of him or anything like that either.

'07 Ó Donnchú was given a half-day pass to go down the town today because he won't be here much longer and when he returned there a while ago, he was 'as drunk as a lord'. I could tell straight away that he'd been drinking just by the cautious way that he crept into the room. He tried to let on that he was fine for the first few minutes, but quickly gave up when he realised that he wasn't going to fool anyone. Next thing, he removed his cap and bowed down before everyone in the room, as if humbling himself before us, then proceeded to reel off the most ridiculous speech ever where he compared the human soul to a bicycle! The Quartermaster's eyes widened in horror. He obviously wasn't used to this kind of blasphemy and poor old Ó Ceallaigh couldn't make head nor tail of Ó Donnchú's blather either:

'It's necessary to oil a bicycle and the same is true for the soul – it becomes rusty in the absence of care,' he says, continuing with his homemade philosophizing.

Next thing, Ó Donnchú threw back his shoulders and launched into 'One Fine Day' from the musical *Madame Butterfly*, following this up with 'In Happy Moments Day by Day' from *Maritana*, I think.

Needless to say, this racket brought the nurse into us and it wasn't Sister Ní Fhearghail who was on duty at all but another nurse who's way stricter. She came charging in through the door, her eyes blazing.

'Ó Donnchú, I was thinking it was you! I've heard stories about you before boy, and if I'd had anything to do with it, you certainly wouldn't have been granted the day pass today. Get undressed and go to sleep now, like a good man. If I hear another gig out of you, I'll tell the Doctor about you tomorrow,' she warned him. Ó Donnchú bent down as if curtsying for a queen, but he was so unsteady on his feet that he promptly fell over.

'Bloody hell,' I said to myself. 'You're rightly screwed now.' The ward sister proved more merciful than I thought however, as all she did was call over the medical orderly and told him to 'undress your man and put him to bed'. 'Drunkards,' she said, in a disgusted voice, 'if that rotten dishwater can leave them in such a bad state, imagine what a good drop of whiskey or gin would do to them!' He might be very good, but the Quartermaster has very little time for '07 Ó Donnchú as a singer, and he never asks him for a song. He'd probably be wasting his time requesting one from him because I doubt if Ó Donnchú would oblige him with a tune anyway. Isn't it strange too – how little the Quartermaster knows about music for a man who's so mad for songs and singing. He's a funny old bird, the same Quartermaster, because I've just discovered that he's as careful with his money as that young recruit from County Clare. I bet he's got a pile of money put away already. Still, his love of ballads got the better of his love of money last night when he handed me two shillings and told me to bring back four bottles of porter from the wet canteen. The deal here was that he hoped to wangle a few songs out of me in return for the porter. Four of us drank a bottle each and the Quartermaster was on such a 'high' that you'd swear it was the best party since the age of the High Kings of Ireland long ago!

Out of politeness more than anything else, I'd say – he handed a bottle to Ó Donnchú – although deep down it really bothered him having to give him one I'd say.

'Let the party begin,' he said, as we quietly popped the corks from the bottles; 'you sing the first song Galway and make it a long one. Here's to your good health, everybody!'

'07 Ó Donnchú made a strange gurgling sound in his throat as if he was choking slightly, but the Quartermaster took no notice of him.

'Good old Galway, sing up now!' he says happily and of course, it was my bad luck that I'd to start off. The session went on very late tonight as Sister Ní Fhearghail was on duty and she didn't mind us so long as we weren't too noisy. I was nearly asleep by the end of it, but the Quartermaster was still going as strong as ever. I could hear '07 Ó Donnchú twisting and turning in his bed in an effort to drown out the racket. 'A night at the opera bejaysus,' he says, before finally dropping off to sleep.

Jim Bullstrom isn't well at all, the poor man. It's tomorrow that Ó Ceallaigh will be leaving and Ó Donnchú will follow him a few days later.

I started growing a moustache a few days ago and I think it suits me fairly well – even if for some reason, no one else has noticed that I'm growing it yet. I was a bit embarrassed initially as I thought the others might tease me about it, but I might as well not have a moustache at all, for all the notice they've taken of it. Sister Ní Fhearghail took my temperature this afternoon and I reddened from ear to ear thinking that she might make some mention of it (i.e. the moustache) – but she didn't make the slightest mention of it. She noticed the flushed look on my face, however and said: 'You're very flushed-looking McCauley; be sure you don't catch another flu now, especially with the Doctor planning on letting you out soon.' (I've shaved off my moustache again since. It didn't suit me somehow). Tonight was my last night in the hospital here as I'm going back to Renmore tomorrow on the midday train. I'd fourteen days' sick leave altogether and I'll have more than seven pounds coming to me on my departure from here. I sent Cuirín Mór a letter saying I'd be going back to Clifden next Wednesday afternoon, and he'll be there to meet me off the bus. We'll have some crack that evening in Clifden, I'm sure. I go back to Galway after that and from there, I'll head for Kilkenny. By then, it'll be nearly Christmas anyway, and I should be able to get permission to spend the Holy Season at home.

I've put on a small bit of weight since I came here, I'd say, although I'm very pale in the face too. In a way, I'm not that sorry at all to be leaving as there were only me and the Quartermaster in the room here for the past week and he'd me tormented singing songs for him. Between the pair of us, we must have sung every ballad and 'come-all-ye' ever composed. I've come to the conclusion now that it's the words of the songs that really fascinate him as one tune is the same as the next to him, from what I can tell. Also, he sings every song in the same air. I tried out a few songs in Irish there for him the other day – '*Anach Cuain*' and '*Céad Slán don Abhainn Mór*', but he hadn't the slightest interest in them. 'Yes, yes, Galway, very nice,' he said impatiently, but do you know 'Kate from Baltimore'?' I'll never forget the Quartermaster, I think. His image will remain engrained on my mind forever – the way he'd be stretched back on the bed, and the warm glow of satisfaction radiating from those two big sad eyes of his as he reaches the eighteenth verse of some old nostalgic ballad. I don't envy the next poor fecker who ends up in the room here after me – whoever he is! Poor Bullstrom's health is getting worse, unfortunately.

I reached Renmore just in time for tea, but a wave of loneliness came over me as I walked into the canteen and counted the number of strange faces there, as compared with all the lads I knew previously and who've now left. The numbers in *An Chéad Chath* have got much smaller, but the story is nowhere near as bad as what Mac Ruaidhrí was making out. There's about half as many lads going to the canteen now as there was before, it seems to me, and you hear a lot more English being spoken now too. Of course, many of the newer lads have no Irish seeing as they're from the east and the south of the country more so than the west. Quartermaster Fawl was very sad to see me going this morning and he gave me one crown as a present so that I can buy a few drinks for myself when I get back. 'Goodbye Galway, the sing-song is over,' he said sadly.

There were two very friendly and talkative women sitting next to me on the train on the way back from Athlone who were travelling home from County Meath where they'd been visiting relatives. As we passed Oranmore, I pointed out the army's firing range to them and the place where aeroplanes used to land long ago.

'And is that it there now, Rineanna?' said one of the women to the other.

'Orah, you fool, sure how could that be it?' said her friend. 'Shur, that place there's where our Cóilín used to be firing the Bren?'

'Oh, and what Bren do you mean?' said the first woman again.

'The Bren gun, you devil. And you bet that Cóilín was a good shot too. I often heard him say that he was so exact that you could mark the hole he put in the target with a halfpenny, once he'd fired a "burst" at it!'

I asked her then whether I might know her son by any chance.

'How long are you in?' she said and I told her.

'Orah, shur you'd only be a rookie by the time our Cóilín was finished in the army,' she replied, as if she too held recruits in a measure of disdain.

By Dad, I said to myself, you know your stuff alright old woman, there's no doubt about that.

I spent last night inside chatting with the Maharajah then got my pay today and left the barracks at one o'clock. Lyons had a half-day pass and the pair of us went for a drink together before I headed for Clifden. Little did either of us realise when we left the barracks that he'd be on the same bus to Clifden with me too when the time came! The pair of us overindulged a bit on the drink. If I remember rightly, we went to Maggie Ann's first and then onto Delia Lydon's, and from there onto Maidhc Uí Chadhain's down in the Claddagh – in that order. And we drank plenty in all three pubs. Lyons was saying goodbye to me up at the bus-stop when he changed his mind on the spur of the moment, and jumped aboard just as it was pulling away from the kerb.

We were 'well-on-it' by then and didn't feel the time passing before we arrived at Peacock's in Maam Cross, where the bus always pulls in for a while. The Carna bus was pulled in there also and, needless to say, we didn't let this drinking time go to waste. Two minutes later we were both sitting at the bar, a half-glass of whiskey apiece in our hands. There was a good crowd from Carna there and Stiofán Mhaidhc was amongst them. He was going home on a weekend pass. The big guard from Recess was with him, a big wild-looking fellow, a man whom Stiofán boasted about his toughness and prowess as a fighter. He told us that he beat Cuirín Mór in a fight up in Cornamona[56] recently.

Cuirín Mór was waiting for us as we got off the bus and he was over the moon to see us. I was fairly tipsy by then and wanted to do *Damhsa na Péiste* right there and then on the road, but the other two told me to cop on and we went into Stiofán King's pub instead. Packie had just walked the full five miles in from Kingstown (where he left the currach) and he'd struggled just getting across the sound in the boat, the sea was so rough. He only left the army a short while ago but he's already got quite thin, I think; he looks healthier around the face though.

I can't remember much about the rest of the night, I'm afraid. I do know that I offered to pay for a 'Bed and Breakfast' for the three of us, after we'd eventually been put out of the pub at the end of the night but that Lyons was horrified at this idea. He said it was way too expensive. 'To hell with the "B&B", Núibín,' he says, 'it's a bad state of affairs if we can't find a shed somewhere around here where we can bunk down for the night. It'd be a sin to waste money like that.'

We left the village and went off looking for a place to sleep in and we'd only about a quarter of a mile walked I'd say, when we came across a shed. There were cattle down below, but there was plenty of dry hay up on the loft. Cuirín Mór and the other two lads climbed up no bother but they'd to pull me up after them as I was out on my feet by then.

Cuirín Mór and Lyons arranged the hay nicely so that it made a big bed and we all collapsed onto it. Before we fell asleep, Lyons told us to take our shoes off because your feet swell when you're asleep – or that's what he thinks anyway!

I woke up in the middle of the night absolutely frozen with the cold, and I found it difficult to get back to sleep after that, but the other two snored away contently till morning. I thought they'd never get up but eventually, Packie, and then Lyons stirred themselves and we climbed down from the loft again. My legs felt numb standing out on the road again and I'd that rotten taste in your mouth that you have after a night's heavy drinking. I would have paid someone a pound right there and then if they'd have given me an apple or an orange to eat, I was so keen to get rid of the taste. I was badly hungover, but the only thing that was bothering the other two lads was that they were starving. They headed down to the lake nearby and washed their faces in the water, but I was so wrecked that I couldn't even bring myself to do that.

Getting some breakfast was our next major concern and we didn't hang around. We went straight back up to King's pub again where the other two lads drank three pints each before eating their breakfast.

It was snowing when we got back to Galway and we went for a few drinks in Curran's pub in Bohermore. We didn't delay, however, as I was tired and Lyons needed to go home so that his wife knew that he was still alive!

I got lodgings in Kelly's pub on Mary's Street, where a strange thing happened to me when I was alone in the bedroom there. I locked the door to have a sleep; the window in the room had obviously been jammed shut for years; even Buddy Bear himself wouldn't have been able to open it, it was that firmly shut. I fell asleep almost as soon as my head hit the pillow and I don't remember anything else until I woke up in the middle of the night when I felt something heavy pressing down on my chest. I was half-asleep at first and I thought that a cat might have got into the room and I put out my hand to pet it. I fell asleep again straight away and didn't wake again until morning. It was only when I woke up properly that I remembered about the bolt on the door and the jammed window and wondered what the hell had happened during the night. I searched the room but there was no living creature there other than myself.

A young girl from Rosmuc brought me breakfast – a big duck egg, something I'd never eaten before. I half-thought of asking her was there anything strange about the house. But next thing, I overheard the 'oul wan' who's in charge there telling the girl to charge me one crown for the lodgings and I didn't bother with it anymore. The journey back to Kilkenny was long and tiring and I eventually got home at eight o'clock that evening. We've moved house since I was last home, and when I first came to the place where the new houses were built, I was lost. I'd to ask a young boy there where my family was living. He gave me a careful stare for a minute as if unsure as to whether he was dealing with someone who was crazy and then pointed his finger in the direction of a house close by. I thanked him and went in.

\* \* \*

I returned here to Renmore Barracks the day before yesterday. I spent four days longer at home than I was permitted, but the first thing I heard on arrival was that I've been transferred to D Company – as have most of the extra men in B Company. It's probably just as well as the old company isn't what it once was. There are just a handful of the old-timers left and most of them live down in Galway town. Another thing – I'll have the Maharajah as a comrade now, seeing as he's been transferred now too, of course. I'd to get a gun and other equipment including new bedding out of the D Company store today, and I managed to get a nice springy bed next to the Maharajah in the upper-level room, where Cuirín Mór and the lads were until a few weeks ago.

The old room we were all in previously has been closed up now and I suppose it'll stay that way until enough new recruits arrive to justify opening it again. A good crowd of new recruits have arrived from the Curragh since I was last here – just before Christmas – half of whom I don't recognise to be honest. It's clear to me that they don't have the same 'go' in them as the lads who were here previously though. Many of them are from east Galway and they are much quieter and have less crack than the Connemara crowd. Hardly any of them drink and they're as 'dry' as a sod of turf, the majority of them. Where we'd plenty of wit and slagging and storytelling before, all you hear now are short, boring conversations mainly almost always in a rough form of English. It's hard to know why these lads were sent to this Battalion in the first place because they've no interest in the Irish language.

I wouldn't mind, but some of them would make fun of the Irish language if they thought they'd get away with it. There are still enough lads from the Gaeltacht here, though, to put manners on them, thank God – if it ever comes to that. You'd notice some of the lads more than others and you'd be curious as to what makes them 'tick'. There are two brothers here named Nolan who're intriguing in a strange sort of way. Although their surname is Nolan, I've privately christened them Hud and Dud. Both lads are big-boned, awkward and untidy and they speak in a slow and plodding way; their intelligence belies the quiet and careful way they go on however, even if you'd need a Ferguson tractor to drag any talk out of them most of the time. Both brothers wear *Pioneer* badges as do many of their friends and the other lads from their locality. They don't drink at all and yet I'm not sure that they're a penny richer for their efforts, because you wouldn't be up with them when it comes to eating sweets. Every time you see them, they're propped up on a kit-box staring silently in front of them and chewing sweets. They aren't twins although they're so similar in appearance that you'd be forgiven for thinking this; they're both the exact same height and build and look

very similar in the face. Máirtín Cúc ('The Teacher') was telling me
yesterday that they refer to one of the brothers as 'Big Nolan' to
distinguish him from the other. This wouldn't work for me I have to
admit. I still can't tell one of them from the other. A small lad from Gort
by the name of Thomas Doyle[57] has his bed next to theirs, inside in the
room. Doyle's a nice lad, and I notice that he has a great respect for the
older soldiers here. Also, he's not 'full of himself', like some of the other
lads here, and the Maharajah was telling me that he'd never let you
down if you asked him for a loan of a piece of soap or a razor blade or
the like. The Maharajah hasn't tried him for the loan of a few bob yet,
but he reckons that Doyle would be just as helpful on that score too.
Seeing as I've served my apprenticeship in the room below already, I
won't let any chance to play pranks on the new recruits go a-begging, I
can guarantee you that. It mightn't be so easy to 'pull a fast one' on some
of these new lads however, as they're the types who've wise heads on
young shoulders – as the old saying goes. They all have big padlocks on
their kit-boxes and keep all their stuff firmly secured at all times. I'd say
Slám Féir and the Horse will be the only two who'll trick them, when
it comes down to it. I'd put money on it!

Not all the lads in this room are new recruits, of course. There's one
very strong block of a man who has his bed just inside the door of the
room on the left-hand side whose surname is Ó Cuirín. He's from
Lettermore[58] somewhere and he already has more than ten years' service
in the army, even though he's only barely twenty-seven years of age yet.
Ó Cuirín is always referred to as '80 Ó Cuirín although you'd rarely see
him in the room here because he's usually up in the Administration
Office or going out with the post to the General Post Office and that
type of thing. Even when he's in the room here, he doesn't talk much
with the others as he's that real lack of respect that older soldiers have
for recruits. Ó Cuirín is a very neat and exact soldier and he's forever
giving out about how awkward and untidy the recruits are – not that he

actually says a whole lot on these occasions. He's always shining and spick-and-span, his shoes carefully polished, his buttons gleaming and a pleat in his trousers that would cut you it's so sharp. They say that he's saved a good bit of money by now and I'd believe it too. Still, despite the jokey façade that he puts on, he looks to me like a man who's anxious about the world somehow, I think. For example, he often wakes in the middle of the night in the middle of a deep sleep and shouts out as if frightened of something. I slept that same deep sleep of the dead a few times previously and I can't but feel sorry for him that he wakes up like this sometimes.

The first time I remember experiencing this dead-weight sleep where you're almost unconscious to the world – not until I first came to this barracks anyway. Whenever it hits me, I know somewhere in the back of my consciousness that I really want to wake up, but it's as if there's something beyond my control that's holding me tight within the realm of heavy sleep and I can't escape it. Sometimes, I feel as if there's something dark standing next to me or flying above me and that it's preventing me from waking or getting free. Needless to say, there must be some kind of rational explanation for these feelings and this really heavy form of sleep. All the same, it's strange how often this death-like sleep affects people here. I've talked to the other lads about it and they say that they've experienced something very similar at times also. I remember one day in particular about or so not long after I arrived here. I was lying stretched out on the bed in the room below (I was Room Attendant that day) when I heard the Bugler sounding out *Fáilte an Aingil* (the Angelus) out on the square. I tried to get out of bed to say the prayer, but I couldn't move despite my best efforts. It was like I was in a complete daze or in a deep stupor and I just couldn't move at all; and yet I'm certain that my eyes were open all the while. The window opposite me was open and next thing I spotted Micilín Ó Conghaile (Maitias' brother) leaning on the windowsill and talking to me. But someone could've given me a golden guinea right there and then, and I still wouldn't have understood a word he was saying. He might as well have been talking Russian instead of Irish for all I could make sense of him. I'm not sure that I managed to close my eyes at all that day, but just a few minutes later (or at least, it seemed like a few minutes anyway) the 'spell' wore off and I was able to get up out of the bed. I walked out to the door and there was a crowd of lads standing outside. I remember saying something like that it must be nearly time for dinner – and one of the men outside laughed. I found this strange but then when I asked them the time, I got a shock. It was half past one in the afternoon and even the lads who were always late had already eaten their dinner! This gave me a right fright I can tell you, and I asked Micilín Ó Conghaile later that afternoon whether he remembered speaking to me. Micilín said he definitely did remember chatting to me and that he'd been confused when I hadn't answered him. Joeen Beag has a great interest in these matters and in his opinion there's something that isn't 'right', some kind of spirit, hanging around the rooms here. Who knows? Maybe a murder or some other terrible crime was committed here long ago when the British were here?

But to move on to something else – the first thing I heard on my return here was the bit about being transferred to another Company. The second thing was that there was a charge against me of course, for being absent for four days without permission. I have a doctor's certificate that I got from the local doctor at home and hopefully, that'll save me. You wouldn't know in this place though. Anyway, all things considered, I've started the New Year fairly well and on top of this, I've begun life in a new company as well. Still, it's probably fairly unlikely that the new Company Captain will prove as patient with me as Captain Cusack was. The entire Battalion went on a slow march today out around Castlegar. It was a lovely outing although I missed the fact that my old comrades like Cuirín Mór and Colm a' tSeaimpín and the rest of them weren't there anymore. We'd great crack all the same and spending the day outdoors helped me shift that downbeat feeling I've had over the last while. The Maharajah and the Sailor were in the same group as me, and the new recruit they've nicknamed Mac a' Scilling ('the Shilling's Son') was in the group following us.

Ó Giolláin[59] is this fellow's proper name and he's from the Aran Islands, but the Horse nicknamed him Mac a' Scilling in much the same way as he renamed Lyons 'Mac a' Leoin' ('son of the Lion'). This Ó Giolláin is the most foreign-looking individual you've ever seen. He looks more like a Basque person or a Spaniard than he does like any other race of people, I think. He's a very friendly lad all the same and he can be very witty when he wants to be. English still sounds a bit strange coming from him – just as it's the other way around in relation to the Maharajah's Irish. We all have great crack listening to these two speaking in what – for the both of them – is their second language. The Rajah makes a right mess of it sometimes when he tries to speak Irish; he pronounces all sorts of words in the most bizarre way imaginable. In the case of Ó Giolláin, he pronounces his English words in such a clipped way that you'd swear they were burning his tongue. You can tell by the Rajah that he's a man who's already bored with army life, even if he's only here a short while compared to the rest of us. He's not a whiner who's always going on about it though; unlike some of the other lads; he just jokes about it.

'You've a lovely life now, Mac an Scilling,' he says to the Aran lad the other day. 'Shur, you've a brilliant life compared to what you had out on the Aran Islands. Back there, you're out slogging away with a shovel all day; either that or *snatching* small fish from the sea …'

'True for you, little brother,' said Mac an Scilling solemnly.

'Don't be talking,' said the Maharajah. 'Don't be talking would you! You crowd are actually worse off than that even. Shur, you crowd were out there making *Novenas* that a ship would break up on the rocks and

184

you'd get all the stuff off it. And you had no mercy in your hearts, you shower! When those poor sailors were in the water, rather than saving them, all you crowd did was start laughing and then bash them over the head with a big plank. Then, once the following morning, you had all the loot for yourselves.'

'Maharajah little brother, who the hell was telling you that rubbish? By my soul, but it's many the sailor that the people of Aran saved down the years.'

'Oh, don't be talking. Shur, don't I know it well. Didn't I read about it in the *Beano* shur,' replied the Rajah.

'Bloody hell, Maharajah, but you've learned lovely fluent Irish since you joined *An Chéad Chath*, so you have,' said the Sailor, winding him up even more.

'Excellent Irish altogether,' added Mac an Scilling.

'It's the duty of every man to speak Irish here,' says the Maharajah, even if the truth of the matter is that he couldn't be bothered learning Irish at all – only that he can have a bit of fun with it.

'It is our national heritage,' I says, imitating the type of thing Gerry Gavanly would say.

'If every man here just picked up a book and went out to teach someone else the language, it wouldn't be long before everyone in the country had Irish,' says the Maharajah; and then, as if as an afterthought, 'but an understanding of the dative case is the most important of all!' And even if he's really making fun of the whole thing, there's some truth in what the Rajah says because he himself is a good example of how quickly someone can learn a new language if they really put their mind to it. When he arrived here this summer, he hadn't even one word of Irish, but now he's even able to tease others or half-mock them in the language, even if he's far from fluent in it as of yet. The Rajah's mockery of the Irish language doesn't bother me in the slightest because I know he doesn't really mean it and that it's all just a bit of fun. I know that he really would speak the language fluently too if it was in his gift to do so. Speaking of Irish, it's hard to gauge the strength of the Irish language around Castlegar[60] and the other villages nearby even if we met many people, both young and old, out marching today and they all spoke Irish. I noticed too that many of the old men out that side still wear more traditional-style clothes like the 'bawneen', even if this area is very close to Galway city. It seemed to me that more men wear older-style clothes out there than do over in Connemara now.

The Maharajah and I were both in good form, if completely exhausted by the time the march was over. We were both lying back on our beds with our shoes off when in walked the new Captain all of a sudden. This man, Captain Breatnach, is barely a year in the army himself, but he's one of those power-hungry types, and he never gives you a moment's peace but is always looking for the next opportunity to assert his authority over others. A tall, thin lad, he's very pale and always has his hair shaved to the bone in the style of the German soldiers during the Second World War. His sole interest in life is in soldiering and in getting ahead in the army, and I'd believe those who say that he has every word of the book *Defence Forces Regulations* off by heart. You can't do anything, but he says that it's an offence under some army regulation or other – according to him, anyway – and he's forever saying that he could spend all day, every day, charging us with this, that and the other – only that he's not so bad-minded as to do this. Indeed, as I pointed out to him myself the other day, he's not shy at all when it comes to charging people with various offences as it is! He was only made a Captain very recently, but he must have more charges issued against men already than all the O.N.C.'s in this Battalion here put together. And despite his unwavering dedication to the army, he still doesn't look half as neat when he's on parade as the likes of Cuirín Mór and Colm a' tSeaimpín did when they were here and in their pomp. Breatnach would spend half of the day getting ready and yet Lyons can get himself spick-and-span and ready for Commander's Parade in two minutes and look better turned out for his troubles too. This is a skill that you can't teach someone; either you have it or you don't. Lyons would often say to me, for example: 'You're in the army now Núibín, but that doesn't mean that you're a soldier yet.' And when I look at some of the crowd who're only here a short while but who already think they know it all already, Lyons' statement makes perfect sense.

Anyway, Breatnach comes rushing into the room like a banshee looking for a lost soul. But there's only the two of us in the room, me and the Rajah. We've managed to hide away when the rest of the Company have been ordered out for Doctor's Parade. One minute we're feeling dead happy with ourselves and then this fellow suddenly appears and we know straight away that we're screwed.

'Aha! McCauley and the Rajah, the two biggest wasters in this barracks,' Breatnach says delighted with himself. 'Why aren't you two on Doctor's Parade with all the others?'

'Get stuffed,' says the Maharajah by way of reply. Oh boy – that's when your man completely blows his top. His eyes widen and one of the veins in his neck looks like it's about to burst, he's that worked up. 'Private MacMahon stand to attention!' he roars. 'Go to hell,' says the Maharajah in what was probably the best sentence of Irish he ever spoke. This time Breatnach lets a half-strangled roar out of him that's a sign of shock. He's momentarily speechless at this level of insubordination on the Rajah's part. Then, when he's recovered himself again: 'I'm charging you immediately, MacMahon,' he says.

'For what?' says the Rajah in feigned innocence.

'For what,' repeated the Captain sarcastically, imitating my comrade's accent. 'For what? I'll tell you for bloody what. For insolence to a non-commissioned officer, that's for what! You're a witness to it McCauley.'

'Yes, Captain, but I don't think he'd have spoken that way to you if you hadn't called him a "dirty thief" in the first place,' I says.

Another roar out of him then. 'A dirty thief! When did I call him a "dirty thief"? Have you lost the plot man?'

'Yeah, you called me dirty thief and a filthy muckbird,' says the Rajah, quickly into the breach again.

'That's your word against ours Captain,' I says to Breatnach as calmly as I could under the circumstances.

This knocked him for six. He was absolutely ripping mad but just about contained himself.

'Right, bejayus!' he says finally, 'this is a game that I can play too, you know. Get up now straight away, the pair of you, and come with me. You're both absent from Doctor's Parade without permission and without a valid excuse – that's one thing I can charge both of you with anyway.'

We'd no option but to follow him out but, just to annoy him more, we both delayed on our way out, pretending to search for our 'missing' caps – everywhere. We were worse than the Marx Brothers the pair of us, like two born idiots arsing around the place pretending to look for the caps and the Captain getting angrier by the minute.

'Soldiers, bejayus! And you've the cheek to call yourselves soldiers as well! You'd get better soldiers than the likes of you at a halfpenny a head down in Glynn's pub in the city below!'

'But Captain, we were soldiers when you were still coaxing the donkey out of the bog. We were trained soldiers while you were still just a red-arse down in the Curragh. The first day you arrived here to Renmore, you asked me – "Where's the swill-barrel for God's sake" – and I showed it to you too!' This bullshit really annoyed the Captain and he let a screech out of him like one of those big pelican birds you see in the Pictures. 'Right, McMahon. I'll sort you out now boy. From now on, I'm going to be down on you like a ton of bricks – until you've paid for all this insubordination,' he said through gritted teeth. He marched us out to the Medical Booth where we'd to undergo a Doctor's exam the same as everyone else, then made straight for the Company Office to write out the charges against us. He had it done quickly too, by God, because he was back again two minutes later with a triumphant look and two of those small ugly Form 117's in his hands. He was in much better form now that he was going to get his own back on us and he was imitating the witty *patter* that some of the older O.N.C.'s come out with, just before they're about to hang you!

'Now, good Sirs, if you can spare a few minutes, the Captain would like to speak to you,' he said, his voice, reeking with false humility. He marched us back up again then and we kept our mouths shut this time. Captain O'Callaghan tried us, hearing both cases simultaneously. He was studying a document relating to me – my 'Behaviour File' apparently – as we came in, and he dealt with me first. O'Callaghan was in the Artillery before this, I think, and his Irish isn't as fluent as some of the other officers here.

First, he placed my file down on his desk and scratched his chin thoughtfully. 'This is a very interesting document McCauley. It tells us a good deal about you. It appears that you have a frequent habit of being (A) dirty on parade, (B) absent without permission, (C) not following orders. These are your main failings. Well, you're beginning anew in this company and I might as well tell you right now that I'm not having any of this crack from now on. As for you, McMahon, there's not much in the notes here against you yet, or at least compared with your pal anyway. Now boys, I'll tell you what I'm going to do with you. The New Year's only just begun and I'm happy to give you both a chance this time. I'm going to give you a 'wiped clean' this time, but I'm issuing you a special warning right now, McCauley. Behave yourself in this company from now on. Your father was a Battalion Quartermaster under my command a few years back. He was an excellent soldier and you're no great credit to him, I have to say. I hope you do better from now on.' We were walking on air when we came out, all the more so at the foul look on

Breatnach's face when he realised how lightly we'd got off. 'Right bejaysus,' he says, when he told us to disperse outside the office, 'you got away with it this time but there'll be another day …'

'Breatnach will have another day,' enunciated the Rajah slowly like a schoolchild reading out a lesson. 'Quiet,' said the Captain, in a poisonous whisper. 'How would it go if I was to charge you two with insubordination and being smart alec.'

'We'd say that you called me a dirty thief,' says the Rajah. 'Dirty thief,' says Breatnach before realising it, then grits his teeth in temper and ordered us to 'disperse'. We were the two happiest men in the army walking across the square that evening, the two of us happy and full of swagger at the fact that we'd won this particular battle. We'll have to be careful with the Captain from now on though, as he'll be watching us like a hawk, you can be sure of it.

For the past week now, I am on Gunnery – *Anti-Tank Gun* (two pound) – myself, Lyons, Colm Carew and Máirtín Breatnach (from an Caoláire[61]) under the charge of Lieutenant Pádraig Ó Siochfhradha[62] and Sergeant Breatnach.[63] Breatnach's one of the nicest and most highly respected men in this barracks and it's no wonder as he's an absolute gentleman. He always speaks to you very politely and if he's ever in bad humour or upset about something (which almost never happens) – he doesn't ever single out individuals for criticism, unlike some of the others here. He's someone who has a strong interest in literature and drama and this means that he has a more humane attitude towards people than others who've no interest in scholarship or learning in my opinion. He's a soldier above all else though, and athletics is as important to him as is literature. He is a very good goalkeeper and always plays for the Battalion team. A big power of a man, he's a good speaker. It's great to listen to him when he is in teaching mode as not only is he an excellent orator, but he also has the clearest and most correct Irish you'd hear anywhere. That said, he's a real disciplinarian and doesn't put up with any shoddy behaviour or anyone who shirks their duties in any way.

Máirtín Breatnach and Lyons are both really fascinated by this anti-tank gun that we've here, but the same can't be said for Colm Carew or myself, I'm afraid. Carew is a great man for music. He's a piper in the Battalion band and you'd stand out in the snow listening to him play a few reels, he's that good, never mind when he plays the flute or the tin whistle. He's from County Clare, a place where good musicians were always plentiful and he knows every Irish tune you can think of. That said, he isn't a very happy-go-lucky fellow for a musician and he's often got a worried or anxious look about him.

Máirtín Breatnach is a very nice lad as well although he can be a bit hot-headed and abrasive and it's easy to get on the wrong side of him. This short-tempered nature of his is a trait that many of the kindest people are prone to however, and he's no sooner lost his cool than he's back to normal again and is as nice a fellow as you could meet anywhere. Lyons and himself are both excellent soldiers and you can't blame them really if they don't rate me or Carew when we make a mess of using the anti-tank gun. Seosamh Ó hUaithnín (Joe Pheaitín Pheaitsí) came in this morning after travelling on the bus from Carna and he had big news for Lyons and me. Packie Cuirín Mór is down in Galway town and he's leaving for England shortly. Packie told him that he'd be in to the wet canteen to see us, before he leaves for Dublin on the afternoon train. Lyons applied for a half-day pass immediately and left the barracks so that he could wish him well down at the train station. I knew that I'd no business applying for one of these passes myself, but I still plan on sneaking out of here somehow when Lyons goes out along the rail-line and into town, no matter what. We were counting down the minutes during training on the anti-tank gun and finally, the bugle sounded to announce dinner. No sooner had it sounded than who should arrive in the gate of the barracks but the old chancer himself,

Cuirín Mór! We 'converged' together (to quote a phrase from Quartermaster Ó Súilleabháin) and to use another of his phrases again, we 'adjourned' to the wet canteen immediately without bothering with dinner at all. A neighbour of Packie's was with him, a quiet fellow who was returning to England and who was 'taking it all in' before he leaves – not that we paid too much attention to this. The three of us were in great form meeting up again, and Packie's neighbour couldn't get a word in, we were that excited about his plans for the future and had so many questions for him. The new lad just stared at us with a dazed expression as if he'd never seen the likes of us previously, we were on such a 'high'. Other than going up to the counter a few times to buy the pints, Packie paid little heed to his neighbour either. I'd have given a thousand pounds there and then if Packie'd changed his mind and decided to re-enlist in the army. People can't always choose what they want in this life, however. You have to use your head and find work wherever you can get it, I suppose. Eventually, the bugle went for 'half-hour' and we'd to get ready quickly for the two o'clock parade.

'I'm probably as well to say goodbye to you now Núibín, seeing as you aren't allowed out on a half-day's leave, but we'll see each other again one of the days in that pub in Marble Arch, I've no doubt. You'll be getting your ticket next October and I'll be expecting you over from that date onwards. Don't forget about our meeting place now, the pub with the big mirrors and the giant clock that hovers over the bottles. If I'm not there when you first arrive in, ask Alfie, that's the name of the barman there (I'm nearly positive about that) – and he'll tell you what time I'll be in.'

The stranger's eyes widened in amazement on hearing this.

'When were you over in London before, Mac Lump?' he says.

This was the first time we'd heard our friend being referred to by this nickname and Lyons and I burst out laughing. Packie gave his fellow-traveller a right dirty look though:

'I don't have to have been over in England before to know my way around the place. That pub exists alright, you can rest assured of that. It has to be there because that's where myself and Núibín are meeting up one fine day from now,' he said.

That shut your man up rightly. He stared at Packie and shook his head.

'Here, let's get out of here. Come on over till you see what our old room looks like now,' I said to them, and we made our way over to Block B.

I undid the bolt on the door and pushed it in, and it was only then I heard the whining coming from inside. Because the room's been empty for a while now, one of the officers locked three greyhounds in there yesterday. He's leaving them there until he finds somewhere else to put them. We stood just inside the door, but Cuirín Mór hadn't the heart to step any further into the room. He took one look around at the high walls and the bare iron beds piled over in one corner of the room now and sighed: 'Oh, look at the state of you now, O little loyal room of old,' he said, 'a pack of dogs in where the finest of Gaelic Irishmen once lived. The snivel and whine of wild dogs where '07 Ó Donnchú's magic singing once rang out. A lonely silence now in the corner there where Colm a' tSeaimpín once told his stories and where mild Mícheál Ó Sé once gave out about the rest of us. Still Núibín, I think we'll do *Damhsa na Péiste* one more time in honour of the old days!' Off we went with the dance and knocked sparks out of the bare, scoured timbers of that old floor, the silent lad from Carna staring at us, his mouth agape. And when the greyhounds saw what we were up to, they increased the sound of their own sad whining music. The *Quarter Hour* sounded on the bugle now and it was time for us to get moving. We said goodbye and good luck to the greyhounds that whimpered loudly as we closed the door.

'Off you go, lads,' I said. 'I'll meet you down on the line.'[64] They headed off and I went back to the room where the other lads were getting ready for parade. I just grabbed a belt and a cap, put on my new army uniform and went out the door. I had to sneak out through the back-gate of course, and I kept close to the wall until I'd no choice but to cut across the field so's to come out near the railway line. I could see the other three lads off in the distance coming to the bridge at Loch an tSáile and increased my pace to catch up with them. The lads were delighted to see me and Cuirín Mór and I stopped and engaged in a quick bout of wrestling on the path. 'Hey, hey,' says Lyons, 'will you cop on for a minute. You've just a few hours left here in Galway now ...' Packie stopped and it was as if this realisation had really hit him for the first time. We walked quickly onwards to the town, each of us a bit quieter in ourselves now that we realised the enormity of what Cuirín Mór's departure really meant. We went into the Corner Bar where we fairly lashed into the drink and we were 'well-on-it' when it came time for us to go down to the train. The 'old wans' in charge of the bar weren't that happy to see us really anyway, as they don't like serving anyone in there who drinks more than three pints in one go, and once Cuirín Mór started prancing around the floor and doing *Damhsa na bPortán* (The Crab Dance) – they told us to get out.

'Aha, you miserable-faced old wans, you won't feel it till Cuirín Mór's back here again and his pockets stuffed with gold coins – wait and see whether he calls into you then at all,' says Packie by way of riposte.

'By dad, Mac Lump,' says Packie's neighbour then (and these were the first words he'd uttered in the space of an hour, I'd say), 'you'd better leave that crack behind you now in Galway if you want to stay in the same lodgings as me, over in England. Ah, there's no way that my landlady will keep you for more than a few minutes if she sees you at that lark. It's strange how we never saw you doing them back in Turbot!'

'I used to dance them alright, you lily-livered buck you; it was just that I danced them when no one else was looking, in case they saw my heart breaking at the thought of saying goodbye to this here royalty.

And as for that old wan of a landlady of yours, I won't be long meeting her before I'll improve her menu for her, I can tell you,' says Packie.

We'd to throw back our 'drink for the road' fairly lively though and make our way quickly down to the train station. Lyons and I shoved a half-sovereign each into Packie's pocket, whether he wanted to take it or not. That was the least we could do for him, needless to say, seeing as he's leaving Ireland. If we'd had ten times more money to give him, we'd have given it to him without a second's thought. We were just on time for the train as it pulled out of the station, and I was just as glad for this because there's nothing worse in my opinion, than a long-drawn-out farewell to someone who's leaving their native land. We all shook hands and I could tell by the cursory handshake from Cuirín Mór's friend that he couldn't wait to see the back of Lyons and me. Packie had tears in his eyes as the train moved off and the long line of carriages crept out past us. He said something about that pub in Marble Arch again but whatever it was was drowned out with the racket from the steam engine and the fact that he was upset. Lyons and myself stood there until the train passed over the bridge at Loch an tSáile and then we went back out onto the street again. And who was waiting for us outside on the street – believe it or not – but one of the Military Police, Captain Mac Néill from Inis Mór! He arrested me immediately. I turned around to say goodbye to Lyons as well now too, but he'd already disappeared into the crowd. He'd slipped back down to the Corner Pub again to drown his sorrows, I'd say. Captain Mac Néill is low-sized yet sturdy, but unlike others in the Battalion, his bite is actually worse than his bark. Just when you think you're safe, he'll nab you for something and the fact that he addressed me in a nice civil manner only made me twice as anxious as I already was! He almost always speaks English because although he was brought up out on the Aran Islands, his family is actually of English background. He spoke to me a in very polite voice as follows:

'I'm frightfully sorry, Mac, old boy, but I've got to arrest you,' he said, as if fulfilling his duty was actually hurting him more than it was me.

'I'm sorry for putting you to so much trouble,' I responded sarcastically in turn, 'but who reported me anyway, if you don't mind me asking?' He gave a short cough as if about to make an excuse.

'Well, as a matter of fact – to be perfectly frank Mac – I saw you myself from the Tower. I hope you won't think too badly of me. Duty first, and all that.'

We started out for the barracks and I wasn't sure which of the three emotions he felt most towards me – hatred, disgust or pity. Because, although he was going to hang me when we got back, he still didn't want me to think badly of him. I knew too that it'd really bother him if I decided not to talk to him anymore after he'd charged me. Even now, as he escorted me back to the barracks, and he trying to make conversation with me as if what he was doing was the most normal thing in the world! Worse still, (and something that I'll never forgive him for) he was praising Cuirín Mór to the skies and saying what a great lad he was, and all the rest of it. I knew as well as anyone that if it was the other way around and Cuirín Mór had gone missing to wish me farewell, Mac Néill wouldn't have had the slightest hesitation in arresting him too. He was some fecker really! The walk back to the barracks felt too long altogether and I was really glad when we finally got back inside the gates again. It was then that your man exceeded himself altogether. He grabbed a friendly hold of my elbow and said in a pleading voice:

'By the way, Mac, I wonder if you'd go a bit easy on the old Gaelic when you're being charged? If you could just speak slowly and clearly – not too much of the 'blas' if you know what I mean. I'm not as fluent as I might be and you know how keen the O.C. is on the language.' I was just dumbstruck on hearing this and didn't say anything to him at all.

I was summoned after morning parade this morning and charged with breaking barracks yesterday. Initially, I was brought up before the Company Captain but these were just the formalities, because I had to be remanded then to see the Commander. He listened to the case attentively all the same, and gave me plenty of time to explain why I'd left the barracks without permission. I felt that I did a good job of 'excusing' myself for breaking the regulations and I spoke in an Irish as eloquent and fluent as anything you'd hear out in Rosmuc – so's to deliberately confuse Captain Mac Néill. I explained how Cuirín Mór and I had always been very close friends and how I felt obliged to see him off at the train station. If army comrades couldn't stand by one another, then who could, I said. When I'd finished speaking, the Captain nodded his head as if in agreement even if he'd a slightly cynical look on his face all the while, however.

'I admire your loyalty to your comrade McCauley,' he says, 'but it's a pity you don't show the same loyalty to the Defence Forces of whom you're a member. I have to remand you to the Commander, I'm afraid.' Even then, I held out some hope of getting a lighter punishment. The Battalion Commander's quite an understanding person normally and he might go easy on me if I explain my situation well to him. I'd no luck on any score today though. The Commander was absent so I was sent to the Deputy Commandant – Commandant Crowe – instead. I can't say that the Commandant and I have ever been too fond of one another really. He's a very strict and uncompromising individual who doesn't put up with any messing and he's given me a fair few dressing-downs before. I remember last year when they put me to work in the Officer's Mess and the Battalion Officers had invited the Bishop to dinner. All of us were at 'high-doe' trying to ensure that everything ran smoothly for his lordship's arrival. The Mess Sergeant had a large number of waiters roped in to help out, and it goes without saying that this son of a gun here was one of them. Commandant Crowe arrived in to inspect us before we were let anywhere near the Bishop and when he saw the state of my white jacket and my finger-nails, he ordered me out of the restaurant altogether. This really hurt me to the quick although I was secretly glad to have got out of the task of waiting on tables and I composed some verses immediately based on this imaginary scenario – in this poem, I pretended that the Bishop was disappointed not to see me working there alongside the other waiting staff:

*'As the ancient Bishop said, 'Where did Núib Mac Amhlaigh go?*
*The man who was the most noted of all the waiters long ago!*
*When I go out to Salthill to visit the bigshots out there,*
*I always met him there, at the head of the table.*
*He'd have knives in his hands and a nice white jacket on him,*
*And I'll put it on the record now that he was the best man at his job.'*
*'Oh, that dirty, ugly old thing, I can't stand him,*
*I wouldn't give him permission to serve you,' was the response of*
*Commandant Crowe.*

*'Even so, I have one request for you, in the name of dutiful Patrick,*
*Tell him to come here now without delay,*
*Because he's the most skilled of the lot when it comes to setting the table,*
*Not like these fools here who haven't a clue about their trade yet!'*
*When they heard his Lordship calling for me so urgently,*
*They were very ashamed and mortified and, not without reason either,*
*And they requested that Mac Amhlaigh be pardoned and told the*
*Sergeant,*
*'Call Núib Mac Amhlaigh in, if he's available!'*

*When he heard this instruction, he thought to himself for a moment,*
*'The cleaning's all done – I think he's cleaned up all!*
*The turf and the timber is tidied, the floor is scoured clean*

*And there's nothing left to do unless he brushes the Hall,'*
*But when he heard that it was his Lordship's request,*
*By my soul, he was quick to go out and get Mac Amhlaigh,*
*And I returned with me delighted and full of joy,*
*And waited expertly on one of Ireland's most important men.*

Whatever about the poem, the Commander couldn't have been tougher on me than he was when I was marched in to him this afternoon. Captain Mac Néill gave evidence first in his broken and stuttering Irish and then I gave my side of the story. I didn't spend too much time on it however, as I could tell by the look on the Commandant's face that I was only wasting my time expecting any mercy or sympathy from him. The Commandant eyed me with those two piercing eyes of his and said brusquely:

'One beetle recognises another. Birds of a feather flock together. It was a good day for the Battalion when Cuirín Mór went out on his ticket and I don't think we'll be crying too much when you leave either Mac Amhlaigh. Will you accept my punishment?'

'I will, Sir,' I says, thinking that maybe he'd go easy on me seeing as his preamble was so angry and terse. I was wrong though. On top of the dressing-down, I was fined a pound.

The drive for new recruits is on again. Here in Renmore is where they're being trained now, rather than down in the Curragh and needless to say, this is a big help for new lads joining from Connemara. There are a good many new lads enlisting too and we've actually reduced the speaking of English again. Still, I can't help noticing that the younger lads coming in now aren't as fine a body of men as those of us who enlisted before them. The new recruits are assigned to A Company and some of them look so young that they couldn't be much more than a few days above enlistment age. There are three lads from the Aran

Islands there at the moment – Micheál Cúc (the 'Teacher's' brother), Pádraig Ó Tuathail and Brian Ó Maoláin. All three of them are very nice, relaxed lads and they still have that innocence that you associate with lads who're living in the city for the first time ever. From Connemara then come, Bhal Ó Loideáin from Carna, Seáinín Ó Cuirín (Seáinín Jack) from Leitir Móir, Tomás Ó Féinneadha from Poll Uí Bhoirinn and Pete Tim from Na Doireadha. Some of them are due to be transferred to our company shortly and it's just as well, as there's been too much English spoken here in recent times.

I received a letter today from Cuirín Mór – the first one I got from him since he left more than a fortnight ago – and I felt a strange mixture of sadness and joy reading it:

> *Hut No. 7*
> *Displaced Persons' Camp,*
> *Corby, Northants.*

Hello Núibín

I'm here as you can see amongst the 'displaced latchicoes' of the Western World – Poles, Ukrainians and Latvians – and it's a tough life I have here now that I never hear a word of Irish or English spoken – just the continuous jabbering of all these foreign languages that I don't understand a word of. I didn't stay too long with my *landlady* because her rotten *spam* didn't agree with me much and neither did the dry bread that she served up. This place isn't much better either though. We earn about a pound a day normally, doing our navvying work. They tell me that you can earn more than this if you head out and travel around the country, something which I am going to do very shortly.

The other people here are big gamblers and sometimes they play cards all night in the prefab I'm in. I join in the cards myself of course, but I haven't been lucky yet in terms of winning anything. They play another game here that you need to have a very strong grip to play also. What they do is light two candles and then place them on the table about a foot-and-a-half away from each other. Then two men sit down opposite one another, placing their right-hand elbows to the table and push against one another trying to force one another's arms down – so's the person who's losing gets burned by the candle. Well, anyway Núibín, I was a while watching them at this crack and especially one big bruiser of a fella who was getting the better of everyone that challenged him. Eventually, he challenged me with a smirk on his face – asking me whether there was much of a man in me. Well, I couldn't refuse his challenge Núibín as I knew that the pride of my country and my island depended on me. Deep down, however, I was worried whether I'd be able to beat this big bastard or not. I sat down opposite him anyway and we began arm wrestling. This fellow had the strongest grip that I've ever felt and he'd a rotten smell from his breath too because he'd been eating onions. Initially, I thought he was going to crush my hand, his grip was that strong, and I'd to grit my teeth to stop myself crying out with the pain. Your man was staring me in between the eyes, a big sneer on his face. 'My soul from the devil Bohunk,[65] but there's no way you're going to get the better of me,' I says to myself, and pushed back against him with all my strength. It was no good though Núibín. This man's grip was as rock-solid and immoveable as Carraig a' Bhalbháin[66] itself, Núibín. Slowly but surely, he forced my arm down and although I pushed back against him with all my strength, I felt the heat of the candle come closer. Your man's smirk grew wider and you could have heard a pin drop in that cabin, everyone was paying such close attention to the contest.

Then suddenly Núibín, an image of my father and my poor Grandfather – the old-King himself – came into my mind, and I knew that they were pleading with me not to let them down. I can't tell for the life of me where the strength came to me from but somehow, I began to force his arm back and straighten it. Next thing, I was forcing his arm downwards and knew that I had him. I had his arm pressed at an angle to the table and it was stalemate like this for a few minutes and I'd to dig deep to find one last bout of strength, but somehow I managed it. He was so close to the candle now that the hair on his right-arm was beginning to singe. The roar of pain that your man let out of him then was sweet music to my ears. I hate that bastard since and I've no time for him because three of those men aren't worth one man from Con![67]

I haven't met one proper Christian since I left Galway Núibín, and not an hour of the day goes by that I don't think of *An Chéad Chath* and the good times we all had there. I haven't been in Alfie's pub yet but with luck, we'll meet each other there before the end of the year, if you come over. Write soon and tell Lyons I was asking for him.

Your old-Patron,
Packie.

* * *

# A Visit to Dublin

Training with the Mortar today and Captain Breatnach instructing us. The Rajah nearly drove the Captain demented with all the ridiculous questions he kept asking him, every two minutes. At first, Breatnach thought that your man was asking him all this stuff because he genuinely wanted to learn, but after a while he realised that the Rajah was only doing it to make the time go by more quickly.

'By God, McMahon but I'll put the skids under you yet if you don't stop this stupidity and concentrate properly on the lesson in hand.'

'But a Dheadí,'[68] says the Maharajah, 'I'm dead serious.'

I presume that what the Rajah meant to say was 'But brother' like all the other lads say in Irish here, but that he got confused. Either way, the Captain went ballistic at this!

'What sort of bullshit is this now with your "O Daddy"? I'm not your father, thanks be to God! And anyway, that's no way to speak to an O.N.C. Address me as Captain from now on boy, or you'll be in big trouble for it. And if you can't say it in Irish, then say it in English so we can bloody well understand you.' The Rajah's brow furrowed as if deeply troubled and he says:

'But Captain, I like to talk Irish. I like to teach the Mortar through the Gaelic. We aren't allowed to speak English when we're on duty.'

'I like to teach the Mortar through the Gaelic,' says the Captain, imitating your man sarcastically. 'I'll tell you what you like really McMahon – you and your bloody sidekick there – except that he's too cute to get caught at it. You like lying back on your bed and snoring your arse off all day and then going back to Seapoint at night, to hop around the floor like an idiot, and tell all the women that you're an army officer. That's what you really like. The pair of you are interested in just one thing and that's causing trouble and acting the gobshite. More's the pity that I'm not the Commandant here and I'd sort the two of you out once and for all – by God, I sure would!'

He continued on with the lesson then and soon forgot the Maharajah's interruptions. He made him go out into the field instead to direct the lad learning to aim the Mortar correctly. In this case, you've to make hand-signals to direct whoever's shooting and make sure he hits the target.

Breatnach sat directly behind the Mortar and began to adjust the sights.

'How's that now?' he says to the Rajah.

'To the right a small bit?' says your man, his face scrunched up as if concentrating very intently.

The Captain re-adjusted his aim and asked the Rajah how it was now.

'To the left a little bit,' says the Rajah, dead serious.

'There isn't anything wrong with your eyes McMahon by any chance is there?' Breatnach says dubiously re-adjusting them.

'Is it alright now?'

'To the left another little bit.'

The Captain cursed and re-adjusted slightly again.

'It must be right now, is it?'

'To the right, a tiny bit.'

'For God's sake boy, you made a shit of it the first time, didn't you! Or d'you actually know the difference between your right and your left at all?'

'I do, Captain.'

'How's it now then?'

'To the left a little bit.'

'To the left bejaysus!' repeats the Captain, angrily jumping to his feet. 'Don't any of you move that Mortar until I've a look for myself now!'

He pushed the Rajah out of the way and went down on one knee to check the sights but was back on his feet a second later, his eyes blazing.

'Right, McMahon, this is all just a bit of fun to you, isn't it. I'll wipe the smile off your face now boy, double-quick. Attention!'

The Rajah did as he was told and Breatnach gave the order – 'forward march.' The minute Breatnach felt wet ground under his feet, he orders the Rajah into a 'forward jog'. Poor Rajah had to jog around the field as everyone looked on and took the mickey out of him.

'Two to wan (one) the field,'[69] says I (I can't deny it!) but Breatnach turns on me with a fierce look.

'That's enough from you McCauley – or, by God, but I'll give you "two to wan" the field. Jaysus. Out you go now there with your partner so and see how you like it. Attention. Forward jog!'

He kept the two of us at this until we were practically dropping with exhaustion, then called us back in. Boy, were we glad when he did. There was no more messing from us and we finished up with the Mortar lesson. Myself and the Rajah were too wrecked to annoy the Captain anymore that day.

There has been a course for the O.N.C.'s on here in Renmore for the last three months and the participants have all completed their qualifications now. They were all awarded their certs the other day and you'd swear that these certificates complete with red ribbons weighed a ton or something the way these men kept admiring them proudly every few minutes. Among the people upgraded were my old pal Maitias Ó Conghaile and '90 Murphy. Both of these men are married and settled down, so the pay increase will prove a big help to them. Although Maitias is in the same company as me, I don't have dealings with him very often and I can tell by him that he doesn't want to be giving me orders either.

Personally, I think it's nearly as easy to take orders from an old comrade like him as it is from a stranger. Many of the other lads here wouldn't see it this way though. They really hate having to take orders from someone who was once on the same grade as them. To be honest, I would have thought this way myself too just a while back, but I've matured a bit as I've got older, I suppose. Acting resentful like this is just a waste of time and energy. '90 Ó Murphy spends most of his time serving the Mess Sergeant these days and working in the Sergeant's Mess. Murphy's a man who'll go far in the army, I'd say, as he's very committed to it and he's well-educated as well. The only people left now from the old crowd who haven't been upgraded yet are me and Máirtín Cúc.

The last two-and-a-half years weren't long slipping by and when I think that I'll be finished with the army myself in seven months' time, I get very anxious about it and even a bit down in myself. I was sick of this place for a short while there just after Christmas, but now that I've got to know some of the new lads, I don't miss the old crowd half as much as before. Even Hud and Dud aren't the worst and they wouldn't leave you short if you needed the loan of a half-sovereign. And now that they've become more familiar with Irish, they don't make jokes about the language anymore. I notice that I've a lot more money in my pocket now too since my old loyal patron, Cuirín Mór left, although Lyons still borrows money off me from time to time. He says that the older soldiers need to stand together and support one another. Unfortunately, I'm the one who nearly always ends up 'standing for' the others.

The Western Command had a big inspection today. *Reveille* sounded at 6 a.m. and two minutes after the last note on the bugle sounded, Captain Breatnach was into us and berating everyone and getting everyone up. He went from bed to bed shaking everyone and pulling the blankets off them, but he still had a hell of a job getting the Rajah out of bed. My comrade was a bit late coming in last night – or early this morning depending on what way you look at it! We were all ordered up on parade then and I came very close to being marked 'absent' I spent so long trying to wake the Rajah. Breatnach didn't hang around. I'd say he was thinking it'd be easier to just charge the Rajah – and I'd to make a run for it myself in the end so's to be there on time. Then, just as we were about to begin marching, the Rajah came sprinting across the square, a big relaxed smile on his face, as to say – 'What's all the rushing and stress about anyway?' That was fine except that I fecked-up badly afterwards during the Main Parade as we passed the statue of Colonel Egan and all the 'top brass' looking on. We were right out in the centre of the Square at the time, all the Companies together, and ready for inspection when we were ordered to 'Affix Bayonets'. On hearing the word 'Affix' you've to remove the bayonet from its sheath and attach it to the top of your musket straight away. I couldn't attach the bayonet to the top of my musket correctly however, no matter how hard I tried. I knew straight away then that the bayonet I had wasn't mine, and didn't belong to my musket at all. I kept struggling with it and thought I'd affixed this bayonet reasonably securely to the top of the musket and that maybe I'd get away with it. Once the order came to 'Lower Arms', disaster struck though! My bayonet flew into the air and struck Joeen Beag's helmet before falling to the ground again! They say that Joeen didn't even blink, it happened so fast, but I wished that the ground had opened up and swallowed me – because that was the only thing that'd have saved me then. You'd have heard a pin drop, the place went so quiet for the next few seconds. A deathly silence enveloped the square and it was worse than any dressing-down you might get from someone. My old teacher Sergeant Red marched up behind me and jammed the bayonet back into its sheath, whispered poisonously into my ear as he did so. We went on with the drill then, every single man and his bayonet raised and in place, except yours truly here! I was sure that I'd get an awful bollocking once the parade was over but strangely, it never happened. I suppose that they were so disgusted by the mess I'd made of it that they decided it wasn't worth their while.

The rest of the inspection went by without further mishap, thank God. I brought a new shirt belonging to Hud down to the market this afternoon, but all I got for it was a half-a-note. The black market's really gone to the dogs these days – no doubt about it. It's these new recruits that are destroying it.

Myself and the Rajah have been anxious since this morning and this is the reason why. I've to go up to Dublin for an ordinance survey course, whether I like it or not, a course that I won't actually have completed until after my stint in the Army is over. What happened was that I applied for this course just after Christmas when I was feeling a bit unhappy about staying here any longer. I didn't hear anything about it afterwards – not until this morning when the Deputy Commander called me in and told me that my application had been successful and that I'd be leaving for Dublin within a few days.

'Well, Sir,' I said, 'I've a completely different outlook on things now and I'm not interested in going on this course now. Is there any chance that I wouldn't have to do it now at all?'

'No, I'm afraid not,' he replied, 'you applied for the course and you were accepted; you have to go on it now.' I got the feeling that he was delighted that I was leaving and I'd no choice other than to accept his decision. When I told the Rajah about this, he got really anxious, the poor man.

'But Núibín, you can't leave like this and abandon me with no comrades at all amongst these bucks here,' he said in a worried voice.

'It's not what I want to do either Rajah, but I've no say in this whatsoever,' then remembering that lovely verse:

*'Nach trua anois mé ag scarúint leat, ag teacht na huaire breá*
*Ó thosaigh an chuach ag goiriúint 'gus an duilliúir glas ag fás.'*
(What a pity that I've to say farewell to you, just now that the finest hour's arrived/Since the cuckoo began calling and the green leaves growing on the trees.)

It's not just the Rajah I was sad to be leaving but Galway too, especially because this city's a great place to be in the summer – travelling back to Connemara, going to all the dances and concerts, boating on the Corrib, and walking around among the tourists in Salthill. While Dublin has its own attractions, I don't have any particular interest in going there. And nor have I much interest in the boring stuff that this course will involve either. What a pity that I ever heard about this course in the first place.

The old barracks looked so fine today that I felt like never leaving. I want to return here again too if I can sometime. They say that once you've been accepted for this surveying course at all, it's very difficult to get out of it, but I'll try my damnedest to get off it anyway. If I managed to get out of that course early and get back, I might stay here for another term and not bother going out on my ticket at all. The faraway hills are green, they say, and when all's said and done, I've had a better life since I enlisted here than I had before that when I worked long hours for little pay. It's easy for Ward to be talking about that nice little pub next to Marble Arch (if such a pub exists at all), but for all I know we mightn't meet each other over there either. Packie is not a big man for letters and I mightn't hear from him at all. Overall, there's a lot to be said for *An Chéad Chath* and maybe I'd be stupid emigrating across the water to another country and to a job that I mightn't like one bit. Yes – I've made up my mind here and now – I'll do everything I can to get back here to Renmore. Maybe then I'll do another stint of army service. Lyons came around this morning asking me was it true that I was transferring to the Survey Corps.

'It is, I'm afraid,' I said and he gave me a curious look.

'Did you put in for a transfer?' he asked.

'Yes,' I replied, my head down. I could see that I'd gone down in his estimation for this. 'I knew well that you wouldn't make a soldier, Núibín,' he said to me by way of judgement. 'I mean you're damned lucky that you're in the best company in the Irish Army and yet nothing'd satisfy you except to apply for a course like that in a place where you'd only meet benders and oddballs. Your soul from the devil, but you're not a real man at all Núib, I swear.'

'Yeah, it's a bad enough show alright,' I said, worried. Most of the lads are gone out tonight, but the Rajah stayed in to keep me company and to cheer me up a bit. Tomorrow night it won't be in this bed or in this room even that I'll be sleeping but amongst strangers that I've nothing in common with, unfortunately.

## Survey Corps Headquarter, Phoenix Park, Dublin

I had one hell of a job today trying to find this place, inside in the middle of this huge park. I walked at least four miles before I found it, and I wouldn't mind but I'd to carry a full kitbag for the duration, never mind the big coat that I was wearing and the shoes, and all the rest of it. It was really warm today and the sweat was pouring off me. At one stage, I found myself a few yards inside the gates of Áras an Uachtaráin before I realised my mistake. I noticed the sign for the Áras on the way out alright, but I suppose I was concentrating so hard on going in the right way initially that I didn't notice it jammed into the grass and didn't realise that it's in there that *Seán T.* himself lives. I asked an old man when I came out onto the road again how far away I was and he gave me good directions. I had to pay a bit of a price for these directions though, because this old man decided to tell me his whole life story and the history of Dublin city at the same time too. The man had a strong Cork accent although he'd been living in Dublin since he was a young man. Like a lot of the older crowd today, he didn't think much of the younger generation. The way he sees it, the Irish race is declining by the day. I was too exhausted by then to disagree with him and patiently listened to his sermon until he let me go in the end. I reached this place then without much delay, and the Sergeant on duty took charge of me and any other 'refugee' who'd the misfortune to land up there too. He took me into a little café first where I got a small bit to eat and then brought me with him to my sleeping quarters upstairs in the same building. 'You can leave your kitbag and your gear there,' he says, 'and we'll go and find a clothes locker for you.' I followed him out across a fine green square that fronts the building and across to the store. The Sergeant opened a big, wide clothes cupboard and he lifted a big heavy locker onto my back and I had to carry it back to my room.

I couldn't understand for the life of me what I needed this item for, seeing as a small kit-box would have done the job just as well.

I didn't feel like talking to the Sergeant much either however, so I kept my mouth shut. Then once I'd moved the cupboard to the room, he said:

'You can put your civvies in that cupboard, son, of course, you've already been told that you wear your own shop clothes most of the time on this course, haven't you?' You wouldn't know here that you were in the army at all, to be honest! I stared a bit gobsmacked at the big heavy cupboard that I'd just lugged all the way upstairs. Shur, I didn't have any shop clothes, not even a tie, never mind all the clothes I'd need to fill a cupboard the likes of it. I was embarrassed to admit this to the Sergeant but then I thought I might as well tell him in case he expected to see me coming to the classes dressed neatly in the latest fashions from Burtons or Hipps.

'You've no civilian clothes, you say?' he said, surprised. 'No Sergeant,' I said. He became a bit distant with me after this but didn't say anything else about it. Since today is Saturday I've the rest of the weekend to myself and on Monday morning I've an interview with the senior officer here after which I'll be put to work. I think I'll head into the city now to taste some of the 'black stuff' in its home-town.

* * *

I'd a good night last night, that's for sure. I spent an hour hanging around the main street looking at Nelson's Pillar and the posters outside all the cinemas. I stood next to the GPO then and listened in on a group of girls from Connemara working as domestics here gossiping with each other. They were only a few feet away from me, but I didn't have the courage to talk to them for some reason. You'd see the same type of girls any night on the halfpenny side of the street in Galway. The only difference was that these girls were dressed more fashionably. It was 8 o'clock in the evening by then and the thirst was getting to me so I walked into a small pub within fifty yards of the GPO and called for a pint. It was only eight pence and, here in Dublin, they give you what they call an 'ex-single' if you don't specify the opposite. And, by God, but this was twice as good as anything that I've ever had in Galway at 10 pence a pint. I'd only just taken my first sip from my pint when I noticed a group of men next to me who were speaking Irish. Needless to say, it wasn't long before I stuck my oar into the conversation. I was nearly broke by then as well, to be honest, and I thought I might as well use my Irish to best advantage if I could. Usually the Gaels are generous, whatever other faults they may have and this was how it proved with these lads too. They bought me so much porter you'd swear I'd just arrived down from heaven to them and they didn't even give me a chance to excuse myself for the poor state of my pocket. They weren't speaking 'book-Irish' either but the finest and most fluent native Irish you'd hear anywhere. They'd a richer vocabulary than me even if I've been listening to people speaking Irish half of my life. We were the last crowd to leave the pub and even then, we spent a good while outside on the street chatting. I was fairly tipsy by then and after I'd said goodbye to these new pals of mine, I managed to get lost again while cutting across the fields after getting off the bus! I was out quite late, but I was still the first man home because the other three beds in the room were empty on my return.

Well – I mightn't have got to know my room-mates last night, but I got to hear plenty of them as they arrived down to breakfast today, one after another, one of them better dressed than the next. They were so well turned-out that they might as well have been going to a wedding. Every man of them had the hair-oil glistening and a shiny wristwatch prominent on their wrists. That was nothing to what they came out with when they started talking though. In fact, I nearly lost my appetite for breakfast when I heard some of the womany shite they were coming out with. If I hadn't heard it with my own two ears, I wouldn't have believed that any Irishmen, never mind soldiers could talk in such a 'law-dee-daw' way. 'What do you think of the dance last night Mick?' says one of them.

'Smashing!'

'How d'you get on with Joan?'

'Tip-top! I think she's a smashing kid.'

'Oh, deffo!'

You'd be waiting a long time before you'd hear the likes of Cuirín Mór or Colm a' tSeaimpín spouting this kind of bollox! Even the Maharajah himself – despite his great interest in new styles of dancing and the sexy women who go to these new-fangled dances – even he wouldn't come out with the likes of that shite!

The food here is very good – not that it's much consolation, given the long, lonely stint I managed to assign myself to here. A hundred thousand goodbyes to the Irish speakers of *An Chéad Chath*. I'm going to die here slowly surrounded by all these smoothies and slick-talkers here.

I was sent back to Renmore Barracks on the midday train today and was back just in time for tea. This is what happened. I'd an interview with the commanding officer this morning, Lieutenant Crowe (the brother of our Commander here, as it happens); it was just after I'd received my papers – *Health Certificate*, *Transportation Certificate* and the like through the post and he wasn't happy with them at all. In fact, he was studying them when I arrived into the room and stared at me coolly for a while.

'I'm afraid that there must've been some kind of a mistake made that you were sent here, Private McCauley,' he said. 'When we accepted you here, we'd no idea what you were like. It's an awful pity that we didn't receive these documents earlier and you wouldn't have had a wasted journey up here. God knows; according to my papers here, you're in trouble most of the time! *Untidy on Parade –Kit Missing – Absent from Duty – Sick* (or at least pretending to be sick!) It's not much of a reflection on you, all of this, is it? Let's not waste our time on this any further. If you hurry, you'll still be able to catch the midday train back to Galway. Good day to you.'

I gave him a bow and walked out of there absolutely delighted with myself. I got my clothes together quickly and headed downstairs, travel pass in hand. On the way out, I met the Sergeant who'd assigned the clothes cupboard to me just the day before yesterday. Needless to say, he was surprised to see me again like this, kit-bag thrown over my shoulder.

'You're off again?' he says.

'Deffo!' I says.

'What about the clothes cupboard?' he said.

'Let Joan have it,' I says as if I was talking about a woman and he gave me a bemused stare, as if I'd lost it altogether! You should have seen the look of joy on the poor Rajah's face when I walked into the canteen here again today! He was delighted to see me and gave me a great welcome. The Horse was very happy to see me back too and same goes for Slám Féir. The pair of them presented me with a big slice of bread as a welcome home present! I got some bedding out of the store then straight away and set up my old bed as it was before. One of the new recruits was sleeping in it when I came in first but myself and the Rajah rooted him out of it fairly lively. I'm lying back here on the bed right now, nice and relaxed, the window next to me wide open and the sweet smell of the sea drifting in on the breeze. My love forever to you Galway! There's no place else like you when all's said and done.

I spent the day over in Knocknacarra and after tea I headed back Spiddal way. I spent a while in Tom Cadhain's house in Cnocán Glas[70] (Tom's wife is an aunt of that girl Margaret whom I was going out with a while back), and then went to down to the pier to have a look at the sea. There were a good few local lads hanging around and we spent a while chatting. Spiddal people are more used to strangers than people in Carna or places back farther west in Connemara. It's more usual for them to have people dropping in for a visit to see them and they aren't a bit shy or aloof. You'd nearly be one of them after a short while in their company. It's a really nice tradition, I think, the way that the men and the young lads all congregate together in the afternoons in Gaeltacht areas. You'd hear some very witty banter and conversation among them too. I get the feeling that the tradition of people visiting one another's houses at night has waned quite a bit in this part of the Gaeltacht and you'd never hear mention of the storytelling that went on in years gone by anymore. I know that some people really bemoan the loss of the older storytelling traditions and folklore but, as long as people are still speaking Irish, they aren't that important, it seems to me. Many of the houses around Cois Fharraige now have a parlour or sitting room, a 'good' room that has nice furniture in it and the like. These new rooms have a cold and uninviting air about them though, and people don't spend much time in them either. Mostly, they use them for when strangers or officials – 'insurance people' and the like – call in.

I called up to the village when it got dark and had a few drinks in *Tadhg Ó Cualáin's* bar before going on to the céilí. In a way, the Spiddal Céilí is now the most Gaelic of all the social events in the Gaeltacht because not only do they not even dance old-style waltzes here, but they also have a notice up on the wall requesting that visitors speak Irish. You'd hear very little English spoken at this dance anyway. The only people using English would be the summer visitors who're actually out here to learn Irish. There's not many Sundays when I'm in Galway that

I'd miss this céilí to be honest, and it's always well worth the journey out from Galway. I usually come out to the dance with Seosamh Bairéad from Baile an tSagairt,[71] who's one of the new recruits here. I usually have a few cups of tea in Seosamh's house before we head to the dance. Seosamh has three really beautiful-looking sisters; Máire, Bríd and Peige are their names. Bríd is teaching school up in Dublin and Máire is due to emigrate to America fairly soon. Indeed, it's an awful loss to this country that so many pretty-looking and fine women have to leave Ireland and go abroad.

We'd a really great night at the céilí, but I was 'deemed absent since morning', on returning to the barracks. I was told that Captain Murphy (or '90 Ó Murchú as he was once known) – is to charge me with being absent from the Officer's Mess.

* * *

*Confined to barracks for the past week*

We were woken at 03.00 hours this morning to go up to Achill Island where a Royal Air Force aeroplane had crashed on a mountain-top there. The Sergeant-Major himself woke us from our slumbers and he had a list of men he wanted for the journey. My name wasn't actually on the list but seeing as it proved very difficult to wake the Rajah from sleep, I asked the Sergeant-Major could I go instead of him. He said that this was fine and I got dressed quickly. I actually felt sorry for the Maharajah, the poor devil, as he wasn't long in from the dance in Seapoint last night and it would've been a crime to have forced him out of his cosy slumber.

Captain Ó Ceallacháin[72] and Sergeant Red were in charge of our work-gang and there were about sixteen of us in the group altogether, I think. It was very cold on the back of the lorry and there wasn't much to see on our way through the surrounding countryside until we reached Ballinrobe anyway. We stopped there and bought a few bottles of whiskey in case we might need them in an emergency for any of the crew of this aeroplane that crash-landed last night and may have survived. Then we drove on again. A short while later and we'd a good view of the Partry Mountains in the far distance and the wild countryside around about. It was seven o'clock by the time we were passing through Westport and I feasted my eyes on the amazing scenery all around that area. It was when we passed over by Achill Sound that the scenery became really spectacular, however, and I was really glad then that I had taken the Rajah's place for this trip – just to see such a beautiful area of Ireland in the early-morning sun. Our destination was the mountain known as Croaghaun,[73] the peak of which is over 2,000 feet. We reached Corrymore House at the foot of the mountain in the lorry. I looked down a few times as we drove through the mountains there, and I felt dizzy at the steepness of the climb and the narrowness of the roads that we were navigating. The mountain was so enormous that you felt the slightest mistake and we'd plunge over the edge of that tiny narrow road and smash onto the rocks below. We reached our destination and were each given a nice sip of whiskey and began the climb at the foot of Croaghaun. They didn't know for sure where exactly the aeroplane had crashed. Local people had heard the crash and the giant ball of fire when it hit the ground the night before but that was all. We knew that if we scoured the mountain-top we'd eventually come upon the wreckage. Our search was a lot more difficult than we'd originally envisaged however, as the mountain-top was shrouded in a heavy mist, a mist so thick that there were times when you couldn't even see the man standing next to you. Every now and then, this mist parted for a second and you saw the mountain peak reveal itself and the ocean like a silver mirror far away. The fog reappeared again just as quickly though, and everything shrouded over again in a thick white blanket. It was a strange feeling walking through the mist; it was as if you were walking into nothingness, the world around about obscured, except for the disconnected voices of the other men.

I was the first to find any of the wreckage. We were fairly high-up on the shoulder of the mountain when I saw what I thought was an old piece of tin or a pot in the ferns. Sadly, of course, it wasn't a pot at all but a piece of the crashed aeroplane's engine. The next time the fog momentarily lifted, the true horror of what'd happened was revealed. There were pieces of that big aeroplane scattered everywhere across the mountain! It was as if a malevolent giant had grabbed hold of that plane and smashed it into a thousand pieces! Far worse than any of the twisted metal was the sight of death itself – the bodies of those poor soldiers that'd been killed when the plane crashed. These poor creatures had been killed instantly on impact, their corpses scattered here and there on the mountain. There was one man whose insides were hanging out, another who'd lost a hand and some of the corpses were torn or burnt in the crash. We found six of the bodies immediately, but it took us a while to find the other two. A few of the lads were so affected by the sight of the corpses that they nearly got sick. Sergeant Red was affected badly by the carnage also. I felt terrible for the poor men who'd died, but strangely I felt no fear whatsoever going near their corpses. Hopes that any of the men might still be alive proved groundless, however, given the force with which the aeroplane crashed to the ground. One man had managed to open his parachute, but they were probably too close to the ground when the crash happened. One thing I found strange was that the men's boots had come off their feet on impact even if their laces were still tied. The sight of their broken and unopened parachutes and the lonely wind billowing through them on that desolate mountainside was very sad. Three of the men had been Irish and the other five were English. One poor man still had an invitation to a party in honour of his own daughter in his pocket, a party that – sadly – would now never take place.

The Captain gave us our instructions. We were to wrap each of the bodies in its own parachute and place them on the stretchers that we'd brought with us. We got to work straight away even if some of the lads found it really difficult.

None of the lads wanted to go near the man whose insides were hanging out, but I stepped forward and did what had to be done very quickly. Captain O'Callaghan must have noticed me because a moment later, he says:

'You're a right "hard-nut" McCauley.' He grabbed the other end of this man's parachute and helped me wrap his body carefully. We all worked quickly and before long we'd all the casualties covered and secured. We'd four stretchers and just enough men to carry them, and so we'd to bring four corpses down first and then return for the other four men. The journey down was a lot trickier than the climb up had been, given the roughness of the ground and the weight of the bodies on the stretchers. At times, during the descent, the feet of one of us would nearly be level with the head of the other stretcher-bearer and we slipped on the rocky shale and moss and had to correct our footing regularly. The bodies were very heavy; they'd been powerfully built men and I was surprised at this as for some reason, I'd always had it in my head that the English were smaller people. Our arms were nearly torn off us with the weight. We reached Corrymore House eventually though, where we found a group of newspaper reporters waiting. There was an officer there whom we didn't recognise and he prevented the reporters from taking any photographs. One reporter verbally abused him for not letting them take photos and this officer went quiet. Although he was absolutely right to stop this man from taking photos we were secretly kind of happy at the way this reporter challenged him – because this particular officer annoyed everyone – whoever he was.

He was very full of himself and secretly, we regular foot soldiers would've loved to have got our own photos in the newspaper. We placed the corpses in the back of the lorry and transported them into Dooagh where they were laid out in a small dance hall. They were left there for identification by their relatives, I think.

Afterwards, our task completed, we were brought to the Clew Bay Hotel where we were allowed into the kitchen to prepare whatever food we liked for ourselves. We had bread, butter, and slices of bacon and eggs to eat, and Pendy Beag from Roundstone did the cooking. We went into the bar afterwards and Captain O'Callaghan bought us each a pint of beer – there were about thirteen of us having a pint there altogether, I think. We were just halfway through our first drink when a Yank who was originally from Achill praised us all to high heaven and stood us all a second pint.

'We'd no army of our own here in Ireland when I left Achill, twenty-five years ago,' he said.

Inspector O'Brien from Westport came in the next minute – he'd been over in Mulraney investigating a case where a man had allegedly killed a donkey with a crow-bar – God between us and all harm – and he called for a pint for each of us also. We also spent whatever few shillings we had ourselves on pints which meant that we were in much better form by the time the meal was ready. Pendy himself appeared out of the kitchen then, and he was gasping with the thirst. People started buying pints for him too and he soon had more porter lined up in front of him than a man could drink in a month. We gulped down the food and were ready for the road again. We heard that another work-group was on its way up from Renmore, but there was still no sign of them when we reached Corrymore House. It was getting late in the evening now and some newspaper-men and a few other curious onlookers had gone up the mountain – whatever good they would do there! In the end, the Captain said to us:

'Well boys, you had a tough job there today and there's no way I'd force any of you to go back up the mountain again to collect the remains that are left if you don't want to. The remaining four bodies have to be brought down before nightfall though, and all I ask is that you volunteer to go back up, only if you wish to do so. Any man who's willing to go back up the mountain again, let him step forward now!' No one moved for a minute and you couldn't blame them either as we were all exhausted after the effort of carrying the first corpses down the mountain; additionally, most of us had only had a couple of hours' sleep the previous night. Then, whatever got into me, I stepped forward. The others followed me in twos and threes then. The Captain was delighted and thanked us for our commitment. 'I knew you wouldn't let me down lads,' he said. We went outside and began back up the mountain again. The climb seemed ten times longer and more difficult than it was the first time. There was a really heavy fog on the hills by now, but we tried to go as quickly as we could since we knew the return journey would be particularly difficult and treacherous. A few of the locals came with us to help including a big fair-haired Englishman who was visiting the islands off the Mayo coast fishing for basking sharks.

Sergeant Red was waiting when we reached the place where we'd left the first bodies shrouded in their parachutes earlier in the day and he was delighted to see us again. He'd had a long and lonely wait since we'd last seen him, watching over the remaining bodies and answering a stream of questions from newspaper reporters and tourists who'd wandered up there to see the crash-site. As soon as we arrived, the onlookers stopped poking around in the wreckage and gathered around us. Do you think any of this crowd helped us carry the remaining bodies downhill though! Not a chance! It was 'Good-morra, Jack!' as Slam Féir would say. Unfortunately, I hurt myself at one stage when John Delia and I were lifting one of the bodies from the ground and placing it on the stretcher. My left foot went from under me and I injured my ankle.

Before I realised it, I cursed out loud with the pain of it. What would you know but didn't one of the local civilians admonish me on this. 'Do you not realise that you're in a graveyard now?' he says angrily. I looked him between the eyes and says, 'I've no reason to know that I am,' I said, 'and I'm not an idle spectator like you either.' I was tempted to add the words 'idle and morbid' to my response but let it go instead. It wasn't what he'd said to me that annoyed me so much as the way he'd said it – as if he was a member of the gentry talking down to one of his servants long ago. We didn't delay and began our descent downhill straight away. There weren't as many of us this time to help carry the stretchers and we'd only gone a short way when our arms felt like they were about to fall off. It was all-hands-on-deck now, and the Captain and the powerfully built Englishman helped us carry the stretchers, fair play to them! We were nearly at the bottom of the mountain again when the other work-gang[74] appeared and we handed the stretchers over to them. They were so late arriving that they might as well have not bothered coming at all – or so it seemed to us at the time anyway. There was a fine meal waiting for us when we reached Corrymore House though and we felt much better once we had some food in our stomachs.

We left the remainder of the operation to the other lads and began the long drive back to Renmore then. It was well past midnight by the time we passed through Mulraney and the local Garda Sergeant invited us into his house where his wife and daughter prepared a cup of tea for us. The Sergeant went out and roused the local publican out of bed and he served us all a few drinks before we resumed our journey home. The people of Mayo are very generous and welcoming, there's no doubt about it. The awful tragedy aside, the one thing I found strange about the area was that I heard no one speaking Irish in Achill at all.

We had a day off from duty today because we were up in Achill yesterday. I spent most of the day in bed and the Rajah brought me my meals back from the canteen. Doheny from Ballingarry (Michael Jim) returned to the Battalion today from the Curragh. Like most of the group who enlisted in 1946, he went out on his ticket last year but re-enlisted again just a few months later.

'Aha, Michael, you came back here again!' says the Rajah, propping his sweeping brush against the wall. 'The shovel was too heavy for you and you had a pain in your back. The pay was good but you were too lazy for it. Then one day, you thought of Renmore again and remembered how soft we had it here and you were filled with regret. And so you wrote to the Minister for Defence and said – "Take me back again in the name of God." The Minister had a soft heart and felt sorry for you. He decided to take you back and you were very happy. The sergeants in the Curragh were delighted to see you return too and so they grabbed you by the head and shaved off all your hair, then assigned you a new number – a number on which the ink isn't dry yet! Now you are the oldest recruit in Renmore!'

'Be gor, McCauley boy, I see you've been indoctrinatin' the Rajah,' says Michael Jim, throwing down his kit-bag and removing his great-coat. 'He couldn't say "Lá breá" (Fine day) when he came here first and now he's like an Election Candidate beggin' votes in Rosmuc.'

Myself and the Maharajah were delighted to see Doheny back again as he's very funny in his own dry way and definitely one of the wittiest lads who's ever been in the Battalion. Michael Jim is a very educated lad and he has really rich Irish also – when he's not too lazy to speak it, that is. The first thing he noticed when he came into the barracks again was how small the new recruits were compared to the lads who were here last year. He was really happy to be back in Galway and amongst his old friends again though, and we've arranged to go out on the town tonight. Myself and Michael Jim wanted to go out for a few quiet pints somewhere, but the Rajah was mad keen to go out 'on the tear' and go dancing in Salthill. 'Stay away from the black stuff tomorrow night,' he counselled us, 'and come out with me to Salthill, to the dance in Seapoint. That's where you'll see some of the finest-looking women around and that's better than swiggin' porter like "sharks".'

The Rajah gets such a kick out of trying to speak the language now that he speaks Irish most of the time. When he's trying to make himself understood in Irish, he's always working his hands and making gestures like a Frenchman, and the pained look on his face as he tries to make himself understood would make a cat laugh, it's so funny! We gave into him in the end though as we were too lazy to continue arguing against his Seapoint 'plan' and the three of us headed out around seven o'clock this evening. Doheny and I were dressed in our army uniforms since these are the only suits we have, but the Rajah was wearing a brand-new suit that he bought recently. It was still early in the afternoon when we reached Salthill and Michael Jim and I were gasping for a pint as we walked past Salmon's pub.

'Why don't we go for just the one here?' says Doheny.

'Yeah, just the one pint each, why not?' I says, but the Rajah put his foot down.

'If you stop for one pint now, you'll stop for plenty more. And the pair of you will be talking a load of bull by the time we get out and you'll both have sore heads tomorrow as well. Be strong and fight off the temptation to go drinking now. C'mon over here with me to Finan's Ice Cream Parlour. We'll have a few fruit ices and that'll kill the thirst. Then we'll head over to chat up some girls.'

'God Almighty tonight! – but if Cuirín Mór or Colm a' tSeaimpín were to see us here eating fruit ices, we'd be shamed for life,' says Michael Jim as we plonked ourselves down on high stools in the Ice Cream Parlour. Anytime I caught a glance of myself and the other two lads in the mirrors of the Ice Cream Parlour, I felt like a right idiot, I can tell you. We looked like a right bunch of gobshites! I was mortified!

The Rajah was very happy and relaxed in himself though and didn't give a damn.

We headed out to the big hall in Seapoint then, even if neither myself and Michael Jim weren't that pushed about it. The entry fee was four shillings each and we soon regretted that we hadn't let the Rajah off on his own and gone to Salmon's instead. But we went in anyway and got some seats in the hall. This Seapoint is a very posh joint and I felt totally out of place there. The band were playing at a nice, relaxed pace when we arrived and a handful of couples were circling the big shiny, slippy-looking dancefloor, nice and easy. The Maharajah came to life the minute he stood inside the hall and why wouldn't he? All the women looked over in his direction and said 'hello' and began flirting with him. He chatted with us for a few minutes and then headed out on the dance floor with one of the most beautiful-looking women in the place. They made a fine sight, no doubt about it, the pair of them waltzing around the floor like two professionals. Not that Michael Jim or myself have much interest in this type of dancing. We'd have slipped out the door again as quick as a flash only that the dance suddenly came to an end and the Rajah brought the girl over to where we were sitting and introduced her. She was a very pretty-looking girl, with lovely blonde hair and a Rita Hayworth[75] look about her. She was nice and friendly to us, but it was obvious that she has eyes only for the Rajah. No sooner did the musicians strike up again but both of them were out dancing again, gliding easily around the floor and doing the Quick-step.

'You should ask one of the women here out for a dance Michael,' I says to my pal, but a frightened look came over him and he looked as if he might make a run for the door. Doheny is a fine-looking man, but he's extremely shy and a bit awkward in company. He's the type of fellow who wouldn't be able to approach a girl at all unless he'd a drink or two in him and even then, he'd find it nearly easier not to meet them at all.

'I wouldn't mind asking one of them out,' I says. 'It's just that I know that I'll be turned down straight away.'

'Of course you'll be turned down, when they see you wearing that army uniform of yours,' Michael Jim says.

'Ah come on. Let's see how I get on so,' I says, with a laugh, getting to my feet and making for the nearest group of women. I was taking a chance really because even if one of them did take me up on it, I can't do the steps of these modern dances, and I'd look a right idiot! I'd a hunch that I'd get nowhere with the women anyway – so I felt safe enough though! The first girl just looked at me and silently shook her head, the second girl said she was tired. 'Get lost' is what the third one said, I think! I glanced over in Michael Jim's direction and he'd a grin on him that went from ear to ear. He nodded his head in the direction of the door, signalling that we should head away and go for a drink somewhere for ourselves. We left the hall straight away before the Rajah had a chance to stop us and headed over to Salmon's and ordered two big frothy pints for ourselves. The warmth and friendliness of the pub was like heaven compared to the dull atmosphere of the ballroom. We were just started on our third pint when in walks the Rajah.

'Aha, the drink was too strong for you in there, was it. You'd the shakes, the pair of you, until you got your hands on two pints of the black stuff! That drink won't do much for you though. You'll keep drinking and drinking and then you'll wake up some day in years to come and you'll both be old lads begging pennies on the street corner to get the price of a pint. Shame on you, old soldier McCauley and recruit Doheny!'

He drank a bottle of lemonade and stayed with us until the sound of the band-music came over loud on the breeze from Seapoint and he was tempted to go back. He became fidgety then and eventually, Michael Jim told him to go back to the Ballroom again for the love of God.

'You remind me of one of Professor Pavlov's dogs, Rajah,' says your man, 'the way you start watering when that ol' music starts up.'

'Aha Micheal, but why don't you speak to me in Irish,' says the Rajah. 'You came back into *An Chéad Chath* to speak Irish but you came back under false pretences, didn't you! You messed up the Battalion with all that English of yours – shame on you!'

'Arah, go to Hell,' says Michael Jim, and he storms off and leaves the Rajah and me without so much as a by-your-leave.

\* \* \*

# Farewell to the Army

My term of service in the army is fast coming to an end. The closer the day comes, the more I keep thinking what I should do after this? I've no problem if they ask me to stay on for another three years, I think – even if I'm not the best soldier in the world. Captain O'Callaghan has a lot of time for me ever since the crash in Achill and not so long ago, he 'rubbed out' some charge or other that I was up on. 'I have to admit that I don't understand you at all McCauley,' he says, 'you did great work up in Achill when you had to, but you're not happy to make any effort whatsoever now that you're back in barracks again.' He let me off this time but warned me not to appear in front of him again soon or there'll be trouble. In a way, I wouldn't mind doing another term of duty here, but then when I think of it rightly, I'd just be wasting time really when I can't honestly see myself having much of a future in the army. The Rajah himself will be leaving here next year and it won't be much fun to be left here on my own with all my friends gone … Maybe I could get some kind of a job around Galway so that I wouldn't have to move back down to Kilkenny at all. If I don't manage to get a job anywhere, I suppose I'll have no choice but to head over to England. If I was sure that Ward would meet me over there then, I wouldn't hesitate for a minute about leaving here, but then I don't know whether I'll actually meet him again either. The last letter I sent to him was returned to me with 'addressee unknown' marked on the envelope. It might be a long time before I hear from him again.

I'm not the only man here who's worrying about what to do next either. Máirtín (Teacher) Cúc is unsure as to whether to accept a second term here or not. We were just discussing this a few minutes ago actually. 'Hey there, Professor,' says Máirtín to me, 'what are you considering doing after this – are you thinking of committing yourself to another term here or will you "go out on your ticket", to use the barbarian slang that's common to this place?'

'That's exactly what I'm mulling over now, Teacher,' says I, 'and to tell you the truth, I'm still in two minds about what to do.'

'My own opinion is that it's better to leave here. I got your letter a little while ago from one of our 'students' over in Birmingham – at the "University of BSA"[76] and, according to him, you can earn up to seventeen pounds a week in that place. They're arriving there in their thousands, he says!'

'Yes, I suppose it's difficult to turn down that kind of salary, Teacher.'


I'm employed as waiter in the canteen these days along with the Horse and the chances are that this is where I'll stay until my term comes to an end in another six weeks or so. God knows, we're given more than enough work to do scouring the floor and washing the dishes and keeping an eye on the F.C.A. lads in case they swipe any knives or anything when they're finished their dinner. The Horse is a mighty worker and he has very little time for people who are lazy. He gives me little enough peace and he's constantly on my case and giving me more work – with every 'Dónall the Lazy Louse' and 'Dónall of the Fleas' anytime I escape from his sight and go on the doss. The Horse remains 'at his post' – as he says himself – most of the day and only joins the recruits whenever he gets paid and wants to play cards with them. 'The Shearing of the Lambs' is how the Horse refers to these games and sure enough, he usually 'cleans out' the recruits and leaves with his own pockets full of money! He returns to where I'm still working in the canteen then and hands me a portion of the winnings – to reimburse me for staying at my post while he was gone!

'Here you go Dónall, oh loyal servant, here's your small fee. The lambs have all been sheared by the old-crook,' he says, handing me a half-crown or a crown maybe. The most recent batch of recruits really love gambling, whatever it is about them, and the Horse never lets any opportunity slip. I suppose he probably picked up a good number of tricks when he was over there in Brooklyn, in the States, because he never seems to lose.

Once we'd all the knives and plates washed, after dinner today, I escaped back to the room here hoping that I could get a little snooze in – unknown to anyone. I'd only just wrapped my coat around me though, when I heard the Horse coming downstairs into the room.

'Dónall the Louse! Dónall of the Fleas! Oh Servant of Laziness, where're you hiding anyway!' he sang as he arrived into the room, but when he saw me stretched out on the bed, he wasn't long changing his tune – 'Oh noble Dónall of the Clean Plates! I bow before you oh Soldier of two Stars! I'd no idea that I'd find you down here now.'

'And there was me thinking that you'd come down here because you needed me for something, Mart,' says I.

'Not at all Dónall. Shur, why would I do that? Now that I have you here however, you wouldn't mind standing in for me over in the canteen as this old-operator here has to go and shear the lambs! You'll be well-rewarded for your work Dónall – don't you worry about that at all!' I had to go with him needless to say, although I would have preferred a few hours' kip more than anything. Máirtín's a funny one alright no doubt about it, especially when he's a few drinks in. You could be inside in a pub with him having a great time and his mood might suddenly change in the space of a matter of minutes. You always know when his mood's about to change however, as he'll go up to the bar all of a sudden and buy a half-cigar. He'll light up and next minute he's talking with this Brooklyn accent and he won't speak another word of Irish to you for the rest of the evening. As soon he starts on this crack, you're better off leaving because you don't know when he might break out and start arguing with anyone near you in the pub. He's a bit of a Dr Jekyll and Mr Hyde that way, God bless him, but I've usually disappeared by then anyway. That said, you won't get a better turned-out soldier in *An Chéad Chath* than him when he's on parade. His buttons will be shining and his shoes would blind you with the polished sheen of them, and he'll have a pleat in his uniform as sharp as a razor blade. One group of the F.C.A.[77] went home last Saturday, but a new group arrived again this morning. Each group does a fortnight's course here. In reality, it's more of holiday by the sea for many of the lads. They spend the day training and learning about different types of weapons but once the training's over for the day, they're 'free agents' and can head off to Salthill or up along the Corrib or wherever. They're well-paid too and it's a 'handy number' for them, that's for sure.

The Tuam Battalion came in here yesterday and amazingly, one of the lads in their group was English! He suffers from poor health apparently because he was sent in to help myself and the Horse in the canteen rather than go out training with the other lads. Sidney's his Christian name. What his surname is I'm not sure, although the Horse has already christened him 'Kynel' because he's always telling us about a Colonel he knew once, some fellow who was in the British Army during the war. The 'Kynel' is a small, weather-beaten fellow who is always incredibly neat. We knew he was English the minute he opened his mouth and we were amazed that he'd be in the F.C.A. The man wasn't long explaining his story to us, however. What happened was that he met a girl from Tuam over in England and they married and moved over here after a while because his wife wanted to be closer to her family. Sidney got a job first in the *beet factory* in Tuam and shortly afterwards, he enlisted in the F.C.A.

I find Sidney a pleasant old devil but the Horse is already sick of him, even if he's only been working with us a short while. Sidney never stops talking, that's the problem. And he's driving the Horse mad with all his blather about the British army, the Colonels, the Tuam beet factory, and all the rest of it. The Kynel is a great worker it has to be said. But God help us – he's the most talkative individual I've ever met and it doesn't bother him in the slightest that the Horse and I always speak Irish to one another. He waits for his chance and then just blathers on like a gramophone, where the needle's got stuck. He's as proud as punch that he's in the F.C.A., the poor devil; you'd swear he was a member of the Military Police back home in England, the way he goes on. Today, he'd a half-day's pass and before he went into Galway city, he called in to us so's we could see him all kitted out and spruced up in his uniform. And to give him his due, he was really well turned-out. You could tell that he'd been in the army before.

There's a civilian in painting the windows and the doors of the barracks' canteen at the moment. He's tall and thin and he'd remind you of a large bird somehow. He's from An Cloch Bhreac[78] originally and he has excellent Irish despite the fact that he's a Protestant. I thought that there weren't any Protestants who were native Irish speakers left in Ireland, but this isn't the case at all. He's not long working as a painter, he says. He worked as a sales rep. before this, hawking bottles of medicine around the country. He manufactured these medical products himself from herbs and his herbal solutions cured many ailments, both human and animal – according to himself anyway.

'My loyal little brothers,' he says, 'there's nothing that grows on this earth that doesn't have a cure in it for some ailment or other. Take some garlic roots for example – they can cure asthma and shortness of breath. Boiled nettle juice cures rheumatism. For every sickness and disease known to man, there's a cure to be found out in the fields or the woods. The Lord has provided all of this for us, eternal praise to Him, and as ordained by His everlasting generosity.' (He removed his cap and looked up at the rafters of the canteen when saying this.)

He gave us a short sermon then on the importance of vegetables as food and claimed that a person could live quite well without ever eating meat at all, provided that they ate enough 'greens'. But then – in the next breath – he enquired whether there was 'any small drop of beef soup left in the kitchen, by any chance!' This 'about-turn' flummoxed the Horse and he told your man to shag off. 'Get out of here quick, you dirty old witch-doctor you, get the hell out of here now,' he says, bundling his dish-cloth in his hands and flinging it at the fleeing painter. 'Bad luck to you, you old-quack! I thought you said someone doesn't need meat to feel full – as long as they ate grass or a bit of sedge, or whatever. Get the hell out of here now before I throw you out through the window.' The poor quack was frightened and he stayed outside after this, supposedly dabbing paint on the window timber-frame but inhaling the lovely aroma of soup all the while. The Horse was 'wound-up' after this brief interlude and it took a long time for him to calm down again. 'God knows this place has been upside-down for the past while – as if we didn't have enough to put up with that gobshite, the Kynel – and now we've this idiot coming around annoying us as well.' Slam Féir arrived in the next minute with an anxious look and wanting to know why the painter had been sent outside.

'Listen here, Mart,' he says, 'what did he do to you anyway?'

'Arah, he was looking for a mug of beef soup, the thief.'

A thoughtful look came over the old cook in that moment and he suddenly disappeared back into the kitchen for himself. A few minutes later and we spotted him quietly dipping a mug into the simmering pot of beef soup when he thought no one was looking. Out the back-door he went then and called the painter over quietly. He probably hoped that the painter'd give him the price of a pint in return for the mug of soup, but no chance! Instead, he graciously accepted the mug of soup from him – not that he ever put his hand in his pocket at any stage.

'Good enough for you,' says Slam Féir, slagging him off. 'You sly fecker you; you thought you'd wangle a few pence out of that fellow by bribing him with a cup of soup, but look what you got for your troubles? Jack-shit, that's what!'

'What harm Mart! Shur, wouldn't I give a small drop of soup to the tinker himself, never mind your man there,' says the cook, letting on that it didn't bother him when secretly, it did. You could tell by him. Mind you, that painter looks like a hardy buck – I'd say he's the type that could survive on nothing. I've never seen him eat anything at all since he began work here and it doesn't seem to have knocked a stir out of him either. He's smart too because he's pacing himself well with the work and making sure to apply the paint as slowly as possible. He should be able to drag the job here out till Christmas, I'd say.

I'm slowly getting my stuff together and packing for when I'm no longer an army-man. I'm leaving here soon. I bought the materials for a suit down in the Woollen Mills the other day and left them into the tailor. If I'd enough to buy a pair of trousers and low-heeled shoes by the time I'm leaving, I'll be fairly well-sorted. Bad as I am, I wouldn't like to be as stuck as poor Ciarraí was when he went out on his ticket last year. He hadn't a stitch except for the clothes that the army had given him. I mightn't be gone yet, but I'm already feeling very lonely at the thought of leaving the army. Still, my mind's made up and I'm not doing another term here. The last three years have been the happiest of my life, but I know that it's time for me to move on now and seek out pastures new – instead of just putting in more time. If I stayed here for another three years, I wouldn't be a penny richer for my troubles by the end of it either. And what's more, I'd still be aimlessly wandering through life without any definite plan. Nearly all the older soldiers here regret that they didn't leave the army years ago and try something else, while they still had the chance – or so they say anyway.

This seems to be the way the younger crowd are going these days too. Heading out into the world to make something of themselves if they can. There's no reason why I shouldn't try my luck, the same as anyone else.

The Horse left us this afternoon to go 'shearing the lambs' and by the time he was back, myself and the Kynel had all the work as good as done.

'Here's your share of the spoils lads, seeing as you remained at your post while the old-crook went off to fleece the punks,' he says, handing me and Sidney a half-crown apiece. He went off then again, laughing quietly to himself.

'What's all this in aid of, Danny boy?' the Kynel says.

I explained to Sidney that the Horse was an expert at fleecing the new recruits when it came to cards.

'I say, t'aint hardly fair is it, old scout?' says Sidney, throwing me an anxious look.

'Don't let the old-crook hear you saying that,' I says.

I've often heard it said that the English are a very straight crowd and I believe it now too seeing the Kynel's innocent reaction there.

Who returned to us today from Athlone but '07 Ó Donncha! I knew well that he wouldn't like the military policeman's life. Himself and Michael Jim went out on the town this evening and I would've gone with them too only that I need to save the pennies now. I had a drink today alright but I didn't go mad. It was the Kynel's last day here and he invited myself and the Horse to the wet canteen at dinner-time where he stood us three pints each. He didn't forget Slam Féir either, fair play to him, as Sidney handed me the price of a pint for him, when he comes in tomorrow. You'd have sworn that myself and the Horse were the best friends Sidney'd ever had, he was that upset saying goodbye to us! I think that the Horse really felt bad about all the bollockings he gave poor Sidney over the past few weeks too. He told the Englishman to make sure to be on the next course that came into barracks and that we're all looking forward to seeing him back here amongst us again. Chances are that I'll be over in the Kynel's country myself when that day comes around. I've spent the last few weeks down in Galway town asking anyone I meet whether I'll have a good chance of finding work or not if I go over to England. I was only wasting my time really though as I'm none the wiser now about the work situation there than I was before. The other day while I was in the Woollen Mills buying the materials for the suit, I asked the supervisor whether they'd any work going in the factory there, but they didn't. With the help of God I might have better luck when I go down to Kilkenny shortly. I returned my kit and various ordinances today. There were a few bits and pieces missing so I'd to pay thirteen-and-ten pence altogether to cover it. This money is taken out of your pay when you leave.

It was when the Quartermaster accepted my stuff back (gun, helmet etc.) that it really hit me. I'm finally finished with army life and it's a lonely old feeling. I went straight back to the room, but I wasn't there more than a minute or two when one of the lads noticed that I was quiet in myself.

'Hey there, Teacher, you look a bit – how would you put it – you look like a right fool in those civvies of yours. Did you ever see any photos of those poor exiles from the Balkans and other places when they've just landed in New York? Well, that's exactly how you look now in that strange rig-out of yours! Maybe you should bring it back to the tailor to see can he put a bit of a shape on it?' says Máirtín Cúc.

I asked '08 Ó Cuirín what he thought of the 'Martin Henry' on me, but he just shook his head and skittered with laughter. He put his head down and kept polishing his uniform buttons. He has such little respect for new recruits or three-year-term soldiers that he barely talks to them. It was the Rajah who liked my new 'style' the most and the minute he strode into the room, he was full of praise for the new suit.

'Aha – the finest suit of clothes, I've ever seen! Leave it to you Núib, to be the one to get it too. We'll head out to Seapoint tonight now, the pair of us, and you'll be wearing that fine suit of yours, and all the girls'll be saying: 'Who's that "man-about-town" there with the fine suit. They'll be fighting amongst themselves to dance with you when it comes to 'Ladies' Choice' – guaranteed. Next thing, your picture will be in the *Connacht Tribune* and the tailors of Galway'll be kept busy all year making suits like your one,' he says.

'Will you listen to the sartorial expert himself,' says Michael Jim, turning over in the bed, 'Be gor – but you're right too! I can't see anything wrong with that suit, Mac, and if the truth be known 'tis better than what a lot of us had on the day we joined up!'

'Don't say another word. Shut it now, I'm warning you,' retorts the Rajah. 'Everyone knows your form shur. Shur, didn't you leave the bogs and the mountains of Tipperary to come up here Michael? You left the bogs where you spent your time jumping from one small hill to the next, chasing rabbits for your breakfast – to land up here! Shur, didn't you wear sheepskin before you came here and every time an aeroplane or bus went by you all went and hid yourselves, you were that scared! Then, one day a Recruiting Sergeant happens to come along and you're so impressed with the bright shine on the buttons of his uniform that you want to become a soldier. Up to the Curragh then with you and as soon as you got the soldier's uniform you thought you were made. So what do you do but take pictures of yourself and send them home to mammy and everyone at home and they're all duly impressed at how well you're doing in life!'

'It's your own county that you're describing now methinks,' says

Michael Jim, 'the one place in Ireland that Cromwell didn't bother his arse with, it was such a wilderness.'

'Come on Núib and we'll head down to the little tailor, in God's name,' says the Professor then 'because you look like something that just escaped prison to be honest.'

I took off my suit, folded it under my arm and quickly headed downstairs, but who should I run into but Lyons coming the other way.

'What's that you've got there Núibín?' says Lyons, spotting the package under my arm.

I told him what it was and his face changed in an instant. Next thing, he's back to his innocent old self, the fellow who's kindness personified. He puts his arm around me and gives me a friendly hug.

'But Núibín, you're not leaving until Friday, and it won't take the tailor below more than half an hour to fix that suit up for you. Here now, hand me that and I'll leave it into the pawn for you until tomorrow. I'm gasping for a pint and I don't even have the price of a bottle on me. I was actually just on my way to ask you for the loan of a couple of shillings when I met you there.'

I thought of resisting for a second, but he'd swiped my suit and grabbed me in a headlock before I'd a chance to think. I wouldn't mind, but I've already got a sports-jacket belonging to the Rajah and a raincoat belonging to Seáinín Jack left into that same pawnshop already and I'll be hit with the full cost for the lot of them now before I leave – you can be sure of it!

I've had shortness of breath and a sore chest for the last few days – it must be the cycling back Spiddal way in the rain to the céilí's and drinking too much of the black stuff while I was at it. The Herbalist brought a handful of garlic in to me today, to try and clear this chest infection. He's a 'character' alright the Herbalist – no doubt about it. Neither the Horse nor any of the other cooks here like him and yet he arrives into the canteen about the same time each day without a care in the world, empty soup-mug in hand, and with the same begging whine of his: 'A small dropeen of beef soup please?' One thing's for sure; if his garlic clears my sore chest, he'll be getting a bucket of soup from me and not just a mugful!

There's been an old raincoat lying in one of the cupboards here for the past six months. No one's using it so I plan on taking it with me when I go out on my ticket. The coat belongs to Small Barry from Mullingar, but he's gone to Dublin now on a piping (music) course and no one knows when he'll be back. It's not a great coat or anything, but it'll do me just fine. And if no one else takes it, chances are that someone'll just pawn it down at the Fish Market and nobody'll ever see it again anyway. You can buy very cheap stuff out in the 'Blackrock' this week too and I'll have to take a scout out there as soon as I get paid.

All I got for pay today was two pounds, one shilling; we'll get the full amount on Friday next, they say. On the day I leave, I'll get three weeks' wages and enough to live on for another three weeks too – seeing as I won't officially have left the Battalion until a few weeks after I've left the barracks.

The Herbalist's been tormenting me with questions the last few days. He wants to know if I'm definitely heading for England as soon as I leave the barracks here. If so, he says he wants to go over with me.

'We could rent a room over there,' he says, 'and make our own meals rather than throwing good money after bad in the direction of some *landlady* or other – the same as I've been doing down in Galway town the past while. If I'd had more steady and sensible comrades with me so far, shur I'd have done way better for myself by now and I'd have left for England ages ago. The problem is that some of the Irish over there are the biggest messers you could meet!'

The Horse nearly went ballistic with me when he heard what the Herbalist was planning. 'Oh, but for the love of God, Dónall, would you cop on to yourself? It would be an absolute disaster if you were to share lodgings with that Witchdoctor there. Imagine the state you'd be in if you were sharing a room with that bloody chancer. You'd probably wake up in the morning to a feed of grass for breakfast, then a handful of herb-roots for dinner! And then some moss sandwiches with you every day for work! Before long, you'd be as thin as a rake, even thinner than he is himself. Get the hell out of here you old-quack you, and don't be putting stupid ideas into my good comrade's head here. If you were half as good at the painting as you are at talking shite, you'd have had the job finished here ages ago. Get the fuck out of here you bollocks – you've the Defence Forces flat broke, so you have.' The Herbalist skedaddled quickly. He's afraid of the Horse. Not that this stopped him from standing outside the window later on and trying to communicate with me using hand-signals!

I was in charge of the canteen this evening after tea. The Horse was gone off gambling again. Whatever it is, this year's recruits are more given to gambling than the crew of 1946–9. And the old-timers love gambling. Shur, they'd bet on anything – two spiders climbing up a wall or a fly landing on a loaf of bread first. I ran into Mícheál Ó Sé as I crossed the square earlier. The poor fellow had lost everything he had playing cards and looked miserable. He was dragging on the butt of an old cigarette – his last one, probably. I felt sorry for him, the poor devil – because he's a real gentlemen underneath it all – so I invited him to join me for a drink. We went downtown and into the Jersey Bar first. Poor Michael was a bit down in himself in the beginning, but he soon shook himself out of his melancholy and we'd a great chat for the rest of the night. He regaled me with all his stories of *An Chéad Chath* in the old days and all the 'characters' and chancers that were there during the Emergency and in the years before that again.

Pádraig Ó Domhnaill arrived in after a while and we had a great bout of conversation and wit. Both Pádraig and Mícheál with their strong Kerry dialects of Irish – and the pair of them as lively and full of crack as the next man. Like me, Pádraig wears glasses and he has a very educated look about him especially when he begins holding forth on something or other. He's got a really great sense of humour and he'd have you in fits of laughter once he starts imitating Slám Féir, the Horse, Mac Ruaidhrí and all the other old-timers. Pádraig loves the old-timers best because they're all unique 'characters', people who're independent-minded even if they've their own idiosyncrasies and quirks about them. Pádraig himself is hilarious and he's always great crack. He's also one of the brightest and most relaxed people I've ever met. There isn't a bitter or jealous bone in his body and he's very generous and always willing to do someone else a good turn. If even half the men in the Battalion here had the learning of Ó Domhnaill from Annascaul, they'd be walking over each other to study for their University degrees. Pádraig doesn't care about all that stuff though. Once he has his books to read, a chance for good conversation, and a minimum of responsibilities to fulfil, he's as happy as Larry!

I got paid today, nine pounds and eighteen pence, and so I went down and retrieved my Martin Henry suit, the Maharajah's sports-coat and Seáinín Jack's raincoat from the pawnshop.

Captain Ó Ceallacháin paid me out my wages. He didn't have the exact money and asked me had I two one-shilling pieces – and that he could give me a ten-pound note. I told him I couldn't do this however, as I didn't have any money on me. A look of horror came over him on hearing this. 'You mean to tell me that you haven't a penny to your name now that you're going out on your ticket – other than the money I'm giving you right now?' He said this in a way that implied it was unusual for a private to leave the army on an empty pocket.

'I haven't a red cent on me, Sir, and that's the truth,' I says.

'Oh, God help us,' he says, shaking his head ruefully. I woke up in the middle of the night last night. My chest felt really tight and I could barely breathe. I felt as if a great weight was pressing down on my chest and I started coughing. I felt a sharp metallic taste in my mouth and for a minute, I thought I might be coughing up blood so I went out to the wash-house to check.

I returned to bed very anxious and worried in myself. All sorts of thoughts, one more worrying than the next, went through my mind. I thought that I might have contracted something terrible like tuberculosis and all sorts of awful scenarios went through my mind. I imagined myself left bed-bound in a sanatorium for ages. I put my hand into my uniform pocket, took out my Rosary beads and began to pray. I recited the entire Rosary from start to finish, all fifteen decades of it. Once I'd said these prayers, my shortness of breath abated and I was less agitated. Slowly but surely, I relaxed. Eventually I managed to doze off.

I went to the doctor first thing this morning to see how bad the situation was. He gave me a detailed examination and removed his stethoscope and called for the medical orderly. I got a right fright when he said that because I didn't hear him right at first and thought he said – 'Get the San'.[79]

A thousand thanks to the dutiful Son of God, but what the doctor actually said was – 'menthol' or something like that. It's some kind of stuff that you apply to your skin apparently so's to make your breathing better. After all my worry, I only had a spot of bronchitis and some accompanying muscle pain in the end. I emerged from the medical booth as happy as any man alive, I can tell you! My heart filled with courage once more and looking down at Loch an tSáile and out over Galway Bay, I was ready to take on the world now that I knew I'd be alright again. I went downtown and bought five feet of cloth (at seven shillings a foot) in Flynn's Woollen Mills – for a suit for my mother. This cloth is very fine material and she'll get great wear out of it. I went into the Corner House then and who was in there but Joe Ó Cuirín ('80) and a man from Whitestrand who goes by the name of Joe Chóilín. '80 Ó Cuirín introduced me to your man and he claimed that he could get me a job no problem in a factory over in Liverpool where he works. Joe Chóilín began to sing the praises of England as a country to me then – how amazing the pubs are over there, how much work is going over there, and, above anything else, how clean the toilets are in the factories over there – of all things! I don't know for the life of me why he thought this was important, but he went on and on about the cleanliness of the public facilities in England for some strange reason.

'Oh, dear little brother,' he says, 'but you'd eat your dinner off the floor of the factory toilets where I'm working, they're kept that spotless!'

'I doubt it,' I says to myself, 'I doubt it very much' – even if I let on to be delighted to have this valuable information. I gave my home address to Joe Chóilín and he's going to write to me and invite me over, if I don't find any work at home. I know this much though. Whatever '80 Ó Cuirín and I spent on the few pints, the man who praised the toilets never put his hand in his pocket once all afternoon!

I returned to the barracks for tea and as I passed over the railway line, the lonelier I felt at the thought of my leaving soon. It's strange how someone becomes so used to the army life and now that I reflect on it, there's a lot of things that I'll never see again once I'm gone from here. The sight of Ó Conchubhair Árann[80] standing opposite the guard-room sounding the bugle; Joeen Beag sitting quietly on his kit-box polishing his uniform; the radiance of the bayonets as the sun glistens bright on them during Commanders' Parade on a Saturday morning – and a thousand other things that make barracks life special. Just thinking of all this now makes me sad and lonely.

I went looking for the Horse and Lyons today after tea because I wanted them to come downtown with me for our last evening together. We went into the Jersey first where we drank five or six pints at a nice relaxed pace; then out to Bohermore where we had another few in Currans. It was around then that the Horse began talking in that American drawl he puts on and the two of us said goodbye and good luck to him and made for the Brooklyn Bar, where we stayed for the rest of the night.

There was a good crowd in from Annaghdown and Claregalway and whenever these people are about, you're bound to hear the old songs. They sang 'Anach Cuain', 'If I was in Claddagh', 'An Draighneán Donn', 'Galway Bay' (the old version), and many others. Lyons has a very sweet voice and he sang 'The Glens of Sweet Mayo' in a fine, hearty voice. I sang 'An Buachaill Múinte' and 'The Rocks of Bawn' and Bean a' Brook[81] (as Cuirín Mór christened her) had tears in her eyes by the time I was finished. I haven't enjoyed a night out as much in a very long time.

Each of us brought a five-nagin bottle of porter with us down to Joyce's in Mary Street where we went to get some food. Normally, they've a great welcome for soldiers in there and give them plenty of the food that they can best afford – a big pot of tea, plenty of bread-loaf and jam. We were a bit late arriving in this evening though and were lucky that they let us in at all in the end.

We sat in anyway and next thing, there was a commotion upstairs where the lodgers live. It's mainly older men who lodge in Joyce's and one of them shouted downstairs for someone to help him at one stage. Another man was giving him an awful beating apparently. Lyons didn't hesitate for a moment. He left down his tea and ran upstairs with me following quickly behind him. At the entrance to one of the bedrooms, a powerfully built young fellow was giving this old fellow a right hiding and the old fellow had just his long night-shirt on. All the old lads inside in their beds were going mad, shouting at the young blackguard to stop.

Lyons stepped forward and floored the young fellow with one punch, then bent down and grabbed the young buck by the lapel and asked him what the hell he was doing battering the poor old lad like that. Looking into one of the bedrooms, who did I see eyeing my five-nagin bottle of porter but an old pal of mine, Micilín Ó hUigín from Ballindooley. I handed him the bottle and he took a mighty slug out of it. In fact, he gulped down two-thirds of the bottle, the greedy yoke! And he still had a thirsty look about him so I gave him the rest of my porter.

Lyons was still shaking the life out of the young thug on the floor and on at him about attacking a poor, defenceless man like that when a shout came from downstairs. It was the woman of the house.

'The Guards are coming – you'll get it now, so you will!' That's when myself and Lyons thought it might be better we made a quick exit. We ran downstairs and out into the yard where we climbed over the back-wall. Lyons kept a firm grip on his bottle of porter all the while and even took a big slug out of it when we stopped at the gates of Saint Nicholas' Church to catch our breath. He must've noticed the questioning look I gave him as he knocked back the porter.

'It's ok. I gave old-Micilín a drink inside in the lodging house and he knocked back the whole lot,' I says.

'Oh, blast you anyway, you bloody rookie,' he says to me angrily. 'You'd probably hand over your bloody gun out on the battlefield! But an army marches on its stomach; wasn't that Napoleon's refrain, wasn't it!' he said, jamming the cork into the mouth of the bottle. He hadn't gone fifty yards though before he felt guilty and gave me another slug of the bottle.

*Wednesday, 18/10/1950*

I rose early this morning and got my stuff ready for leaving. This didn't take long seeing as I'd very little in the way of possessions anyway – other than my Martin Henry suit, a few army shirts, and a pair of shoes. I was unsure whether I should take Small Barry's raincoat with me or not, but I decided to take in the end and put it on! None of the other lads here knew who owned it – apart from me – and Barry had probably forgotten it anyway. He was a small fellow, who was always a bit crazy and liked his drink the same as the next man.

I said goodbye to the lads and stood in the doorway of the room one last time. A lump of sorrow came into my throat. I managed to hold back the tears until I went out to say goodbye to The Maharajah who'd gone out for a shave. I couldn't look him straight in the eyes, I was that bad. How's it that we always have to say goodbye to the people we get on the best with in this world? How come we often end up in the company of people we aren't that keen on really at all?

After leaving the Rajah, I went down to have one final look at Company B's old room where we all lived last year – this is the room that once housed Cuirín Mór, Colm a' tSeaimpín, Ciarraí, Sonaí Mhichil, Joeen Beag and all the others, the room where I spent the best days of my life. I gave it one last look and turned away. Inside, I knew I was leaving a big chunk of my life behind me forever.

I hit out across the Square, the other fellow's old raincoat on me and my kit-bag slung over my shoulder. The morning parade was underway, but the officers had yet to emerge from the barracks. Major-Sergeant Mac Aodha had taken over the parade-stand from the other captains, but when he spotted me, he signalled over and told me to wait a moment. He walked over to me then, nice and slow.

'Well McCauley, you're finally leaving us?' he says.

'I am Sir,' I says and then, for the crack – 'but I'll come back if you need me in an emergency!'

He opened his mouth to say something and I thought I might have annoyed him. But he just burst out laughing instead!

'May God keep you and mind you lad,' he says and turned away. I went out through the gate and down along the railway line and when I came to the first arch at the bridge, I glanced back at the big grey barracks that looked a bit foreign to me already. At the second arch, who did I run into but Small Barry, his kit-bag on his shoulder and he just returning from his course! We stood and chatted for a while and I wasn't sure whether to say anything about the raincoat or not. 'I like your taste in raincoats,' he says then, and we burst out laughing.

I spent the morning wandering around Galway town and met up with my uncle Joe who'd come the few miles into the city on his donkey and cart. We went into Johnny Folan's and drank a few pints back in the West and then I went up-town to the train station. It was a lovely autumn day and it reminded me of my childhood days walking home from school. The smell of burning stalks in the potato patch and the sea that lay in front of you, vast and smooth stretching all the way to the horizon, all the way back to the three sentries – the Aran Islands. You'd hear a cow lowing in the west over in Barna back then, it was so quiet, the sound drifting across the afternoon. You might hear a donkey braying far away and the sound of a woman calling her hens to order up in Rahoon – 'Chuck, chuck, chuck'. I felt a sense of happiness and peace in that moment that I've never felt since.

I stood at the corner of Eyre Square and looked around me, then walked up the road to the station. Two elderly men sporting old-fashioned hats and tweed clothes stood against the wall of one of the hotels there chatting in Irish. Farther down the road from them was Old Rainey the piper, squeezing some tunes out of a worn-looking chanter that'd seen better days. The heavy-sweet smell of porter and the light scent of the wood-chippings came across the air to me from the Corner House.

'A thousand farewells' to so much that is beautiful, I says to myself. 'A thousand farewells ... to the sweet melody of the Irish language and the last remnants of the old Gaelic way of life here in Ireland. Galway might have its faults, but it's the last city on this earth where you'll hear the old language of the Gael still spoken on the street and in the market-place. A thousand farewells to the Corrib and the rowing boats on a golden sunny afternoon, all the nights of music back west in Connemara, and the finest bunch of honest men you'll ever meet – the men of *An Chéad Chath*! My love is yours forever, sweet Galway!'

I walked down to the station and boarded the train, and I was filled with the same emotion that I've felt so many times before. I hate the bloody sight of that great, lonely, empty shed of a place and the train with its impatient spumes of smoke and the porters lugging baggage onto the platform. I hated the place now because I was leaving my native home that I've loved since the beginning of time – the place I love more than anywhere else in the world.

The engine gives a high, sharp blast and we're slipping out through the dark tunnel and out of the station. We're chugging more quickly as we go over the bridge at Loch an tSáile and I press my face against the window to get one last glance at the old grey-brick of Renmore Barracks before the train takes me away. I give it a quick glance and then Ballyloughane disappears from sight. I stay at the window for a long time until Galway Bay fades into the distance. Then I lean back in my seat, my eyes fixed straight ahead as the countryside disappears behind me.

*89383 Private Dónall Mac Amhlaigh*

# Glossary

1  Doire Fhatharta, Carraroe, County Galway.

2  Daideo – 'Grandad'

3  *Eanach Mheáin* – Annaghvaan

4  *Galway Races* – The Galway Races is an Irish horse-racing festival that begins on the last Monday of July each year. It is held at Ballybrit Racecourse in Galway, Ireland over seven days; it is the longest of all the race meets that occur in Ireland.

5  *Dev* – De Valera

6  C.B. – 'Confined to Barracks'

7  *'Faillitheoirí'* – Dossers. Those who make mistakes.

8  *An Chéad Chath* (or *An Chéad Chathlán Coisithe*) was the 'The First Infantry Battalion'. It was first established as an Irish-language speaking unit in Galway, in 1924. All the armed forces' units other than *An Chéad Chath* functioned exclusively through English.

9  *Alp luachra* - a species of lizard found on the bogs and the moors. It's said that you should never sleep outdoors with your mouth open in case this lizard might sneak into your mouth and eat whatever food is in your stomach.

10  *Buckshee* – British military and naval slang – meaning 'anything you can get easily/for free'. Origin unknown but possibly from *baksheesh* – 'money given as a tip, a present, or alms' – Middle East (Persia).

11  James McCauley, Dónall Mac Amhlaigh's father, was born in Limerick and served with the Munster Fusiliers in the First World War. He subsequently joined the East Clare brigade of the IRA, after which he served in the new Irish army (1922–57).

12  Maurice Francis 'Mossy' O'Riordan (1926 – 27 August 2008) was an Irish hurler who played as a right corner-forward for the Cork senior team. He played with the Blackrock club. O'Riordan arrived on the inter-county scene at the age of twenty when he debuted with the Cork senior hurling team during the 1946 championship. He immediately became a regular member of the starting fifteen

and won two All-Ireland medals, three Munster medals and two Railway Cup medals. He emigrated to New South Wales in Australia where he died in 2008. He's buried in East Maitland cemetery (NSW) with his wife, Molly (née Fennell), and his two sons Eoin and Sean.

[13] *Breac-Ghaeltacht* – an area where the Irish language is gradually disappearing or very weak as a spoken language.

[14] *Ireland's Own* is a family magazine published weekly in Ireland. It specialises in lightweight content, traditional stories, and uncontroversial family content, including puzzles and recipes. It was launched on 26 November 1902 by John M. Walshe of *People Newspapers*, and originally cost just 1d. The magazine was designed to offer 'wholesome Irish Catholic fare' to challenge the appearance of British newspapers in Ireland, such as the *News of the World*, that were seen to have lowered the moral tone during the early-1900s. The magazine's appearance coincided with a new stress on Irish identity and Irish nationalism and a bigger reaction to British imports. Two other influential examples were the creation of the GAA (Gaelic Athletic Association) to promote Gaelic games and the appearance of the Gaelic League promoting the Irish language. To this day, *Ireland's Own* continues to combine a sense of patriotism, pietism and national news with a wide range of interesting historical and cultural pieces.

[15] *Our Boys* was a magazine published on a monthly basis by the Irish Christian Brothers in Ireland. At a time when there was a growing sense of national self-identity in Ireland, the purpose of *Our Boys* was to compete with British boys' magazines, which were in the main pro-British Empire and pro-Church of England. It specialised in adventure stories, school stories and historical stories featuring Irish protagonists, competitions and puzzles, as well as lightweight family content. This magazine was sold through Christian Brothers' schools worldwide and in many newsagents throughout Ireland. The magazine had a large circulation in Ireland and was also made available to Irish communities in England, Australia, the US, and even in India, where it was distributed through the network of schools run by the Christian Brothers.

[16] Brian O'Higgins (1882–1963), also known as 'Brian na Banban', was an Irish poet, politician and a founding member of Sinn Féin. He was President of Sinn Féin from 1931 to 1933 and took part in the 1916 Easter Rising where he fought in the GPO. O'Higgins was best known for the anti-recruitment poem *Who Is Ireland's Enemy?* He was elected unopposed as a Sinn Féin MP for Clare West at the 1918 general election. He opposed the Anglo-Irish Treaty and voted against it. From the late 1920s onwards, he ran a successful business publishing greeting cards, calendars etc. decorated with Celtic designs and often with his own poems. From 1935 to 1962, he published the *Wolfe Tone Annual* which gave popular accounts of episodes in Irish history from a republican viewpoint. He was a devout Catholic and critical of those who believed all republicans had also to be socialists.

[17] 'scutters' – diarrhoea.

[18] *Martin Henry* suits were bespoke tailored. This company was set up by Joseph Henry who started off his own business in 1895 in Sligo making breeches. His son, also named Joseph Henry, in turn learned his trade in Savile Row, after which he expanded the company's reputation throughout the UK and the US. His grandson, Joseph Martin carries on the tradition to this day.

[19] *Shoneens* – People who were ashamed of their Gaelic backgrounds and aped English manners and ways, including in terms of speaking English very frequently.

[20] *Mass* – The Mass or Eucharist is the central act of worship in the Catholic Church. Many of the other sacraments are celebrated within the framework of the Mass.

[21] *Inis Toirbirt* – Turbot Island, off the coast of County Galway.

[22] *Joeen Beag* – (Little/Small Joe)

[23] *Colm an tSeaimpín* – Colm, the Champion

[24] Known as a '*roscadh*', this is a set piece of colourful rhetoric inserted into a heroic narrative of valour. This type of narrative poetry, as originally performed, was not intended to be translated literally.

[25] *Gobán* – 'Jack of all trades' or 'incompetent tradesman'

[26] *Mac a' tSeaimpín* – 'Son of a Champion'

[27] A 'rissole' from the French, is a small croquette, enclosed in pastry or rolled in breadcrumbs, usually baked or deep fried.

[28] *Ceannaire Ó Sé* – Leader Ó Sé

[29] 'old lad' – father

[30] *Carraig an Bhalbháin* – 'The Mute's Rock' – probably out in the sea somewhere.

[31] *Cuirín Mór* – 'Big Curran'

[32] *Ó hIceadha* – 'Hickey'

[33] *Ó Condúin* – Condon

[34] *Tearmann* – Sanctuary, reservation

[35] *Thomastown* – County Kilkenny

[36] *Tá sé's* – Lit: The 'He is's' – i.e. 'He is here' etc.

[37] *Modh Coinníollach* – In Irish – 'Conditional Mood'

[38] 'glasses' – i.e. 'spectacles'

[39] 'herself' – the woman bar-owner.

[40] *ceann* – head/top.

[41] *eile* – another

[42] 'cat' – cat

[43] *mo* – my

[44] *leithéide* – the likes of …

[45] The *Astaire Ballroom* was upstairs in Victoria Place with the entrance on Merchants Road.

[46] The *Commercial Boat Club* was founded in 1875 and is still going strong in Woodquay in the heart of Galway city. The many societies which continue to meet there today include fishing, snooker, darts, bowls, table tennis and pool.

[47] *Aon Déag* – eleven

[48] The *Joyce Country* includes the areas of Maam, Cornamona, Clonbur, Cloghbrack, Finney, Tourmakeady, Cong, Cross and The Neale. The area is called 'Joyce Country' after the Joyces who are said to have migrated from Wales to live in the barony of Ross in the early-1400s.

[49] *Coill Sáile* – Kylesalia, Ballnahinch

[50] 'quenching the candle' – i.e. calling it a day (on the drinking).

[51] *Mac a' Leoin* – lit: 'son of the lion' in Irish – really, Ó Laighin (Lyons)

[52] *gimmick* – word of unknown origin but possibly an approximate anagram of 'magic', the original sense being 'a piece of magicians' apparatus'. An ingenious or novel device, scheme, or stratagem, especially one designed to attract attention or increase appeal.

[53] The Raineys were a Traveller family who wintered in a house in Tuam but toured the fairs and markets of Connemara during the summer. They consisted of Paddy, known as 'Big Rainey', and his brother Stephen (who went by the nickname of 'Spare Parts') and Paddy's wife Bridie who was the singer. The two brothers played the fiddle, though Paddy's instrument was somewhat decrepit and his bow 'was strung not with horse-hair but what looked like carpet-thread, fastened to the heel through a cotton-reel nailed on it'. Luckily, visiting Englishman and university lecturer Tony Knowland taped the Raineys in a session in Freeneys in Letterfrack in the mid-1950s. A full half-century later, the Raineys music was made available for the first time on the album simply titled *The Raineys* issued in 2006.

[54] *Pioneers* – The Pioneer Total Abstinence Association of the Sacred Heart (or PTAA) is an Irish organisation for Roman Catholic teetotallers. Its members are commonly called 'Pioneers'.

[55] 'old fellow' – father.

[56] *Corr na Móna* (Cornamona) – Irish-speaking townland in North Connemara.

[57] *Tomás Ó Dubhghaill* – Thomas Doyle

[58] *Leitir Mór/Leitir Móir* – (Lettermore) is a Gaeltacht village in Connemara, in Galway, Ireland. The name derives from the Irish 'Leitir Móir' meaning 'great rough hillside'.

[59] *Ó Giolláin* – 'Gillane/Gillen'

[60] Castlegar is a village and parish in County Galway, Ireland, located just outside of the city of Galway. The name derives from the Irish 'Caisleán Gearr', meaning 'Short Castle'. The annual Galway Races are held at Ballybrit Racecourse which is in the parish of Castlegar.

[61] *An Caoláire* – Killary

[62] *Pádraig Ó Siochfhradha* – Patrick Sugrue

[63] *Breatnach* – Walsh

[64] 'line' – i.e. the train-line between Renmore and Galway city.

[65] *Bohunk* originates as a slang/derogatory term directed specifically at those of Bohemian descent. Bohemians are from the region now known as The Czech Republic. It is a term used to describe Eastern European immigrants and Slavs. It was the equivalent of calling an Irishman a 'Mick' or a German a 'Kraut'.

[66] *Carraig a' Bhalbháin* – ('The Mute's Rock')

[67] *Con!* – Connemara or Connacht.

[68] *A Dheadí* – Daddy

[69] *Two to wan the field* – i.e. the betting odds are at 'two to wan' (one). Horse racing/gambling jargon.

[70] Máirtín Ó Cadhain (Kyne) – (1906–1970), one of the most prominent Irish-language writers of the 20th century, was from an Cnocán Glas, near Spiddal. Perhaps best known for his 1949 work Cré na Cille, Ó Cadhain played a key role in bringing literary modernism to contemporary Irish-language literature. Politically, he was an Irish nationalist and socialist, promoting the renewal of Ireland through Gaelic culture. As with famed Dublin writer Brendan Behan, he was a member of the IRA during the Emergency.

[71] *Baile an tSagairt* – lit: 'the Priest's Village' – townland next to Spiddal, County Galway.

[72] *Ó Ceallacháin* – (O'Callaghan)

[73] In June 1950 a *Hanley Page Halifax* from the British Army's RAF base Aldergrove in Belfast was returning to base having completed a survey flight west of the Kerry coast when the weather conditions deteriorated badly. A thick fog caused the plane to crash on very high ground on Croaghaun, on the west mountain of Achill Island with the tragic loss of 8 crewmen.

Squadron crew list

*Pilot* ........ Ernest George Hopgood
*Navigator* ........ Joseph Kevin Brown
*Co-Pilot* ........ Michael William Horsley
*Engineer* ........ Harold Shaw
*Air Signaller* ........ Cornelius Joseph Rogan
*Gunner* ........ Martin Gilmartin
*Meteorological Observer* ........ James Charles Lister
*Airman* ........ Bernard Francis McKenna

[74] This work-gang removed all the wreckage of the crashed aeroplane from the mountainside.

[75] Rita Hayworth (born Margarita Carmen Cansino, 1918–1987) was an American actress and dancer who had Spanish, Irish and English heritage. Known to the press as the 'love goddess' she achieved huge fame during the 1940s as one of the era's top stars and screen idols. She appeared in a total of 61 films over 37 years and was also the top pin-up girl for American GIs during World War II. She acted and danced alongside many of the major male stars of her era including Glenn Ford, Gene Kelly and Fred Astaire. Astaire, with whom she made two films, called her his favourite dance partner. One of her most famous films was the technicolour musical *Cover Girl* (1944).

[76] The *Birmingham Small Arms Company Limited* (BSA) was a major British industrial conglomeration. It incorporated a group of businesses manufacturing military and sporting firearms, bicycles, motorbikes, cars, buses and bodies – steel, iron castings, hand-power and machine tools, coal cleaning and handling plants, and sintered metals including hard chrome process. At its peak, BSA (who also owned *Triumph*) was the largest motorcycle producer in the world. It went into decline in the late-1950s and early 1960s, however, when much of its market shifted to the U.S.

[77] F.C.A. – *An Fórsa Cosanta Áitiúil* is the reserve force of the Irish Army.

[78] *An Cloch Bhreac* – Cloghbrack, Cornamona, Co. Galway

[79] 'San' – a word similar to 'sanatorium'.

[80] *Ó Conchubhair Árann* – (O'Connor from the Aran Islands)

[81] Bean a' Brook – (i.e. the Landlady of the Brooklyn Bar)

# PARTHIAN TRANSLATIONS

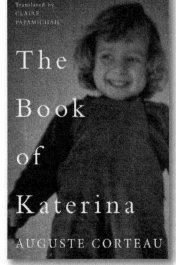

## THE BOOK OF KATERINA

Auguste Corteau

Translated from Greek by Claire Papamichail

Out 2021

---

£10.00
978-1-912681-26-6

## HANA

Alena Mornštajnová

Translated from Czech by Julia and Peter Sherwood

Out October 2020

---

£10.99
978-1-912681-50-1

Creative Europe

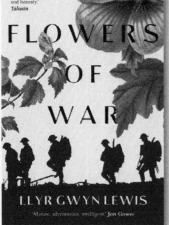

## FLOWERS OF WAR

Llyr Gwyn Lewis

Short-Listed for Wales
Book of the Year

---

£9.00
978-1-912681-25-9

## MARTHA, JACK AND SHANCO

Caryl Lewis

Winner of the Wales
Book of the Year

**Out October 2020**

---

£9.99
978-1-912681-77-8

# PARTHIAN TRANSLATIONS

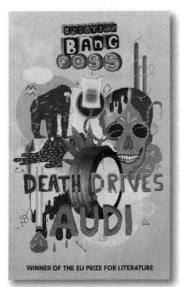

## DEATH DRIVES AN AUDI

Kristian Bang Foss

Winner of the European Prize for Literature

£10.00
978-1-912681-32-7

## FEAR OF BARBARIANS

Petar Adonovski

Winner of the European Prize for Literature

£9.00
978-1-913640-19-4

Creative Europe

ENGLISH PEN

FREEDOM TO **WRITE**
FREEDOM TO **READ**

Supported using public funding by

**ARTS COUNCIL
ENGLAND**

This book has been selected to receive financial assistance from English PEN's Writers in Translation programme supported by Bloomberg and Arts Council England. English PEN exists to promote literature and its understanding, uphold writers' freedoms around the world, campaign against the persecution and imprisonment of writers for stating their views, and promote the friendly co-operation of writers and free exchange of ideas. Each year, a dedicated committee of professionals selects books that are translated into English from a wide variety of foreign languages. We award grants to UK publishers to help translate, promote, market and champion these titles. Our aim is to celebrate books of outstanding literary quality, which have a clear link to the PEN charter and promote free speech and intercultural understanding.

In 2011, Writers in Translation's outstanding work and contribution to diversity in the UK literary scene was recognised by Arts Council England. English PEN was awarded a threefold increase in funding to develop its support for world writing in translation. www.englishpen.org

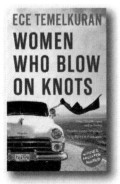